EDUCATION AND THE COMMON GOOD

EDUCATION
and the
COMMON GOOD

A MORAL PHILOSOPHY OF THE CURRICULUM

by Philip H. Phenix

**PROFESSOR OF EDUCATION
TEACHERS COLLEGE, COLUMBIA UNIVERSITY**

GREENWOOD PRESS, PUBLISHERS
WESTPORT, CONNECTICUT

Library of Congress Cataloging in Publication Data

Phenix, Philip Henry, 1915-
    Education and the common good.

    Reprint of the 1961 ed. published by Harper, New
York.
    Bibliography: p.
    Includes index.
    1. Moral education--Curricula. 2. Education--
Philosophy. I. Title.
[LC268.P46 1977]   370.1   77-22594
ISBN 0-8371-9728-7

EDUCATION AND THE COMMON GOOD

Copyright © 1961, by Philip H. Phenix

Originally published in 1961 by Harper & Brothers, Publishers,
New York

Reprinted with the permission of Harper & Row, Publishers, Inc.

Reprinted in 1977 by Greenwood Press, Inc.

Library of Congress catalog card number   77-22594

ISBN 0-8371-9728-7

Printed in the United States of America

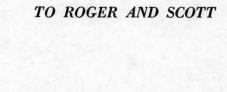

TO ROGER AND SCOTT

CONTENTS

PART 1 * INTRODUCTION

This introductory chapter will state the theme around which the whole book revolves and on which the widely diverse topics considered are so many variations. This will constitute the text upon which the succeeding chapters are commentary, illustration, and elaboration. In order that the central theme may stand out clearly, its statement will be followed by a discussion of the context in which the text is set, indicating some of its sources and relationships.

A glance at the chapter headings reveals at once the need for such an introduction. The subjects treated cover a wide range, from table manners to international organization, from scientific methods to the tax structure. How can the treatment of matters so different within the compass of one short book be justified?

There are several common concerns by which the topics are united. These concerns move successively to deeper levels, finally culminating in certain principles which are the organizing center of the entire analysis.

The first unity lies in the fact that this is a book about education. The study grows out of the practical problem of deciding what should be taught in our homes and schools. If we ask what should be the content of instruction, it is evident that anything like an adequate answer must include many different topics, because a person living in the complex modern age must know and be able to do a multitude of things. So it seems reasonable that a book about the content of education should treat subjects covering a wide spectrum—not exhaustively of course, but only so as to show why each one is important

3

and to indicate something of the knowledge, skills, and attitudes that need to be developed in each area and how this may be done.

The next unifying concern is that of finding a common perspective from which to consider the content of instruction. Shall it be the traditional subject fields? Shall it be current issues in education, like federal aid to schools, education of the gifted, and so on? Instead of such perspectives, the *major problems in contemporary culture and civilization* have been elected as the basis for the choice of topics. What should we teach our children? We must above all teach them to meet the problems of our time with courage and competence. And what are the problems of our time? Are they not such matters as the role of intelligence, the mass media, standards of taste, sex, race, politics, and religion? The fifteen subjects considered in chapters 3 through 17 cover most of the major problem areas in modern life. Thus, the question, "What shall the young be taught?" is answered by saying, "Teach them to meet the challenge of these problems."

The traditional formal schools taught subjects—the three R's and their higher elaborations. The progressive schools were concerned more with the individual child's interests and needs. The premise of this study is that neither the organized subject fields nor the psychology of personality furnishes the criteria for deciding the content of instruction. The clue to choice in the curriculum lies in the demands that are imposed by the development of modern civilization. Hence the chapters to follow range over what appear to be the principal problematic fields in present-day culture.

This leads us to the third level of unity, deeper than the concern for the curriculum and for the problems of civilization. Problems appear and their solution is believed important only because people have values, that is, purposes that they wish to realize. Race, social class, the use of leisure time, and the like are problems only because values are at stake, because people care about the outcomes, because these are questions on which decisions of moment must be made. They are real problems because most people are not neutral toward them but, on the contrary, hold firm convictions about them. Thus, the use of genuine issues as the criterion of what shall be taught affirms that education is a moral enterprise, where the term "moral" refers to purposeful conduct based on consideration of values. Intellectual and esthetic responsibility, right choice of work and recreation, conservation of natural and human resources, and so on are all moral issues. With respect to each of them every person is faced with the demand to make choices between better and worse. Hence the present array of topics is bound together by the common thread of moral concern. Each matter considered, from the choice of food to the worship of God, is examined from the standpoint of the values at stake and with regard to the betterment of conduct through education.

Questions then arise about which values shall be chosen. Whose purposes shall the curriculum reflect? What moral standard shall govern teaching and learning? It is in attempting to answer these questions that it is necessary to move to the fourth and deepest level of concepts that unify the many subjects comprising this volume.

This fourth level is concerned with the nature and source of values. The essential idea is that a distinction must be drawn between values based on interest or desire and values based on objective worth. There is a decisive difference between *wanting* something and *affirming its worth,* for about any want it is always possible to ask whether or not it is worthy, about any desire whether or not it is desirable, about any interest whether or not it is right. The position taken here is that the moral enterprise makes sense only if there are objective excellences that invite the loyalties of men and constitute the standard and goal of human endeavor. It is not claimed that anyone knows what the ultimate good is, nor that it is always actually possible to secure agreement about moral questions. But it does seem clear that any serious concern to discover and to do what is right rests on the premise that there are objective standards of worth upon which universal agreement is in principle possible.

Objective standards of worth do not mean abstract moral laws to which all particular instances should conform. Judgments of value are always concrete and particular. They always have reference to circumstances and context. For example, it is unlikely that there are any rules that define the ideal economic or political system for all people at all periods in history. Similarly, excellence in works of art or in games is a specific quality of the concrete object or game. But to affirm the concreteness of values is not to make them subjective and relative to the appraiser. The moral enterprise presupposes the potential universality of judgments about values that are individually objective.

Why are we so far from common understanding about what is really good, and why are we so slow to serve the right? There are three causes. The first is ignorance. The problems that present themselves for decision are often extremely complex. It is difficult to take proper account of the myriad relevant factors in making decisions on even relatively minor matters like diet, let alone such major concerns as foreign policy or population control. The antidote to ignorance is research and education. By increased knowledge, widely disseminated, judgments of value can at least be made more intelligently, for a just appraisal of any situation requires that the facts of the situation and the consequences of alternative decisions be understood.

The second cause of difficulty is the boundless depth and richness of reality. The world is constantly changing, every moment presents new problems, and old solutions seldom apply to fresh situations. Furthermore, every judgment of worth is necessarily tentative, for no insight or system of knowledge contains the whole truth about anything, and no finite act or object embodies perfection. The dynamism and infinitude of the world forbid any final state of consummatory equilibrium, in which all truth is known and absolute right is done. It follows that education should be primarily not for accumulating information but for learning to learn and for readiness to meet new demands and make new choices imaginatively. The quest for finality and absolute certainty must also be abandoned in favor of the adventure of boundless discovery.

The third and most important cause of confusion and conflict in the moral enterprise is the human tendency toward self-centeredness. People disagree on good and evil, not mainly out of ignorance nor because of the changefulness of the world, nor because perfection is beyond reach, but primarily because they are self-centered. They then reinforce and entrench this selfishness by adopting a philosophy in which values are reduced to interests, desires, or wants, and in which all notions of objective good and right are rejected. Thus, theoretical warrant and support are given to self-serving.

If this chief cause of moral failure and confusion is to be remedied, the central aim of education should be the transformation of persons so that they will serve the good instead of pleasing themselves. The focal point around which the entire argument of this book revolves is that the cardinal goal of instruction in whatever field, from physics to etiquette to race relations, should be the development of loyalty to what is excellent, instead of success in satisfying desires.

This ideal of commitment to what is right further proves to be the key to the meaning of democracy. Fundamentally democracy is a social system in which in some significant sense all citizens are accounted equal. In what respect are they equal? Surely not in abilities, wants, interests, needs, qualities, or circumstances. They are equal in being human, mortal, possessed of body and mind—but from these elemental equalities no significant direction for conduct follows. The significant equality upon which democracy rests is moral. Democracy presupposes the equality of all persons with respect to truth and right. There is not one standard of worth for certain persons and another standard for others, but a single standard under which all are comprehended. Goodness is no respecter of persons; rather, all persons are obliged to respect goodness.

Thus, democracy is the social expression of belief in objective qualities of goodness and of common loyalty to them. It is not to be assumed, of course, that the content of the good is fully known or agreed upon. On the contrary, the continuing task of democratic man is to seek ever fuller disclosure of the truth, through study, reflection, experiment, and dialogue, moved by shared devotion to a goodness that forever escapes complete finite embodiment and universal consensus. Education for democracy, therefore, should encourage the habit of sustained inquiry and the arts of sincere persuasion, and above all should confirm and celebrate faith in the priority and ultimate givenness of truth and goodness, in which the moral enterprise is grounded.

In contrast with this ideal of democracy established in common dedication to a given order of worth and excellence is another concept of democracy growing out of the interest, or satisfaction, theory of value. Here the common good is defined as that which maximizes satisfaction and minimizes destructive conflict; that is to say, democracy is regarded as a means of organizing for the greatest possible harmonization of desires. The position taken in this book is that such a democracy is inherently self-defeating, in part because the unrestrained pursuit of satisfaction tends to breed conflict rather than harmony, but more importantly because human nature is such that persons and cultures do not grow in beauty, strength, and virtue when people strive only to get what they want. The fulfillment of existence comes not from grasping for it, but by indirection, as a by-product of self-forgetful and loving devotion to the good.

These, then, are the several levels of unity that bind together the diverse topics of the chapters to follow: first, the curriculum of education; second, the major problems of contemporary civilization; third, the values by which education is seen as a moral enterprise; and fourth, a concept of value as devotion to worth rather than to satisfaction of desire, together with an ideal of democracy as the social expression of basic moral commitment. This is the text upon which everything to follow is commentary. Each chapter discusses an aspect of the one theme that the central purpose of all education—whether in homes, schools, churches, business organizations, community agencies, or the mass media, and whatever the area of learning, whether science, art, health, or international relations—should be the transformation of persons from the life of self-centered desire to that of devoted service of the excellent, and at the same time the creation of a democratic commonwealth established in justice and fraternal regard rather than in expediency.

To make the basic perspective as clear as possible, a few comments about the relation between desire and devotion are needed. *First, it would be a misunderstanding to assume that desire is in itself wrong. The truth is quite the contrary. Most of the ordinary objects of human interest—such as food, companionship, vitality, and security—are good.* The point is that the desire for anything is not a *criterion* or a *measure* of its goodness. That which is really excellent may or may not be wanted. Through good education, however, it is possible to a large extent to help people habitually to want what they should want, thus effecting a happy reinforcement of devotion by desire. But that something is desired, whether intelligently or not, is no indication by itself that it is really valuable.

Thus, *desire as such is not here ignored or condemned.* No grim, joyless, ascetic obedience to duty is advocated. Rather, the way is indicated to the abiding enrichment, fulfillment, and joy of life that follow from abandoning self-will, the quest for success and power, and the demand for autonomy, in favor of dedication to the right and good. With such devotion, satisfaction will usually abound far more than if it is directly sought. But this is not its justification, for true love demands no compensation and is sometimes not so rewarded. *What is desired and what is of worth may often, in fact coincide.* In the long run, loyalty to the good should bring with it rich fulfillment of many of the heart's desires. Pleasure and happiness are commonly associated with the good life; but they are not its inevitable goal or standard.

Augustine once offered this ethical prescription, "Love God and do as you please," by which he meant that a person who is really devoted to the good experiences no conflict between desire and duty, for his wants have been transformed to accord with the supreme object of devotion. Such a person, however, is not necessarily successful or secure in the ordinary society of self-centered people.

Development of the central theme of this book through a variety of separate areas of learning has been guided by four concepts which are usually given somewhat restricted meanings but which prove to be widely applicable to the analysis of the moral enterprise. These concepts are: democracy, economics, science, and religion.

First, democracy is here taken to refer not simply to political organization, but to all aspects of civilized life. For example, the canons of valid scientific knowledge are as much a matter of democratic concern as are the principles of representation in government. Similarly, democratic ideals are as pertinent to the use of the mass media, to appropriate manners, and to health education as they are to the conduct of elections. Democracy has this comprehensive relevance because it has to do with the establishment of *universal* principles of conduct. Democracy is a way of life in which everybody counts, and not only a privileged few. The significance of this way is contained in the detailed setting forth of what it means for everybody to count, in intellectual life, in creative pursuits, in the realm of conscience, and in religion.

Second, economic considerations are important throughout this analysis because they are the source of the idea that values are interests. Economic life is concerned with the production, distribution, acquisition, and use of goods and services that are in limited supply. The economic man is conceived of as one who has wants that he seeks to satisfy as fully as possible, with due consideration for the competing demands of others. This economic outlook has come to dominate all phases of life. Knowledge is considered a commodity to be accumulated and consumed, and intelligence is viewed as a tool for prosecuting vital interests. Taste is a function of sales appeal, work is done for profit, and even play is a means of gaining success. Nature and people are regarded as resources for efficient exploitation, and religion is seen as the ultimate form of life insurance.

Third, the fundamental presupposition of science is taken as a model for the moral enterprise in all its phases. The scientist assumes that there is truth to be progressively discovered, that acknowledgment of truth is a universal obligation, and that knowledge of it is everyone's privilege. It is here assumed that judgments of worth in the esthetic, moral, and religious fields require a similar presupposition of the givenness of an order of value which is to be discovered and universally recognized and honored. Truth is one kind of value, different in quality from esthetic excellence, justice, or holiness, but like them in being part of an objective structure of worth. To be sure, knowledge in the natural sciences has become precise and universally warrantable to a degree not realized in the other realms of value; and this disparity has led many concerned and competent scholars to deny that esthetic, moral, and religious values are anything more than relative and culturally determined preferences, without any basis in a universal and objective order of worth. Despite the evident difficulties in securing agreement on such values, one can take the position that the moral enterprise requires loyalty to values that in their own realms have an authority comparable to the value of truth in scientific inquiry.

The fourth basic concept is religion. In the final chapter it will be shown how the whole range of topics exemplify a religious point of view, provided religion is understood as ultimate devotion and is not restricted to the conventional sectarian sense. Thus, our guiding theme is that the primary aim of education should be conversion from the self-centered striving for advantage to a life of loyal dedication to excellence. This accords with Whitehead's belief that "the essence of education is that it be religious." Perhaps also this book not only may throw light on the fundamental purposes by which education should be directed, but may at the same time suggest the outlines of a relevant and mature faith for modern man—a faith that grows directly out of the daily struggle to make responsible decisions.

Having thus stated the text that governs this book, it may be helpful now to say a few words about context—to indicate some contrasts and kinships with other movements and writers past and present.

It has been said that all philosophy is but a footnote to Plato, who raised all of the major philosophic questions and indicated most of the possible answers. The present work certainly belongs in the Platonic tradition, with its emphasis on the primacy, reality, and transcendence of the good and on the unity of truth, beauty, and goodness within a supreme source of light and love.

More generally, it stands within the "realist" tradition in affirming the objective reality of the orders of truth and other kinds of excellence, as against nominalists and subjectivists who believe that knowledge is essentially a human construct and values are nothing but human preferences. In the manner of the realists, the competence of reason to understand the intelligible structures of the world both as fact and as value is affirmed. This analysis is in line with the view of those who, like the Stoics, conceive of a natural law of moral obligation as well as of physical existence, though not with the position of legalists who suppose that an actual code of law may be an absolute statement of the right.

At many points the influence of John Dewey and other pragmatists will be evident, particularly their belief in democracy as a comprehensive way of life, their confidence in the wide relevance of the scientific spirit and methods, and their commitment to education as a moral enterprise. However, in other respects the position taken in this book differs substantially from that of the pragmatists. They base their philosophy on the concept of man as an intelligent adaptive organism and regard reason as an instrument for solving problems of adjustment to the natural and human environment. They hold that to be moral is to be social, and that the ideal of social life is democracy, in which the fullest possible harmony of interaction is realized. This position is most compatible with what is hereafter designated as the "democracy of desire," in which conduct is conceived of as guided by desire disciplined by reflection on the consequences of various courses of action.

The pragmatists rightly emphasize the intelligent charting of consequences, but such concepts as satisfaction, adjustment, problem solving, growth, and harmonious interaction do not provide a sufficient basis for judgments of worth. These may or may not be good, depending on circumstances. Sometimes frustration, dissatisfaction, and conflict are preferable. The sole criterion in respect to values is what is true, right, and excellent, apart from how satisfactorily personal or group interests are served. The pragmatists hold that man is the measure of truth and goodness, that ultimately something is worthy *because* intelligent human beings want it. The position here taken is rather that man is himself judged and measured by an antecedently conceived goodness, and that it is the proper goal of man to discover and be fashioned after the image of that excellence.

As an account of how human beings actually do behave, pragmatism is reasonably adequate. For the most part, people are more or less intelligent adaptive organisms, and they *do* aim to solve their problems of interactive adjustment. The pragmatists also rightly warn against dogmatism and absolutism, making clear the dynamic nature of human existence, the particular contexts in which judgments of value must be made, and the need for intelligent appraisal of alternatives. Their concern with the processes of rational inquiry and their rejection of easy and premature certainties are entirely in accord with the position set forth in this book. But pragmatists tend to swallow up values in process: they are so determined to banish fixed traditional codes of value and so absorbed with the methods of reconstructing them that the transcendent ground and goal of the moral enterprise are obscured, if not explicitly denied. For the conduct of life and the guidance of learning we need a firm commitment to truth and goodness which men and their processes subserve but do not create.

For educational purposes and for the health of civilization we require a new accent on values that transcend human wants. The various behavioral sciences have performed a valuable service in describing the factors and conditions shaping human conduct. Why do people act as they do? And how can conduct be improved? Harold Lasswell's celebrated *Politics* analyzes human life as a struggle of people to get the most of what there is to get, and the various objects of striving he designates as "values"—that is, what people want. We cannot safely guide education on the basis of a Lasswellian picture of human beings.

We need to be wise enough to know that people do largely live by acquisitive striving, and we should take account of this fact in educational planning, but we should also know the more urgent truth that there is another more authentic human way—the way of loyalty, devotion, and love—in which the urge to get is transmuted into a contrary dedication, to give. The knowledge of this possibility and the acceptance of this goal constitute the major premises for educational policy.

The theme developed here may be regarded as a broader application of the ideas set forth by Tawney in *The Acquisitive Society*. The standards of the marketplace have become dominant in all phases of culture. It is largely taken for granted that success, power, wealth, and position are the goals of living and that education should be organized to serve these purposes. Tawney argued for the subordination of gain to function and of economic life to principles of justice. This parallels the objective of the present work, which is to show the destructive consequences of a desire-dominated philosophy of life and to point the way to a restoration of culture and learning through the reaffirmation of standards of excellence.

The present book may also make a contribution to what Walter Lippmann calls "the public philosophy." Lippmann's view is that there are universal principles, accessible to men of dedicated reason, by which the life of the commonwealth ought to be governed. Democracy is misconceived when it is regarded as the rule of the people, in the sense that the wants of the people are to be carried out as fully as possible. Democracy ought rather to be conceived as a way of approximating the practice of justice by insuring that no individuals or groups arbitrarily and irresponsibly exercise authority over others. The public philosophy is the claim that the objective law of right, written into the nature of things, makes on citizens, as contrasted with the claims that the citizens make on the natural and social reality on which they depend.

The context in which the spirit and intention of the present book are most clearly revealed is that of the religious traditions of mankind. For example, the central teaching of Buddhism is that the misery and frustration of existence are due to attachment and desire, and that release comes from understanding this basic cause of suffering and from taking the necessary measures to become free. The way to emancipation is through renunciation, detachment, and compassion.

This is similar to the thesis that the proper goal of education is conversion from the life of self-serving to the life of devotion.

The same basic idea is found in the contemporary Jewish philosopher, Martin Buber, who contrasts the "I-Thou" with the "I-It" orientation. The former is a truly personal relation manifesting love and reverence. The latter is an external connection established for purposes of manipulation and control. This is the contrast suggested in the succeeding pages. The way of interest or desire is the "I-It" approach to life—the acquisitive, managing, using, consuming attitude. The way of devotion is that of the "I-Thou"—of reverence, appreciation, humility, and service. The central task of education in every field of study is to effect a "turning" (in Buber's phrase) from the life-destroying struggle to get and to hold, toward the life-giving path of reverent devotion.

In a different context, there are similar insights in classical Chinese culture, particularly in Confucianism, with its concern for the right ordering of life in accord with the Will of Heaven. The message of this book is that democratic life should be conceived not as an enterprise of autonomous men, no matter how clever they may be in organizing to pursue their interests, but as a way of realizing the Will of Heaven—that is, of doing the truth and serving the right in which man's proper being and destiny consist. This is another manner of signifying the "public philosophy" earlier mentioned. In every field of endeavor—in scientific inquiry, manners, family life, politics, and all the rest—man is not his own judge and master; he is "under orders," he is answerable to principles of "propriety," he is responsible for the preservation, improvement, and perpetuation of the "traditions of civility." The fulfillment of human existence is thus not in the mastery of life, but in glad obedience to the right.

More than from any other source, the position here set forth derives from the Christian tradition. In its theoretical basis much has been drawn from Paul Tillich. One guiding principle is what Tillich calls "theonomy," which means a situation where the divine ground of being shines through the finite conditions of historical existence and where man sees the orders of truth and right as the law of his own being. This is the meaning of the life of reverent devotion, as opposed to the self-sufficient finitude of autonomous man and to servile subjection in what Tillich calls "heteronomy," which may be interpreted as the essence of undemocratic authoritarianism.

If a single text for the present work were to be selected, it would be: "Whoever would save his life will lose it, and whoever loses his life for my sake and the gospel's will save it." The striving for success, security, and influence may be regarded as the losing attempt to save life—an attempt in which contemporary civilization, with its promise of material abundance and of power to control the conditions of existence, is deeply involved. This anxious and strenuous effort is a consequence of the widespread doubt or denial of any worthy object of loyalty. It is to the establishment of faith in the reality of infinite goodness made manifest in the conditions of finite existence that the work at hand is directed. It aims to redirect education away from grasping after the life that is but the prelude to death, to self-forgetful dedication to goodness itself, through which alone true and enduring life comes.

The theme, again, relates to two ways of love. One is the love that springs from the desire to possess: "the lust of the flesh and the lust of the eyes and the pride of life." The other is the love that leads to loyalty and sacrifice: "greater love has no man than this, that a man lay down his life for his friends." The one is concupiscence in all its manifestations. The other is charity—the responsible, concerned love which issues in caring and sharing. The objective of all learning should be the transformation of personality from one centered in acquisitive love to one grounded in self-forgetful love of righteousness.

Finally, the chapters to follow do not so much argue a case conclusively as bear witness to a fundamental outlook and orientation toward culture and education. Reasons are given for the positions taken, and it is hoped that they are good and convincing. But it is doubtful that anybody will be persuaded solely by the logic of the argument. It is a spirit and a way of viewing things that is more likely to be communicated. Every author is in search of an audience whose vision he may help to clarify and confirm.

Perhaps more can be done, however, than to bear witness to a viewpoint. A further objective is to encourage discussion of the purposes that should guide contemporary education. This is a discussion into which all should enter, whatever their philosophical or religious po-

sitions. This book may hopefully stimulate even those who differ
sharply from its position to greater concern for the moral issues in
teaching and learning.

In treating so wide a range of problems as appear in this study,
adequate documentation and scholarly support of the statements
made would require erudition that the author cannot claim. Specialists
in every one of the fields considered can doubtless find many faults
with what is said—faults that could have been avoided had each field
been treated by an expert. The present overview is nevertheless offered, with all its shortcomings, as an illustration of the kind of integration that every person must attempt in his own way. Everybody
must come to terms in some fashion with the whole sweep of human
concerns. Every citizen, every parent, every teacher and administrator
must make decisions about what shall be taught in homes, schools,
churches, industry, and community. Everyone must somehow put together his convictions about such matters as knowledge, the mass
media, art, manners, work, play, nature, health, sex, class, race, economics, politics, international relations, and religion into a pattern
for the formation of character through the curriculum.

This is, then, an essay in synthesis. It is an illustration and an
invitation to integral thinking about education. It is a call to each
reader to new perspectives on the curriculum, to the end that the
high calling of education in democracy may be better served.

Every human being needs goals and principles by which to direct his life and shape his conduct. To be a person in any satisfactory sense is to have a characteristic way of life—a system of ideals and values that one has adopted as his own or to which he has declared his allegiance. Not only the quality of life, but also its intensity, creativeness, and persistence are dependent upon the possession of definite aims. When such principles are lacking, personal existence loses its zest and meaning, life seems stale and unprofitable, and personality decays for want of an integrating objective.

The need for a clear set of values holds for societies as well as for individuals. Social groups have ideals and regulations that comprise their reason for existence and their basis for effective activity. Productivity and progress by the group require commonly accepted aims. Societies, like individuals, deteriorate when the characteristic patterns of group life are no longer understood or accepted. When the binding power of shared goals is dissolved, harmony and cooperation give way to discord and antagonism. Corporate life loses its vigor and appeal, traditional symbols are emptied of their meaning, and confusion and anxiety arrest social advance and condemn the culture to stagnation and decay.

The need for goals in individual and social life sets a clear and exacting task for education. It is through education, not only in schools but also in homes and in other institutions and by a variety of agencies, that individual character is formed and social patterns are propagated. The most important product of education is a constructive, consistent, and compelling system of values around which personal and social life may be organized. Unless teaching and learning provide such a focus, all the particular knowledge and skills acquired are worse than useless. An "educated" person whose information and ability are directed to no personally appropriated worthy ends is a menace to himself and to society. A highly sophisticated society educated to no coherent way of life is likewise by its very learning made the more prone to disease and degeneration.

Parents, teachers, writers, ministers, and others responsible for education are, of course, not solely accountable for individual and social values. These people inevitably reflect the influence of large cultural and social forces beyond their power to control. Compelling purposes cannot be created at will by concerned individuals. Guiding ideals for life for the most part grow out of complex cultural conditions which are not deliberately produced. Nevertheless, those who teach do exert an influence on those who learn, and often the effect is profound enough to counteract other, more impressive forces. Furthermore, in times of prevailing doubt and confusion, even a few voices speaking with clarity and authority can contribute measurably to the restoration of purpose.

Regardless of what other forces may limit the success of their efforts, it remains true that the teaching of values is a fundamental obligation of educators. All special knowledge and skill derive meaning and justification from the purposes that persons and societies should seek to promote. Education is not a neutral enterprise. It is permeated with convictions about what is important to know and to become. Educators have unparalleled opportunities for the promotion of desirable personal and corporate objectives which will heighten the significance of life and fortify the will to progress.

The essence of the curriculum—whether considered formally in schools or informally in other agencies of education—consists not of the objective lessons to be learned and courses to be passed, but of the scheme of values, ideals, or life goals which are mediated through the materials of instruction. The really significant outcome of education is the set of governing commitments, the aims for living, that the learner develops. The various subjects of study are simply means for the communication and the appropriation of these values.

Never before in human history have the requirements of education been so exacting as today. This is clearly evident in view of the staggering volume of new knowledge and technique which is being continually produced and which must be put to use in the management of the indescribably complex mechanism of modern civilization. Less generally recognized is the still deeper crisis in values. The rapid pace of change in what we know and can do has caused pervasive unsettlement of traditional values. The introduction of wholly new modes of living as a result of invention has greatly widened the range of available choices and thrown into question the superiority of long-established ways.

Our greatest danger is not the avalanche of novelties with which the industrial age presents us, but the loss of direction that exclusive preoccupation with the problems and pleasures of innovation entails. The fresh opportunities presented by a world made over through science do not bear with them instructions for their proper employment. Enlarged potentialities magnify rather than diminish the responsibility for making wise decisions among possibilities and intensify the difficulties of such choices.

It is particularly important that the work of education shall not be consumed with the effort to deal with the complexities and superabundance of modern cultural products. Some kind of radical simplification is essential if mankind is not to be smothered by the endlessly multiplying mass of things to be known and done. Expansion of educational opportunities cannot begin to solve the problem. Nor can specialization, which involves a relinquishment of general human responsibility for the sake of mastery in a limited field.

The answer lies in focusing education upon values. Worthy purposes, goals, meanings—these are what need to be acquired by every person. These are the foundation of every good society. If education is designed with regard to these objectives, the particular tasks to be accomplished will fall into perspective. Criteria will be available for distinguishing essential from nonessential subjects of study and for wisely apportioning available resources of time and talent.

Today we are lacking in sustaining purpose; many individuals are beset by a gnawing sense of meaninglessness. This prevailing lostness is reflected in the confusions and contradictions of organized society. With all our knowledge, our troubles multiply, and we see no way through the tangle of domestic and international problems. Despite having attained the highest "standard of living" in the history of the world (measured by production and consumption of goods), Americans have not found the secret of happiness. Having conquered the wilderness and built a nation unparalleled in power and wealth, we seem to have lost our clear vision of a future worthy of sacrifice and struggle. We only fear the loss of what we have, as ambitious peoples everywhere importunately clamor for a larger share in the riches of the earth.

The malady of meaninglessness is not peculiar to America. It is the predicament of modern man everywhere. It is the sign of a profound spiritual sickness brought on by the wholesale dislocation of traditional values, the development of mass society, and the spectacular increase in available material power. The special position of Americans in this situation is that we have succeeded so well in the game of acquisition that we are now forced to face our spiritual sickness openly and directly. Many other peoples "on the way up" are temporarily finding ample direction and purpose for life in their effort to win prestige, power, and possessions. The world-wide rise of nationalism is the dramatic evidence of this fact. The people of the nations that have newly won independence from imperial control are exhilarated by the prospect of a brighter future in the political firmament, and peoples whose resources have long been exploited for the enrichment of others now see their own prospects for material improvement happier than ever before. For such people there is no present problem of motivation or direction. Their goals are simple, concrete, and compelling.

Most impressive of all on the contemporary world scene is the growth of the communist movement as a system of meaning and value. Communism is not unrelated to nationalism, as the development of great communist nations such as the U.S.S.R. and China well demonstrates. Nevertheless, the system of ideals and principles upon which communism is founded far transcends the rather simple motives of national ambition. Communism is presented to mankind as a total way of life, complete with ideological justification. As such, it promises to all who accept it a solution to the problem of meaning and provides definite goals by which to live.

Communism, like nationalism, actually affords only a temporary escape from the basic spiritual predicament. Its proponents claim more for it, advancing it as a complete and final answer to human problems. In fact, communism is based on an untrue conception of human nature and of values. Its present success is due to the fact that the collective effort and strong centralized authority associated with it are producing dramatic improvements in the economic, political, and military position of nations hitherto impeded by traditional systems unsuited to industrial civilization. As long as this tangible progress in modernization continues, sufficient goals for living are provided. When these immediate objectives—of affluence and power —are reached (and at the present rate of progress, barring total war, this time is not far off), the communist peoples will feel, even if they may not express, the emptiness of their system as a framework of meaning for life, and they, too, will experience the need for direction and motives for conduct.

The appeal of the communist movement today is at root the same as that of the ill-fated fascist movements of the 1930's and 1940's in Germany, Italy, and Japan. When individuals are united in a totally controlled drive for national power, they are proud to belong to a successful organization. They gain satisfaction from being on a winning team. The collective effort supplies the larger system of reference by which individual purpose and progress are measured. The price exacted for these benefits is the loss of personal freedom.

That millions of people have deliberately or by default preferred the ordered life of the police state to the hazardous blessings of liberty is striking evidence of the vacuum of meaninglessness into which modernity has plunged mankind. Freedom without direction and purpose is an insupportable burden, from which even the tyranny of a successful state is a welcome escape.

Nationalism, communism, and fascism are not the only ways in which men attempt to escape from freedom and to regain security and purpose in living. They do it in every appeal to arbitrary authority. The giant corporations or professional organizations to which individuals give allegiance and with which they identify their lives supply a temporary pattern of meaning. The resurgence of religious orthodoxy and the revival of traditional religious supernaturalism and institutionalism are further evidences of the struggle for reassurance in an age of disintegrated values. Many people try to solve this basic problem by simply condemning the typical products of the scientific age and by reasserting the values of the past—that is, by a resolute renunciation of modernity in favor of the "classical" tradition.

In all of these approaches to the recovery of purpose, education has played a pivotal role. The nationalism of many of the newly independent states can be traced directly to the leadership of a few men who have had the benefits of extensive education. The possibility of technical development by such nations depends upon the rapid expansion of educational opportunities to produce the necessary skilled workers. Political stability and military security also presuppose well-developed provisions for education directed to the national interest. Education was a key factor in the growth in power of the fascist states, with their assiduous cultivation of state-controlled youth movements, ideological reshaping of the school curriculums, and their hostility to the traditional teaching of home and church. The communists are even more thoroughgoing in their employment of education for the purposes of revolutionary socialization. Not only is the program of the school wholly designed to fulfill the aims of communism, but newspapers, radio and television, advertising, book publishing, and even the arts are marshaled by the central government as tools in a comprehensive and continuous program of indoctrination.

Similarly, though perhaps less impressively, education is the key to every other form of social movement with a determinate set of guiding principles. In the advancing of business and professional interests, continuing institution-oriented education programs make an important contribution to the creation and maintenance of "organization men." The renewed emphasis on religious orthodoxy has been associated with a vigorous upsurge in theological education, in the growth of church-controlled schools, and in concern for religion in public education. Finally, the New Conservatives make their most vigorous attack on modern education and seek above all, through the restoration of traditional learning to the schools, to secure the values they believe essential to civilized existence.

Thus, individuals and societies need a system of values by which to live; the nature and pace of modern cultural transformations have cut men adrift from the security of established ideals. Men have sought in a variety of ways—through surrender to central authority or retreat to the past—to recover meanings and motives, and in all of these conditions and developments education is centrally implicated.

We now move to the issue toward which this analysis points. Are there discernible principles and ideals which can supply modern man's needs for personal and corporate energy and guidance, without surrender to arbitrary authority or retreat into the past?

This book affirms that the principles of democracy, rightly understood, provide an answer to modern man's predicament. Democratic ideals, the finest flowering of two and a half millenniums of Western civilization, have provided the vision and the wisdom necessary to build enduring commonwealths established in liberty, justice, and love. The American Experiment has been a great adventure in democracy. The dominant note of our aspiration as a people, the central direction of our efforts, the authentic measure of our success, has been the democratic faith. The United States is, of course, not the only nation with this heritage. Other nations have in certain respects achieved a higher perfection of democratic aims and practices than have Americans. However, our country has the special distinction of having been founded on democratic principles and having maintained unbroken allegiance to them for nearly two centuries.

In the growth of democracy both in the United States and elsewhere education has been of great importance. The development of universal free public education, beginning at the elementary levels and rising within recent years to the college and university levels, has been a direct consequence of the democratic impulse. Methods of teaching, courses of study, and administrative procedures in the schools have been fashioned in the light of the democratic vision. In democracy American parents and teachers have found significant goals for the guidance of individual conduct and social development.

Yet today there seems to be evidence that democracy has lost some of its power to inspire and direct. Even when democratic ideals are still affirmed, they often appear to be dull platitudes rather than energizing aspirations. Democracy does not always generate the enthusiasm that nationalism, communism, and the other collectivist and authoritarian gospels produce. Americans and other democratic peoples are beset by doubts and uncertainties. Instead of the progressive spread of democracy throughout the earth, they see antagonistic systems on the march while they seek anxiously to save themselves from outer conquest and inner disintegration. Amid unprecedented prosperity and power, many Americans and other free people are haunted by feelings of emptiness and forebodings of unavoidable defeat.

Is democracy a failure? Is it now evident that democracy is not truly adequate to the predicament of modern man? Does democratic education have a future, or must we find other patterns by which to direct the course of learning? Are there actually resources of abiding worth in the democratic way, or must we now discover post-democratic standards for our personal and corporate life?

The answer to these questions depends upon what is meant by "democracy." Two contrasting types of democracy need to be distinguished. In this contrast may lie a clue to the fate of democracy in the modern world.

The first kind of democracy is founded on the principle of organizing life to insure maximum satisfaction of human interests or claims. According to this conception, the highest good is independence, or autonomy. Human beings are regarded as continually in pursuit of happiness, and the goal of this democracy is to help people as far as possible get what they want. Thus, the determining authority in human affairs is the desire of the people; they are not to be governed by anything or anyone beyond themselves. Man and man alone is the proper measure of all things. Each individual is expected to seek his own welfare and to cooperate with others in forms of social organization that will enable everyone to gain what he desires without interfering with the corresponding pursuits of others, and also to increase his own and others' satisfactions by such joint efforts. This type of democracy is here referred to as the *democracy of desire*, since the image of human nature upon which it is based is that of an intelligent organism striving single-mindedly to fulfill its desires.

Under the democracy of desire, education is governed by the twin principles of self-realization and social accommodation. Teaching should be directed toward helping the learner to gain maximum satisfaction of his interests, with due regard for the demands of others. Skills of every kind, particularly those of trained intelligence, are to be acquired as tools for the more efficient acquisition of what is desired. Education also serves to transform and refine desires, so that one does not simply seek immediate gratification of animal hungers, but gains the ability to postpone present satisfactions for the sake of more lasting benefits and to enjoy the "higher" pleasures as well as ordinary bodily delights.

According to this first view, values are neither more nor less than what people want. The value system of a person is the set of desires that govern his conduct, and the values of society are the will and preferences of the people as expressed in customs and through the activities of government. The "good" and the "right" are simply values arrived at through the refinement of desire by critical intelligence. In other words, the desirable is what is desired by one who takes account of circumstances and consequences. The purpose of such critical appraisal is to avoid frustrations and disappointments due to unreasonable expectations and to open up new and richer fields for want-satisfaction. Thus, the general aims of education are to intensify and extend human desires through the charting of possibilities for enjoyment, and to supply the tools necessary for the effective exploitation of these possibilities.

The democracy of desire is the dominant conception of democracy today. As we shall see in later chapters, this is the prevalent view in every sphere of life—in scholarship, in the arts, in work and play, in politics, economics, and international affairs, and even in religion. It is assumed that the gift of democracy is the emancipation of man from all higher powers, so that he may at last build according to his heart's desire the world of which he is now the master, thanks to science and invention. This form of democracy is man-centered. Its emphasis is on acquisition, on efficient production for large-scale consumption. The good society is regarded as one of material affluence, where a wide range of desires are powerfully stimulated and abundantly satisfied.

The other type of democracy centers around devotion or loyalty to the good, the right, the true, the excellent. It is referred to as *the democracy of worth.* Devotion is different from desire. It is primarily other-regarding rather than self-interested. It invites sacrifice and loyalty instead of conferring gratification. It is concerned with giving instead of getting. One honors and respects things of value instead of using and consuming them.

The watchword of the democracy of worth is responsibility, not autonomy. Its objective is not to maximize satisfactions but to establish and increase what is excellent. Universality and equality in the democracy of worth refer not to privileges but to obligations and opportunities to serve the right. In this view, the democratic way is a means, not for securing to every person as much as possible of what he wants, but for minimizing the injustices caused by self-centeredness.

If the American way of life is to be worthy of survival, and if democratic societies are to offer any lasting solution to the problems of men, the solution lies with the democracy of worth. We should not chart our course and determine our destiny primarily by reference to what people want, whether intelligently or not. The history of mankind and the facts of personal experience suggest that the health and fulfillment of life spring from release from self-centeredness in loyalty to the good. Authentic democracy is the means of making such commitment most likely.

Under the democracy of worth, education is directed toward the learning of what is excellent. In such democratic education the learner's desires are relevant only insofar as they reveal the nature and extent of the transmutation that must be effected through teaching and learning. The cardinal principle of teaching is, then, to subordinate considerations of learner interest and satisfaction to those of transcendent qualitative worth. This does not mean that the wants and inclinations of the learner should be ignored, but only that they should never become the criterion of value.

Education in a democracy of worth is opposed to much so-called democratic education of the progressive, child-centered variety. In the latter, desires have been nourished and fed, and when they have conflicted with the interests of others, they have been redirected by intelligence—that is, socialized—so that the sum total of want-satisfaction might be increased. When desires are frustrated, measures are taken to remove the obstacles, or, if this is impossible, the unsatisfied wants are replaced by ones that can more surely be fulfilled. Teachers and parents have been cautioned against repression and warned of its dire consequences for the emotional health of the young. In short, such education has been directed to the intensification, elaboration, and harmonization of desire. Instead of this, education should be dedicated to the civilizing function of exchanging natural wants for human loyalties.

Although the self-regarding character of desire is opposite in direction to the other-regarding character of devotion, the two are subtly interlinked. *Devotion to what is good does not necessarily negate pleasures and satisfactions; in fact, it often heightens them.* Thus, eating for health and for the loving celebration of life usually does not diminish enjoyment, but generally intensifies it. The point is that these subjective rewards are by-products of the activity of eating, and not its main objective. While in some cases the dedicated life, instead of yielding dividends in pleasure, requires pain and sacrifice, which the truly devoted person willingly suffers, love and loyalty generally impart to life an incomparable sweetness and zest, far transcending the pleasures of self-centered satisfaction.

In the democracy of worth, education follows a value principle and not a principle of want-satisfaction. Furthermore, a value is defined not as what yields pleasure, either immediately or in the long run, but as what evokes continuing self-transcending dedication. Only such a way of life can supply the directives and energies for regenerating and advancing civilization, the meanings required for healthy life individually and in association, and adequate foundations for teaching and learning.

The basic assumption of the democracy of worth is that the values that emerge in human experience are not in the last analysis determinations of human will, but discoveries of antecedent possibilities. This assumption does not require any belief in "absolutes" in the ordinary sense of known values that are independent of time and circumstance. The excellences toward which mankind gropes are manifest in a great variety of forms. What is true, right, or desirable is not determinable in the abstract, but only within each particular situation. Generalizations are, of course, possible, but can never capture the full truth or right in any one case. This complexity of the evaluation situation does not negate the basic assumption that values are discovered and not man-made. They may be made in the sense that by human activity conditions are created in which the values become manifest. But the experienced quality, the "being of worth," is not itself a matter of human decision, for the essence of value, as distinguished from desire, is precisely the power of evoking devotion and of transforming persons in conformity with its own pattern.

In the democracy of worth it is further presupposed that these discovered excellences are *universal,* not in the sense of being abstract generalizations, but in that of being of relevance and appealing concern to all human beings. Universal values are those that are potentially capable of eliciting every person's loyalty. Obviously desire, which (as we are using the term) is self-interested, cannot claim universality, for private wants do not take account of others, except as others limit the acquisition of what is desired. Only values that can reconcile the forces of egocentrism (individual or collective) by their power to attract allegiance are suitable ideals for a commonwealth for all mankind.

The use of scientific methods and of "democratic group process" does not guarantee freedom, when human autonomy is the governing principle, for these techniques only cover the impulse of some men to manage others and thus make the resulting subjugation of mankind more rapid and more irremediable. The true basis for democratic freedom is devotion to excellence. Through loyalty to what is true and right, without regard to individual and group wants or calculated advantages, release is gained from both external compulsion and the more insidious tyranny of desire. Devotion in its essence is a free, uncoerced self-giving, the fruit of which is the enrichment of personality, the flowering of individuality, and the advancement of the enlarged community.

The present work is not intended as a definitive statement of the values toward which the democracy of worth should be directed. Truth and rightness are forever beyond full and final formulation or realization. Every claim to universal perfection turns out to be tainted with self-interest. Yet we cannot escape the necessity for specific decisions about what is worthy of devotion. The values suggested in what follows are offered in illustration of the kind of objective that might follow from commitment to excellence. The really crucial task is not recommending any given set of values, but establishing the fundamental principle that there are values worthy of our devotion and suggesting ways of developing personal and social disciplines based on that principle.

Four pivotal values to be developed in a democracy of worth are here proposed. These are: *intelligence, creativity, conscience,* and *reverence.* Intelligence will be analyzed first with respect to intellectual competence in general and then with particular concern for the problem of truth in the mass media of communication. The ideals of creativity will be discussed in relation to esthetic standards, manners, work, and recreation. Conscience will be treated in relation to problems of conservation, health, sex and family life, social class, race, economics, politics, and international affairs. Finally, reverence will be set forth as the value that encompasses and undergirds all the rest, as the key to the principle of devotion upon which the democracy of worth rests.

PART 2 * INTELLIGENCE

There are at least four reasons why intellectual life supports democratic ideals. First, intellect is a universal human property; all human beings have the power of reason. It is this power that sets mankind off into a separate species, *homo sapiens*. No individual or class of people can claim a special position by virtue of a rational capacity that others totally lack. No human beings can be excluded from the family of man because they have no intelligence, for rationality is the mark of our common humanity.

To be sure, intellectual abilities differ greatly from one person to another. The range of capabilities is impressive, reaching from the genius of an Einstein or a Leonardo to the near-vegetative mentality of the feebleminded. Such obvious differences make it evident from the outset that if intelligence is to have any place in democracy, it cannot be on the basis of intellectual equality. Particular powers of mind are not universal. The ability to compose great music or to invent useful new machines is a rare endowment. What *is* universal in mankind is the potentiality of engaging in the characteristic activities of mind—such as remembering, imagining, conceptualizing, and purposing—regardless of the rate or quality of the actual intellectual performance.

Second, intellectual life is crucial to democracy because it is the source of the human community. The power of reason is developed in and through communication. A person thinks only insofar as he learns to employ the meaning-bearing symbols of language, which arise in social intercourse. Man is not defined only as the reasoning animal:

he is also the talking animal, and this is not a mere coincidence; it is due to the intimate connection between thinking and speaking.

Communication is important for any society in which all the people are to have a share in the control of the common life. Participation in a democratic commonwealth depends upon the ability of every person to make his intentions known to others and to take account of the well-being of others. In short, there can be no democracy without common knowledge, and common knowledge is founded upon the universal human power of reason manifest in speech.

In the third place, intelligence is the source of human freedom. Decision among different possibilities presupposes their imaginative envisagement and evaluation. The very idea of "possibilities" rests upon the assumption of a conceptual domain or dimension that in some sense transcends the realm of realized fact. Furthermore, the process of judging is a distinctively intellectual function, for it involves a kind of standing outside of both actualities and possibilities in order to take their measure. When the people in a society are denied freedom, they lack the privilege of guiding their lives by intelligent choice among possibilities; since decisions are made for them, reason is reduced to the subordinate role of directing activity along prescribed lines. On the other hand, democracy advances when reason ventures beyond the bounds set by arbitrary authority and proposes different possibilities for consideration and decision.

Fourth, intelligence is the foundation of individuality, which is another central ideal of democracy. It is by virtue of mentality that the significant differences between persons are effected. Having a self or being a self is a consequence of intellect, for a self is reflective in essence: it has the distinctive power of being aware of its own being. Only by virtue of human mentality does a person become more than an object, a thing. He is a unique *somebody*, like every other person in having the power of thought, but different from any other person in the singularity of personal identity. This is the soul of democracy —this combination of universality and individuality—and the life that animates it is intelligence. Reason not only unites all mankind into one intelligent species but also negates that undifferentiated sameness of interchangeable human units which—often parading in the guise of a "people's democracy"—constitutes a denial of true democracy.

Democratic education is founded upon the nurture of intelligence.

Everyone needs education to make good his membership in the common humanity, to participate in the responsible conduct of corporate life (through the power of communication), to exercise wisely the obligations and privileges of choice, and to achieve identity as a person. In the democratic commonwealth, therefore, education should be universal, socially oriented, aimed at the development of mature judgment, and cognizant of individual differences.

For the contemporary human situation, the most serious issues go beyond these general democratic principles. The critical problems concern the proper function of intelligence and the appropriate object of rational activity. It is here that the contrast between the democracy of desire and the democracy of worth becomes evident.

In the life of reason the decision in favor of worth rather than desire takes the form of a *commitment to truth*. The principle of devotion to truth, whether or not anyone's interests are served by it, is the cardinal presupposition of intellectual activity. Truth is not something that is fashioned in response to human wants. It is not created, but discovered. Neither individuals nor groups can will the truth into being, for truth is what is so, whether or not anyone wills it. Truth is not determined by popular assent. Hence the notions of popular sovereignty, of human autonomy, of the will of the people as the ultimate authority—all of these ideas cherished by exponents of the democracy of desire—are alien to the concept of truth. Even complete consensus does not determine truth, for it is implicit in the idea of truth that any persons or all persons may be in error. The truth is not something that conforms to mankind, but that mankind is obliged to acknowledge and respect.

This priority and givenness of truth are often summed up in the concept of *objectivity*. Truth is not what anyone subjectively wishes or determines, but what objectively is. Right thinking is said to be objective rather than based on personal desires or preferences. However, the idea of objectivity must be used with caution. While truth is not made by persons, neither is it wholly independent of them. The forms of knowledge are necessarily conditioned by the structure of the human apparatus of perception and cognition. All human knowledge arises from a relationship between intelligent creatures and the world of intelligible objects. Therefore, knowledge is never purely objective, nor purely subjective, but a product of object-subject relationships.

In calling attention to the human components in knowledge, pragmatists and other critics of naive realism have performed a valuable service. They have convincingly shown that knowledge is not an absolute representation of the objective world, but that it is relative to the particular conditions of observation and conventions of language. The content of human knowledge is therefore to some extent subject to human interests and determinations. But it does not follow that truth is man-made. Within any particular humanly chosen context of observation and discourse, the outcome of inquiry is not subject to human volition, but is a revelation of fact. This is what is meant by the truth, which everyone is obliged to acknowledge and which is not subject to the will of any person or of all the people, but to which all are subject.

Thus, the relativistic critics of simple objectivism and absolutism in knowledge do not by any means establish complete human autonomy and sovereignty in the intellectual sphere, nor do they alter the priority and authority of truth. Their analysis serves to show that man himself is an essential ingredient in the truth. Knowledge is hypothetical and conditional rather than absolute, in the sense that any true statement is an assertion about what is the case under certain specified circumstances of observing, experimenting, and language usage. Instead of negating the idea of truth, these insights enrich it. They refute only the pretensions of those who prematurely claim possession of complete and infallible knowledge.

The democratic nature of the intellectual life is evident in the universality of truth. Universality is not intended here in the absolutist sense—as independence of all conditions—but rather as confirmability by any and all persons. Truth is in principle public, not private, property. Knowledge is not to be accessible only to a favored few; it is open to everyone. Yet care is necessary in interpreting this public character of knowledge. There are many facts that relatively few people understand, and much knowledge that most people will never comprehend. No simple egalitarian rule applies in matters of knowledge. If truth were limited to what everyone knows, there would be no truth at all, and if it were circumscribed within the domain of "common knowledge" or "public information," the depth and scope of truth would be disappointing indeed. The great ideas, through which civilization is lifted to new levels, are grasped by comparatively few people. High intellectual attainment is the achievement of only a small proportion of people.

Does a realistic appraisal then force us to abandon intellectual democracy in favor of aristocracy? Not at all, provided we affirm the democracy of worth. For the universality of truth means only that knowledge is no respecter of persons, that anyone who will meet the necessary conditions and undertake the necessary disciplines may test facts to see if they are actually as represented. In practice few people have the patience or the ability to undertake the tests required to confirm any but the most ordinary and simple claims to knowledge. The wish and the will to know are not sufficient to establish truth. Knowledge is not subject to desire or to demand. Anyone who would understand must take upon himself the yoke of truth, acknowledging its worth and devoting himself to the disciplines requisite to the mastery of truth.

For example, knowledge of the grammar and syntax of the obscure and long-extinct Akkadian language is certainly not public in the sense of being common knowledge. But it is nonetheless in principle public, in that anyone may study the language and investigate the evidence for assertions made about it. The Einstein formula "$E = mc^2$" is more generally "known," but it is not really understood thoroughly by most people. It is confirmable only by the few trained investigators who have the theoretical insight and experimental skill required by modern physical science.

Intellectual democracy does not mean that everyone is entitled to his own opinion and that opinions are equally valid. Nor does it hold to the principle of equal hospitality to all beliefs. The only equality is that of obligation to the truth. The demand for public confirmability is made in the name of that requirement. Esoteric knowledge, guarded from public scrutiny, is subject to distortion arising from personal bias and private interest. Openness to investigation of truth claims is essential to counteract the tendency to utilize the powers of reason for private purposes.

In the democracy of worth, intellectual authority is not eliminated, as extreme egalitarians would have it. Nor does the authority reside in the people, but only in the truth itself. In such a democracy, experts—men of high learning and unusual intellectual skill—play an important part. They are not privileged persons, exercising authority autonomously over less gifted people. Nor, on the other hand, are they merely servants of the people, using their knowledge to fulfill the purposes of the majority. They are properly custodians and trustees of the truth as always becoming revealed, and representatives of the people in the dedicated pursuit of knowledge.

This picture of intellectual democracy suggests the intimate connection between democracy and science. A fundamental tenet of modern scientific investigation is the public nature of valid knowledge. In the advance of enlightenment the tyranny of untestable traditional authority was thrown off, and the unwarranted pretensions of private revelations were brought to light. Superstitious beliefs, tenaciously held because they were incapable of verification, were widely abandoned in favor of more reasonable convictions. By insisting on public confirmability, the scientific movement to a considerable extent has freed mankind from the burdens and confusions caused by self-proclaimed authorities and seers. At the same time it has demonstrated the unparalleled truth-revealing power of inquiry which is in the public domain and in which everyone with the requisite ability and concern cooperates in the common cause of the advancement of understanding. In such an enterprise persons with special gifts make their special contributions to the knowledge that belongs to everyone.

The implications of the foregoing analysis for democratic education are far-reaching. First, democracy is inconsistent with the exclusive, aristocratic type of education, in which intellectual accomplishments are reserved for a privileged class of "gentlemen." Such education belongs only in a slave society, where learning is a mark of freedom from the burdens of manual labor. Second, the democracy of worth also excludes the opposite extreme—education designed primarily for the pursuit of success and satisfaction through knowledge. Both the aristocratic and the utilitarian forms of education subordinate knowledge to human wants—of a class, of individuals, or of a whole society. Instead, democratic education should foster concern and respect for the truth.

In the truly democratic school or home it is not assumed that the ideas of everyone are equally valuable, nor is it assumed that what is so is determined by voting or "group process." Nor is the parent or teacher regarded as the ultimate source of authority. Everyone stands under the same authority, that of truth, and everyone is both responsible to it and welcome to make it his own. Since truth is for each and every person, it should be the goal of education to teach every person to appropriate knowledge, not in order to grasp it for his private purposes but to make it really his own. In democratic education, knowledge should, therefore, as far as possible be gained first-hand rather than taken on the word of someone else. Hence the importance of direct experience in contrast to purely verbal instruction. Obviously much, if not most, knowledge cannot be acquired through immediate personal experience, but must be mediated through language.

This restriction on direct knowledge makes it all the more imperative that the learner secure a thorough grounding in the ways of inquiry, so that he understands how he should go about testing the truth of what must be acquired at second-hand because of limitations of time and resources. It is far more important to know well the methods of investigating the truth of alleged facts than simply to accumulate information, for it is solely by having this ability to verify, or to comprehend the process of verification, that a person really understands the meaning of any information and thus makes it his own. Instruction centered about the *methods* of inquiry, rather than about its *products*, is the basis for education that fulfills the democratic ideal of the universality of truth.

For all who teach, the public character of knowledge entails a further responsibility—namely, *the will to communicate* what is known. It is not enough that knowledge be confirmable by anyone with the requisite ability and training. The growth of a democratic community of shared meanings depends upon a sustained effort to enlarge the company of those who understand. In a democracy there is a clear duty for novices in the mysteries of knowledge to take the initiative in bringing still others within the fold. They should not have to be urged or persuaded to yield up their secrets, but should freely, gladly, and continually serve as missioners of the truth they discern.

This will to communicate has at least four implications. First, skilled professional thinkers—scholars, scientists, learned men in all fields—have an obligation to render their knowledge in the most intelligible possible form; they should not glory in obscurity. Specialists who seek to secure special power and prestige for themselves and to protect their group from possible competition and criticism, tend to create their own secret societies which are not open to the people at large. The approved method of insuring this exclusiveness is to develop special techniques and vocabularies that outsiders cannot understand. While the necessity for technical methods and languages cannot be denied, this is no warrant for calculated obscurity. Intellectual democracy requires no leveling of knowledge for effortless popular consumption. It does demand of those with great insight the true teacher's sense of mission—to impart that insight to others.

Second, in the division of labor in a complex civilized society this diffusion of insight requires not only the devotion of the key men of learning to the common good, but also the development of a corps of interpreters, whose special skill lies in translating the knowledge of the specialists into more commonly understood thought forms. These interpreters must work in close cooperation with the specialists and must themselves have a high degree of technical competence in the fields they intend to mediate to the wider public. While the frontier thinkers in a democracy should possess the spirit of the teacher, the interpreters are by the nature of their work wholly concerned with teaching. Often they are not specifically designated as teachers, since they may function best as writers or lecturers and they may not serve in any of the regular institutions of formal education. They are nonetheless educators by vocation, and they are essential to the democratization of learning through the widespread mediation of intellectual values and the evocation of popular loyalty to truth. They also provide excellent models and resources for parents, schoolteachers, and others engaged in the more formal work of instruction.

Third, the will to communicate involves serious concern for the teaching of language. Communication takes place through meaning-bearing symbols, which are the foundation for shared cultural life. The most important phase of the curriculum is the provision for the mastery of these symbolic systems. No other skill is so crucial for the maturing child as the ability to use language easily, accurately, and forcefully, for it is this power that opens up to him the boundless riches of the cultural inheritance and is the key also to mutually significant associations with other people.

Fourth, concern for communication should lead teachers to emphasize the process of critical analysis. The purpose of intellectual criticism is to discern meanings and to make symbolic usage more effective as an instrument for imparting meanings to others. Analysis can be employed, and often is employed, to denigrate what others have said, but this is ordinarily not its proper purpose, which should be the improvement of understanding. When analysis is central in education, the student is expected always to interrogate what he reads or hears, to make certain through the exploration of related ideas that he really understands what is meant. He is not expected merely to accept and store knowledge received from his teachers. Everything must be tested so that, as a proud citizen in the democracy of inquiry, he may recognize and hold fast to that which is true.

Most of what has been said above about the primacy of truth and the public character of knowledge may appear to negate the democratic ideals of freedom and individuality. It is a fact that those who insist most on truth often believe they are in possession of it and all who differ from them are in error. Champions of the truth have frequently engaged in acts of tyranny and oppression in the name of truth. The democratic concern for freedom forbids any such perversion of this ideal. Democratic truth is the object of free and glad allegiance. It wins solely by persuasion and never by coercion. To be free is not to believe anything one wants to believe. Such a condition is one of enslavement to shifting impulses and impressions, which may be even more oppressive than doctrinaire authorities. Truth is the source of freedom only as it has commended itself to the inquirer as worthy of devotion.

The principle of freedom in inquiry means not only that assent must be by uncoerced persuasion, but also that arbitrary limitations on the domains open to investigation are excluded. Truth invites its devotees to follow the path of argument wherever it may lead. No map of presently accepted facts is to be used to set bounds to thought and experiment. Of course, other than intellectual considerations may make certain investigations undesirable. For example, scientifically valuable full-scale testing of nuclear devices may be excluded on moral, political, economic, and medical grounds. The point here is that there should be no orthodox prescription of the content of truth which on intellectual grounds predetermines the areas accessible to study. This does not mean that men are free to make of truth anything they will, but means rather that no human agency is to prevent the persuasive power of the truth itself from acting.

Just as devotion to truth is the ground of intellectual freedom, so is it the source of individuality. Being an individual is not simply a matter of being different. In the personal sense it means having a determinate and dependable character rather than being controlled by a mass of inconstant and inconsistent impulses. Living by reference to truth is the means of achieving such character. The universality of knowledge is in no way incompatible with personal uniqueness, for the individual personality is marked by its own special content, organization, and creative uses of knowledge. If the whole of truth were contained in some limited set of doctrines, the ideal of universality might be in conflict with individuality. But actually the domain of truth appears to be boundless. It contains resources for the endless enrichment of unique lives and for generating an infinity of personal individualities. Significant forms of human character emerge through devotion to truth, as release is gained from stultifying self-centeredness, which cuts off the creative springs of personal life.

Furthermore, human individuality draws strength from the human community, not from estrangement and isolation. Private, esoteric, nonpublic knowledge might create human differences, but it could not contribute to genuine individuality, which thrives on association. Universal knowledge, on the other hand, not only provides resources for the growth of unique persons, but also (because of its public nature) constitutes a powerful and enduring link with other persons.

The emphasis on democratic ideals of freedom and individuality is important at the present time, because of the tendency for new intellectual orthodoxies to arise, cutting off inquiry and restricting experience, usually in the name of science. Some positivists and other types of empiricist have defined certain criteria for testing the validity of assertions and have excluded all other criteria as inappropriate. In this way they have greatly narrowed the content of truth, for example, to those propositions that can be tested by the methods of natural science. While it is important that means be devised for making good the public nature of knowledge, in order that orderly progress in investigation may be assured and irresponsible subjectivism may be eliminated, it is just as important that the many kinds of knowledge and the wide variety of symbolic forms by which it may be expressed and mediated should be acknowledged and utilized.

There are as many modes of truth as there are ways of defining the means of potentially universal confirmability. Moralists, art critics, and theologians, for example, propose truths that they believe can be verified by anyone following the appropriate procedures and with the requisite competence—just as do physicists and mathematicians. Granted that the truth criteria of the former groups are frequently less serviceable than those of the latter and may need to be partially abandoned or modified, it would be a mistake and undemocratic to declare one particular method of inquiry, such as the current procedure in physical science, the only road to truth. We are less in danger today from the restrictions imposed by religious orthodoxy or a revered philosophic tradition than from those imposed by the dogmatism of certain scientists or scientific philosophers who make ex *laboritorium* pronouncements about the canonical tests of truth.

Languages, concepts, and theoretical structures in each field of inquiry are devices to coordinate and interpret sharable human experience. There is no single public with a body of knowledge. There are many publics, each consisting of all those persons for whom a given set of symbolic forms provides a shared body of meanings. Each of these publics is limited, but in an open society is *potentially* unlimited, in that all who can and will are welcome to enter. Some of these communities are faulty, because the entrance conditions are not clear, so that many who try earnestly to understand the language of the initiates fail to do so. These publics need to be reformed by the revision of their symbolic structures. But, in order to avoid these faulty systems of language, democracy would not be served by the creation of a single vast public with a single admissible language of truth. To be faithful to the truth in its infinite depth and variety, an unlimited plurality of symbolic modes and communities of meaning is essential.

In regard to education, the considerations above suggest the proper meaning of academic freedom. It means neither academic license, nor unrestricted teaching of whatever one wishes. Academic freedom presupposes loyalty to the truth and should be granted only for the sake of the truth. There is no reason why scholars and teachers should receive special privileges making them immune from ordinary social regulations and enabling them to do and say whatever will advance their own purposes. What is important is that they be free to study and teach the truth, so long as they demonstrate their good faith through willingness to examine and present evidence which is open to all qualified persons to consider.

Education should also be so organized that belief is coerced not by external influences, but only by its own intrinsic power of conviction. For the teacher this requirement presents a high challenge. The easy way of instruction by giving answers must be avoided, as must the use of those grading systems and other forms of reward and punishment that focus attention on "right" conclusions rather than on the process of investigation and fidelity to the evidence. Responsible dissent from majority findings should be welcomed, and those who differ should be given an opportunity to explain the grounds for their convictions. But the conflict of beliefs should not simply be accepted as a result of the relativity of all knowledge. Differences should be used as a stimulus to further investigation, with a view to reaching deeper understandings in which all may share.

The individuality of students should be encouraged, not by releasing them from the discipline of responsible thought in order that they may think what they please, but by opening to them the inexhaustible resources of truth by which they may be formed and transformed. Paradoxically, the source of student conformity today is not the imposition of standard traditional beliefs but the triviality of much in our variegated curriculums. This superficiality stems partly from overemphasis on a restricted problem-solving which limits inquiry to matters relating to personal demands and their satisfaction. Real individuality thrives rather on dedication to truth. The inveterate problem-solver often attempts to reduce the truth to man size, while the devotee of truth wants man to be expanded to truth size.

The superficiality of much in the curriculum also comes from a narrow view of what comprises valid knowledge. There is no single admissible method of thinking to which all must conform. If individuality and freedom are to thrive, the plurality of valid intellectual disciplines and ways of inquiry must be asserted and defended, and administrative policies in academic institutions must foster this pluralism.

We turn, finally, to a consideration of the uses of educated intelligence. Democratic ideals are opposed both to education that creates an exclusive intellectual aristocracy and to a sharp class distinction between those who think and those who work—a distinction that has become meaningless in the age of technology, where most work demands considerable intellectual competence. What, then, are the proper uses of trained mentality, and what purposes does education for intellectual excellence serve?

The answer lies partially in the disinterested pursuit of truth in and for its own sake. Devoted scientists, scholars, and teachers are to a considerable extent inspired by a pure love of truth. There is nothing undemocratic about such single-minded dedication, provided the principle of potentially universal accessibility is honored in the process. But the discovery and the contemplation of truth do not exhaust the purposes served by the development of intellectual powers. None of the values that are the objects of loyalty in the democracy of worth is independent of any of the others: each value contributes to all of the others, forming a unified complex of objectives.

Accordingly, the proper uses of educated intelligence are to discover the truth *and* to advance the realization of other forms of excellence. In short, reason should be devoted to serving whatever is of worth.

The importance of the mass media lies in the fact that for the first time in human history the means exist for speedy *total* communication. The mass media provide the channels for full publicity. They constitute the basis for the rapid creation of a public, or of publics. This is the literal meaning of "publication." The mass media of communication must be of crucial significance for democracy. These techniques make it possible to define "the people" with new clarity, for they constitute an effective source of common experience. They greatly multiply the interconnections between individuals and among groups and correspondingly increase the need for conduct that takes account of other people. In nondemocratic forms of social organization the privileged ruling classes are protected by a curtain of privacy which shields their actions from general view. To be sure, mass communications may be used by tyrannical individuals or groups to increase deceptions and to compound injustices. But in the long run it would appear that these new media work in the direction of some sort of democracy, by making information available to everyone. This may not be ideal democracy, but it will be a form of social organization in which all the people must be reckoned with. Since under modern conditions the actions of all people in key positions of power and influence are thus likely to be known almost immediately by nearly everyone, these people cannot make decisions without reference to the reaction of the public. Hence the mass media produce a society in which all the people are at least tacitly consulted in the making of decisions of public consequence. In this sense they constitute an important democratizing force in the modern world.

It is not enough, however, that the mass media contribute to democracy. The crucial question is, what kind of democracy do they serve and promote? There is no doubt but that radio, television, newspapers, and all the other potent modern means of public-making create forms of association in which each person counts, in a way hitherto unknown. But to what end does he count? What is the animating spirit of those great new publics generated by the magic of the mechanical and electronic arts?

Three answers may be given to these questions. The first answer is that the mass media are tools for advancing the interests of those who control them. This concept of the purpose of mass communication is probably the one most widely held today—though usually tacitly rather than explicitly. The channels of publicity, according to this view, are means of exerting influence, of getting people to believe and to act in ways the publicist desires. They are techniques for amplifying the power and range of the user's words, so that he may (quite literally) have a greater voice in the conduct of human affairs. They are impersonal agencies for manipulating other people.

This first conception of the function of publicity is democratic only in the limited and perverse sense that the mass media create and influence whole publics, and that presumably every person is entitled to advance his interests in this way. But the publics thus created are not communities of free persons; they are masses of more or less identical psycho-physical objects pushed this way and that by the powerful purveyors of propaganda.

A second conception of the purpose of the mass media is, apparently at least, more benignly democratic than the first. This is the view that the function of the agencies of mass communication is to create and sustain a "popular culture." Now the goal is to serve the public's interests, by supplying the people with what they want; it is not manipulation and control of the public by special interests. From this standpoint the people are consumers to be satisfied, rather than objects to be managed. There is always an author, an editor, or a performer who can represent every person and every kind of life, thus creating a great company of others who remind one that he is not alone and who give him assurance that what he does and approves is right. In this manner the powerful techniques of public-making have provided a major answer to the democratic demand for self-determination. While it is still not practicable for each person to do exactly what he wants, the mass media do contribute immeasurably to that self-justification which is the mainspring of the autonomous spirit. In this mass society every person—a few misfits excepted—can at last find *public* warrant for being or becoming whatever his heart desires.

Actually the craving for collective support for oneself is a sign of misgivings about one's worth. Multiplication of this same self through mass identification does not produce personal strength, but only magnifies weakness. The pandering function of the mass media merely weakens human personality by fostering self-deception. The truth is that man is not and never can be really autonomous. He is not and never can be free to order existence to his heart's desire. When he tries to do so, he is both resisted by the outward barriers to his asserted sovereignty and beset within by the sense of meaninglessness which comes from having no correspondence with the health-giving laws of life.

There is a close connection between the use of the mass media to advance special interests and their use to give the people what they want. When people live by the principle of want-satisfaction, they will employ any available means for acquiring the wanted objects. They will give honor, prestige, and power and will gladly subject themselves to those who will supply their cravings. In a society pervaded by the goals of consumption, those who seek power for themselves can also, by skillful psychological manipulation, create new wants, which they then proceed to satisfy, at a profit to themselves. A people whose highest goal is the freedom of personal gratification is thus most likely to be enslaved to those who produce and distribute the so-called "good things of life."

The third answer to the question about the purpose of the mass media and the nature of the publics created by them comes from affirming the democracy of worth instead of the democracy of desire. In this case the basic premise is that the organs of publicity exist to advance neither special interests nor public satisfaction, but solely the cause of excellence. Both those who publish and those who see or hear are committed to act and to judge in devotion to what is right and true. The process of communication is not simply a bipolar one between the publisher and his public, but is a triadic one involving also the controlling reality of truth, which transcends the participants and transforms the relationship between them.

The character of the mass media of communication and the purposes by which they are directed are, of course, of profound educational significance, chiefly because today they are among the most, if not the most, powerful and pervasive of all educational influences. Young people—and older people, too—are caught in an almost continual and inescapable barrage of sights and sounds from the various organs of publicity. Until recent years the average person had to seek out sources of information and entertainment. Now he has to seek refuge from their omnipresent importunity. Whether he wills it or not, every person is, as it were, bathed in a flood of symbols pouring in from the mass media—music, news, sports, weather and market information. Onto the time-honored stimuli of the natural and social environments have been superimposed the more insistent stimuli of this new symbolic environment.

To a considerable extent the broadcasters and publishers are the leading educators of our day. It is they, perhaps more than schoolteachers and parents, who set the intellectual and moral tone of the society and suggest the values that shall govern the conduct of life. Perhaps the mass media are the real public schools—the institutions in which the public is not only taught but brought into being as a public.

The public channels of communication are educationally important also because they provide a wealth of teaching materials and models for parents and teachers. The teacher is no longer one whose main function is to impart information, which is so abundantly available and attractively arranged in a variety of published forms. The function of teaching has become one of selection, evaluation, interpretation, application, and individual guidance. To put it another way, the mass media have shifted the emphasis in education from teaching to learning, because they offer at least the possibility of such rich resources of well-organized, authoritative, and cogent materials for learning that students need only the time and the incentive to learn. Again, this is to say that the most influential and important teachers, to some extent today and even more so tomorrow, are those who speak and write for the mass media. Nonetheless a continuing and increasingly important task of ordinary teachers and parents will be to develop in young people the trained perception and critical judgment that will enable them to use published materials profitably and responsibly.

One further important link between education and the mass media is the fact that authors, broadcasters, advertisers, and others who speak through the public channels are nurtured in homes and schools. Thus, the traditional institutions of education may help to determine the character and the purposes of what is done via the newer agencies. In a healthy society the influences of homes and schools should complement and sustain those of the mass media, and vice versa, replacing the chaotic and frequently antagonistic relationships that now so largely prevail.

We turn now to a consideration of some of the principles that need to be observed if the mass media of communication are to contribute to a democracy of worth. As a preliminary to this analysis, however, it will be necessary to discuss the major antidemocratic consequences resulting from the use of these techniques. Along with the democratization of sorts inherent in the creation of comprehensive publics, there are also contrary, potentially undemocratic tendencies. These follow from the high cost of production in the mass media. Considerable equipment is required to print and market newspapers, books, and magazines, to make radio or television broadcasts, and to produce motion pictures. While per capita costs of mass-produced items are low, because of the large numbers of people involved, the cost per issue or per program is normally high. As a result, considerable concentrations of wealth and power are required by the mass media of communication. It is not possible for anyone who wishes to do so to create a public. The privilege of publication is limited to those who command the requisite resources of money and position.

These simple economic and political facts underlie the antidemocratic potentiality of the mass media. The ability of a relatively few already powerful people or organizations to exert still further pervasive influence introduces the possibility of tyranny and misuse of power in some respects even more devastating than that accomplished by physical compulsion. To hold the mind and imagination of a public in subjection is more injurious to their dignity as free persons than bodily restrictions would be.

These undemocratic tendencies and dangers can be counteracted. The mass media are not necessarily contrary to democracy. They can and should contribute to human freedom and justice in a democracy of worth. What is required is the public regulation of the mass media, by reference to standards of worth, in such a manner as to prevent their arbitrary employment for the advantage of private interests, either through deliberate manipulation or through giving the public what it thinks it wants.

The use of the mass media in a democracy of worth is based on four principles. The first principle is *freedom of speech*. If truth is to be known and right is to be done, there must be opportunity for exploration and for search, hence for diversity of beliefs and for the public expression of this diversity. The basic assumption of the free and open society is that no one can speak about the true and the right with final and full authority. There must be no official public view to which all are obliged to hold and from which no variance is to be permitted. It follows that the mass media should be organized so as to permit and encourage the creation of many publics. A single system of production and distribution, resulting in the making of a single public, would destroy the contrast and the variation that are the source of cultural enrichment and social progress. In other words, democracy should be pluralistic. A monolithic society, consisting of only one public, is a threat to truth and justice. Freedom of publication is a prerequisite for this necessary pluralism.

Freedom of speech is not, however, without its conditions and limitations; it is not absolute and unconditional. It is founded on the presumption of good faith in those who publish. It is one thing to defend plurality on the ground that no one can claim complete knowledge of the good and the true. It is something else to uphold it from the point of view of the demand for individual autonomy. To stand for freedom in the name of a truth that is beyond mortal reach is different from defending it for the sake of personal license. In this contrast lies the clue to what is meant by "good faith." Good faith is faith in the good. It is action predicated on loyalty to the good.

Thus, to the first principle must be added a second—namely, the *principle of regulation*. It is in tension with the principle of freedom of speech, not as total contradiction, but as partial limitation. It sets bounds to freedom. While plurality of published influences is desirable in order to allow for criticism and improvement, not any and every influence may be permitted. Any society needs some minimal standards which prescribe in broad terms the range of permissible public communications. Such definite judgments are necessary because even people who are committed to the good are never completely devoted to it. A society organized on the basis of dedication to excellence as an unargued presupposition is made up of people none of whom actually fulfills that ideal. There are also people in such societies who do not even nominally profess or assume any such allegiance to values and who pursue their autonomy, relying on the good faith of those who are dedicated to the right.

Whether the regulation shall be narrow or broad depends chiefly upon the degree to which the members of the society are actively and consciously devoted to the good. When such devotion is nominally assumed but is actually weak, it is necessary to set up stringent legalistic regulations which define within a narrow range the allowable forms of published and broadcast materials. When loyalty to the good is actually widespread and strong, social controls on what is communicated may be correspondingly relaxed.

Regulation of the mass media is not practiced solely in a democracy of worth. Such controls are also the main reliance of non-democratic social orders—the means by which the techniques of public-making are reserved for the special purposes of those who hold the reins of power. Regulation is likewise essential in the democracy of desire, as the basis for insuring the social peace and cooperation necessary to satisfy the maximum number of interests. Though undemocratic societies, democracies of desire, and democracies of worth all must regulate the mass media, the nature and source of the regulations are different. In the first two, the controls are based on considerations of efficiency and expediency: in the one case for maintaining inequality of power; in the other, for distributing and equalizing power. In the third society the controls are based not on preservation or accommodation of interests, but entirely on value considerations—on right, justice, and qualitative excellence.

Every society censors communications that would immediately endanger the security and safety of the public. For example, use of the mass media to incite rebellion against the established government or the publication of military or diplomatic secrets are obviously inadmissible in any kind of society, on the grounds of corporate self-preservation. Other matters that would be repugnant to most people, such as gross misrepresentation of facts important to health and safety, or public displays of vicious and immoral conduct, would also normally be prohibited by law.

The question then arises of who should do the regulating. Ultimately the responsibility lies with the agencies of government. The courts may adjudicate complaints brought against publishers or broadcasters, legislatures may prescribe the limits within which freedom of speech is allowed, and other government agencies may exercise regulatory powers through the granting and withholding of licenses.

The extent to which such government control is required depends upon the degree to which regulation is privately and voluntarily effected. In a society where the people are widely committed to the right rather than to the advancement of their own interests and the satisfaction of their own desires, the censoring functions of government can be reserved for the occasional serious offender who escapes other controls. When voluntary private regulation is weak, strong government restrictions are required.

The producers of the mass media may regulate themselves through their own associations, both on an advisory basis and by invoking sanctions on those who stray beyond the bounds agreed upon. Individual producers may also regulate themselves, in the light of standards of excellence to which they have pledged their loyalty. Such self-control does not really belong under the principle of regulation at all, for it is simply the responsible exercise of freedom. This indicates that ideally freedom and regulation are not in any way opposed to each other. In fact, to be truly free is to regulate one's conduct in accordance with the good. The principle of regulation is contrary to the principle of freedom only when freedom is taken in the sense of autonomy.

The distributors of the materials of mass communication are another important means of control. For example, subscription agents and booksellers can to some extent choose what they will and will not sell and to whom. Motion picture theaters can sometimes determine the films to be shown, and they can in certain cases restrict the viewing of films to appropriate persons (for example, to adults). Since television and radio programs, on the other hand, are open to everyone without limitation, it is necessary to maintain a more broadly applicable standard of public propriety than applies to the other forms of mass communication.

Finally, voluntary regulation of the mass media may be exercised by the receiving public as individuals and as groups. Voluntary associations such as churches and clubs may adopt their own standards of quality and may employ their own corporate disciplines to enforce the observance of these standards. Of special importance in this respect are families, in which books, newspapers, magazines, movies, and broadcasts may be chosen with reference to standards of worth considerably different from and higher than those generally prevailing. Family standards are continually subject to erosion from the inflow of debased materials from the mass media—as in the brutality and immorality of many of the so-called "comic" books, the triviality, sensationalism, and distortion of most journalism, and the preoccupation with crime and violence in many television programs. It is the obligation of parents to maintain at least minimal standards in the home by appropriate regulation of the reading, listening, and viewing diets of their children.

Similarly, libraries and museums may regulate the quality of the materials acquired and the manner of their use by the public. Schools, too, play an important part in the selection of published materials, both in choosing what is used in regular instruction and in influencing students' habits of seeing and listening.

The ultimate goal of control of the mass media is to educate the public in self-regulation—to develop in all the people, whether producers or recipients, a reliable sense of what is worthy and what is not worthy of being made public. In this manner the principle of regulation supports and confirms the principle of freedom.

The third principle for the mass media in a democracy of worth is that of *social support for excellence*. In a democracy of desire or in an undemocratic system, where mass communications are used to advance the interests of individuals, of groups, or of the people as a whole, excellence is at best a by-product. There is no necessary relation between true worth and the satisfaction of wants. It is not often likely to be to the advantage of a newspaper publisher, for example, to print the whole truth or to present the most searching analyses of the news. Nor, apparently, can movie, radio, and television producers normally afford to offer a steady flow of high-level programs. Under these conditions, while materials of great worth may be produced, their appearance is fortuitous and sporadic and their tenure precarious. Furthermore, the very excellence of the offerings is compromised and tainted by their subordination to the interests they are used to serve.

The predominance of commercial support for the mass media in the United States is evidence that in this field a democracy of desire prevails. Newspapers, magazines, radio, and television are largely supported by the sale of advertising. Hence the nature of what is communicated is mainly determined by what will sell products. Each commercial sponsor tries to present whatever will please the most people among those who are in the market for his product. If he can make use of snob appeal to sell automobiles, washing machines, or beer, he may sponsor a symphony orchestra, but if a sordid murder drama would commend itself to a larger public, he will present that instead. Under this system there is no commitment to excellence as such, but only as it may happen to be a useful tool of product promotion.

By contrast, in a democracy of worth, excellence is the direct and primary aim, to which other considerations are subordinate. In such a society the means of mass communication are given direct social support for the publication and broadcasting of excellent materials. The money and the manpower are provided specifically to accomplish these beneficent purposes, which are of such great importance for public well-being. Thus, dependence upon organizations whose primary purposes are entirely other than public communication is avoided.

The principle of social support for excellence may be carried out by a number of different means. The most obvious way is for the government to operate its own general press, radio, and television services for the public good. This has not been done in the United States by the federal government, presumably because such activities are not included among the powers specifically assigned to it by the Constitution. However, some of the state and municipal governments have entered the broadcasting field in a small way. In many other countries government-controlled mass media are the rule. In some cases—the British Broadcasting Corporation, for example—great contributions to public well-being have been made. In other cases the dangers to liberty in government-operated press and radio have become evident. This peril is most ominous when the government has a monopoly of the mass media. As pointed out earlier, democratic freedom depends on a plurality of public-making agencies. Even though the official media of communication may in principle be devoted to the good, those who operate them are never wise enough or good enough to be the exclusive architects of the public mind. Thus, while a case for government-supported mass media may be made, other independent agencies should coexist in the field with them, and safeguards should be provided in the system of government to insure that high professional standards prevail and that the media are used for the general good rather than for partisan advantage.

A second means of providing social support for excellence in the mass media is through private, nonprofit organizations devoted directly and exclusively to the mass production and distribution of high-quality communicated materials. Examples of such agencies are the noncommercial educational radio and television stations and certain nonprofit publishers and film makers.

Third, there are commercial mass media devoted to excellence and supported by direct consumer purchase of the materials produced rather than indirectly by the sale of unrelated advertised products. The highest-grade newspapers, magazines, and books are supported by a reading public dedicated to excellence. The success of such publishing enterprises depends upon a widely diffused will to truth and a widespread interest in significant cultural attainments. The plan of subscription television rests on the application of the same rationale to this newer medium of communication. Whatever its shortcomings in other respects, the idea has the great merit of establishing a direct relation between product and purchaser, thus creating the means of responding to a substantial demand for programs of consistently high quality.

Finally, the social support for excellence can be accomplished through the various institutions of formal education. As pointed out earlier, the mass media are now in fact, if not in name, the most powerful of all the agencies of education. Their function is to disseminate widely the resources of culture by means of words and images. This is also the primary function of schools. By long tradition the schools are deliberately responsive to the claims of truth and of other ideals of excellence. The mass media, as now organized, have no such generally acknowledged objective. This is understandable in a society organized on the basis of expediency, but not in one dedicated to the realization of values. In a democracy of worth mass media ought to be frankly regarded as agencies of education and should be made an integral part of the work of the institutions of education. The making public of information and even of entertainment is a natural and proper extension of the function of regular educational agencies.

A growing recognition of the educative role of the mass media may result in profound changes in both the schools and the agencies of mass communication. There is no reason, for example, why outstanding teachers cannot make valuable materials for learning at every level available by press, radio, and television to the public at large. With such public accessibility of the materials of instruction, the emphasis of teachers in school classrooms may shift considerably. Guidance, testing, and individual application can largely take the place of presentation of learning materials by the teacher. The primary function of most teachers should be to stimulate and channel the students' dedication to make use of the abundant resources available through modern techniques of symbolic reproduction and distribution.

The great universities should become centers of public education in a new sense. They should not merely cherish their own intellectual life, serving only those who come to them for instruction. They should become major centers of mass communication, carrying on a continuous work of adult education of the public in the letters, sciences, and arts, by printed publications, by motion pictures, and by radio and television broadcasts. For this work they should receive the substantial material support that would be required to do the job at a high level of competence. In this way the institutions of education could admirably exemplify the principle of social support for excellence.

The fourth principle of democracy in mass communication is that of *criticism*, or of evaluative response by the receiving public. Only by criticism can the one-directional nature of mass communication be overcome.

Criticism may be accomplished in several ways. The first way is direct communication of the individual with the author, publisher, or producer. A relatively small number of thoughtful letters or conversations may have a significant influence on the quality of what is published. A second mode of criticism is the regular publication of reviews by expert critics. Evaluations by such reviewers have considerable effect upon the professional standing of authors and producers and in the formation of public opinion. They are particularly essential in a society devoted to values, to keep before the public a clear vision of ideal ends to be served and to show explicitly in what respects materials offered for public reception do or do not measure up to these standards. Third, criticism can be accomplished implicitly by the publication of material that acts as a countervailing influence. Fourth, indirect and inarticulate, but nevertheless effective, criticism may be effected by giving or withholding support for the agencies of mass communication. With commercial mass media supported by advertising, the individual consumer may respond by purchasing or not purchasing the advertiser's products. This is obviously a cumbersome and uncertain mode of expressing evaluations. With government-controlled media, criticism must take place through the regular political channels. In the case of mass media supported by private philanthropy or by the sale of materials to the public, criticism is exercised directly and powerfully on an economic basis.

It is with respect to the critical function that the pertinence of the institutions of education to the mass media of communication is perhaps most evident. Criticism is integral to the educative process. It is an essential feature of good practice in schools, colleges, and universities. When mass communication occurs under the auspices of non-school agencies, criticism is an extrinsic function—an activity carried on by interested outsiders who wish to have a part in determining the nature of what is made public. When the mass media are an arm of the schools, the critical function is intrinsic, since self-appraising, reflective activity is an essential feature of education. It is this self-evaluative function that makes the institutions of education uniquely appropriate as centers for mass communication in a democracy of worth.

PART 3 * CREATIVITY

The preceding two chapters have been concerned with the value of intelligence—first, with respect to the general principles of intellectual excellence and, second, with respect to the standards appropriate to mass communication. It has been argued that ideal democracy in the intellectual life rests upon the premise of universal truth to be discovered and shared, and that the proper aim of democratic education is to foster dedication to this truth.

In this and the next three chapters the major emphasis will be on the value of creativity. Intelligence is at issue in this aspect of life, too, but in a somewhat different fashion than in the aspects previously discussed. Now the center shifts from man the knower to man the maker, from the abstractions of rational discourse to the concrete products of his handiwork. But the thesis is still the same—namely, that there are standards of worth by which these products can be evaluated and that a proper goal of human life is to engage in creative activity in loyalty to these standards. The criteria of excellence in this domain are not the same as those in the sphere of ordinary discursive knowledge—though careful examination reveals an essential continuity between the processes of evaluation in the sciences and in the arts. Suitable criteria of worth in a work of art, for example, can be developed, but they are not the same as those that apply to mathematical propositions or to the generalizations of the natural sciences.

The discussion of standards for the mass media has already to some extent foreshadowed the forthcoming analysis, since the channels of mass communication are not restricted merely to the transmission of literal information. Their function is not only to convey knowledge but also to influence feelings and actions. They are, therefore, to be judged not simply by standards of truth in the usual sense, but by much broader criteria of qualitative worth. The public atmosphere—the cultural tone—created by books, magazines, television, and the other media, is generally even more important than the factual exactness of the information communicated.

How can goals for democracy and for democratic education in the domain of human creativity be formulated? Let us begin to answer this question by considering the difference between aristocratic and democratic views of esthetic experience. The aristocratic position is that refinement of taste is for an elite class of "gentlefolk"; in fact, it is regarded as a mark of status and belongs only to a select few. The great mass of "common" people are expected to be crude and simple, neither understanding nor caring for the "higher things." Furthermore, the select few are regarded by themselves and usually by others as the authorities in questions of taste and style.

Two assumptions are implicit in this aristocratic view. The first is that esthetic experience is a special, separable kind of human activity, and that esthetic judgments are relevant only to certain kinds of activity. For instance, making or listening to music, executing or viewing a landscape painting, or preparing or eating exotic foods would be considered appropriate occasions for esthetic evaluation, while ordinary pursuits like operating a lathe, feeding a baby, or painting a house would not. These special esthetic pursuits are customarily reserved for the aristocrats, and ordinary people are not expected to have the ability, the resources, or the presumption to engage in them. The second assumption is that esthetic experience belongs to man not as a human being but only as a member of a special social group. It is not integral to being a person, nor a part of everyone's birthright, but simply an aspect of special privilege.

A democratic position rejects both of these aristocratic assumptions. First, from the democratic standpoint there is no experience that does not have its esthetic aspects or dimensions. Human activities may not be classified exclusively into esthetic and nonesthetic categories. Judgments of qualitative significance apply to the commonplace as well as to the unusual and to utilitarian as well as to leisure-time pursuits. In fact, in a democracy the ordinary events of existence are matters of particular esthetic interest and concern, simply because their quality has such widespread and continuous influence on the general level of individual and collective life. Second, from a democratic viewpoint the esthetic life belongs to every person as an essential part of his being. It is not an optional mode of existence but is integral to the human status.

These differences between aristocratic and democratic esthetic ideals have clear consequences for education. In an aristocracy, special disciplines are developed for the cultivation of taste. The "liberal arts" are regarded as studies for gentlemen, who have the freedom to enjoy things for their intrinsic perfection and without regard to practical utility. Aristocratic gentlemen and gentlewomen are also trained in arts of speech and behavior that serve to mark them as superior to ordinary people. They are taught high discrimination in food, clothing, and architecture, so that their style of life may comport with their status. The common people are educated to know their place and to perform the duties laid upon them by those who rule, without concern for elegance or distinction.

In democratic education, on the other hand, there is a pervasive concern for the quality of experience. All studies, whether "general" or "special," "liberal" or "vocational," "theoretical" or "practical," are subjects of esthetic concern. A major goal of teaching is the elevation of life through the improvement of taste and the sharpening of discrimination in whatever one does. Furthermore, the opportunities to grow in this grace of life are a part of everyone's education, and each person is held responsible for the quality of his thoughts and acts.

Esthetic experience in a democracy is not only a matter of universal concern; it is also a sustainer of the twin democratic ideals of individuality and freedom. Individuality in the full sense pertains to persons. It is more than particularity, which grains of sand and blades of grass also have. It is a depth of meaning, a qualitative richness, which marks the highest levels in the order of creation. Since esthetic experience is concerned with individuation, which is consummated in personality, it follows that esthetic excellence is an important goal for democracy. In an age of machine mass production of identical items, individuality is in danger. In pre-industrial society everything that was made bore the mark of the person who fashioned it and who thus confirmed and communicated himself in the thing. Today persons tend to be obscured and submerged by the impersonality of the identical things their machines have made. While there is no need to forgo the advantages of mass production, it is important that in other ways the realization of individuality through esthetic activity be fostered. In aristocratic societies it is only the elite who are allowed to be true individuals, and this privilege they make good by their esthetic pursuits, while the common people remain in collective anonymity. In a democracy it is the right and the privilege of every person to realize his full individuality, through the development of qualitative discrimination and construction.

Esthetic experience further reinforces democratic ideals in its emphasis on creative freedom. Art is making, producing, fashioning. When esthetic concern is felt, life as a whole is a work of art. Conduct is directed by considered design. Experience is fashioned in accord with standards of excellence of form or pattern. To live in this way is to live as a free man, for freedom is simply the exercise of deliberate choice. There is no "art of living" without freedom, and freedom is fulfilled through significant creative activity. In esthetic experience a person is liberated from the bondage of mere organic existence and becomes aware of himself as a spiritual being who is heir to and trustee for a whole world of meanings.

We come now to the question of esthetic standards. According to one view, characteristic of the democracy of desire, esthetic evaluations are nothing but indications of subjective feeling-states. There are no objective or universal criteria for esthetic excellence, and there is no way (or need) to resolve differences in opinion about esthetic values. The creative nature of esthetic activity, it is held, itself indicates that these values are made rather than discovered, and the fact that the creation is individual and free means that everyone in such matters is wholly autonomous.

Such a view destroys any basis for effective esthetic judgment. It amounts to an abandonment of the concept of qualitative excellence. The result is a thoroughgoing relativism which makes value judgments dependent on the accidents of circumstance and temperament. Evaluations can, of course, be made by statistical enumeration of preferences. It is characteristic of democracies of desire to make popularity the criterion of worth. Modern advertising depends heavily upon this fact.

In the mass society, where value is determined by popular appeal, the situation is in sharp contrast to the aristocratic societies, in which standards were set by a few connoisseurs, and in which the larger the number who approved of something, the lower was the value likely to be accorded it. The notion of determining values by popularity is unsatisfactory. At this point the aristocratic society was right. Judgments of excellence cannot be made by statistics, because quality is not a function of quantity.

In a democracy of worth, standards of esthetic excellence are presupposed. These standards are not regarded as fully known, nor must they be explicitly stated, but they are assumed to exist. All striving toward qualitative worth is founded on this assumption. All people and all forms of activity are regarded as subject to judgment by the standards of worth. The people are not the source and measure of values, as they are when popularity rules, but the people are themselves measured by these values.

The principle of worth further presupposes that esthetic experience is an act of *discovery*. From this standpoint, esthetic "creation" is seen as discovery through experimentation and through insight into hitherto unrealized possibilities. Creativity is not claimed in the radical sense of complete origination. New things are made and new things are done, but values are not arbitrarily given to them; rather, formerly unseen excellences are manifest in and through them. Thus, creativity does not necessarily imply autonomy. It does require active personal engagement in the exploration of possibilities for concrete embodiment of meanings. Human creation is not the invention of values, but the revelation of values by means of imaginatively constructed objects.

Serious esthetic education makes sense only when dedication to qualitative worth is acknowledged. If esthetic judgments are simply expressions of subjective feeling, there is no point in trying to change or develop tastes. Then the notion of improvement in taste has no meaning, for a liking simply *is*. It can be criticized only by a standard that transcends subjective preferences. Under the subjective view, esthetic education can, of course, serve two purposes. First, it can show ways of increasing the intensity and widening the range of personal enjoyments; and, second, it can assist in the socialization of tastes—that is, in developing shared preferences and in helping individuals to adjust to prevailing social expectations.

In contrast, under a philosophy of worth the major purposes of esthetic education are: first, to enable individuals to respond to *higher orders* of qualitative significance and insight; and, second, to stimulate criticism of popular mediocrity and to discourage uncritical conformity to mass convention.

Up to now no indication has been given of precisely what constitutes esthetic excellence. In the nature of the case no general rule can be given, because each thing is judged in its concrete individuality. Nevertheless, some suggestions can be offered concerning the criteria that are appropriate for the evaluation of esthetic worth. Such criteria are the object of esthetic education, and they are guides for the discipline of individual creativity.

One standard is *unity*. A good book has some central theme which relates the various parts to one another. It is not simply a collection of unconnected episodes or isolated arguments. An excellent musical composition is more than an aggregate of separate sounds; there is a musical argument, so to speak, which runs as a thread upon which the individual notes are arranged. The rooms of a lovely building are organized according to some idea of the whole. Its architect had a single concept of the structure, which he then analyzed into component parts each of which would contribute to that concept. If he was a true artist, he did not merely adjoin space to space in a heterogeneous assemblage. Unity is an essential esthetic feature of any well-fashioned thing, whether it be a painting, a poem, a tree, a conversation, a meal, or a machine.

Affirming the ideal of unity is another way of asserting the concreteness of the esthetic mode of experience. Esthetic understanding is synoptic. It is synthetic, rather than analytic. Clearly, no synopsis or synthesis can be attained without an idea of the whole. There must be coherence among the parts, which is to say that the parts must be seen as differentiations from the whole and as contributory to the unified entity. In fact, the notion of a "thing" presupposes unity. A recognizable object has a definite form, or character. A formless mass, a heap of odds and ends, is literally nothing—that is, no thing. So to be really something, to be worthy of notice and admiration, an entity must have unity of form, some organizing idea, plan, or purpose. This is the most fundamental measure of esthetic worth.

Significant esthetic unity is of a special kind. It is not the unity of sameness, but the unity of *variety*. There is obvious unity in the repetition of a single note, but that does not make it a beautiful musical composition. A canvas covered with one shade of paint has unity of a kind, but it could never be called a significant work of art. Esthetic unity is the organization of different parts into a single whole. It is the weaving together of a variety of contrasting strands into a consistent pattern. Mere sameness or repetitiveness lacks interest. A true esthetic object represents an imaginative achievement, resulting from the ability of the perceiving mind to discern relationships between separate and distinct things, so that together these many things constitute some greater single thing.

An esthetic object is a complex, a unity of contrasting elements. The whole is thus qualitatively different from the parts. It is the parts compounded into a new totality to which both the likenesses and the unlikenesses of the parts are essential. Without the likenesses there could be no ground of relatedness; without the unlikenesses there could be no new and higher levels of complexity, which are the source of esthetic interest and creative progress.

The need for both unity and variety could be illustrated by any number of examples from contemporary culture. Much modern painting fails to present any clear unity of idea; it appears to be an arbitrary, and sometimes even accidental, medley of colors and shapes. In contrast, popular music is often esthetically deficient in variety; a single simple theme or rhythmic pattern is repeated many times over with none of the elaboration and variation which lend interest to good music. On the other hand, modern "serious" music, like painting, frequently seems to have no thematic structure to give coherence to the whole. The main esthetic threat of machine civilization is the suppression of variety through the multiplication of identical mass-produced items. However, this tendency is counteracted by the virtually endless outpouring of new products by an inventive and affluent society.

The proper coordination of unity and variety constitutes *harmony*; that is, unity and variety are not separate qualities of an esthetic object, though each may separately be made the focus of analysis. Harmonization is the blending of different but mutually compatible elements into a whole. In a harmonious object the parts enhance rather than negate one another. Harmony must not, however, be interpreted as simple concordance. In music, dissonance is often a useful effect, which can be appreciated by those who have become accustomed to it, just as seasoning adds zest to food for those who have acquired the taste for it. Similarly, drama would lose its reason for being if conflict were eliminated. In fact, the main function of tragedy is to exhibit the inescapable and usually unresolvable conflicts which are the substance of the human predicament. So if harmony is a desirable esthetic quality, it cannot mean a serene, untroubled unity of the parts. It does mean that the elements are so organized that each contributes to, and does not detract from, the effect of the others.

Closely related to harmony is the ideal of *balance*, or *proportion*. Each component should be given its appropriate weight or importance in the whole. This is admittedly a vague conception, yet it is not without meaning. For example, a vase is commonly given symmetrical proportions around the central axis, while another kind of balance prevails vertically, such as an alternation of wide and narrow segments. Balance always presupposes some recognizable formal measure. In the case of symmetry, the measure is simple equality, but balance is obviously not necessarily symmetrical. It is determined by the character of the whole to which the constituent elements contribute. A building has balance in its design when the number and sizes of the rooms are in accordance with the purposes for which the structure is intended. A novel is well proportioned when the various episodes are related in such a way that the author's story is told with greatest clarity and economy. Imbalance in anything is due to an excess or a deficiency of parts in relation to the plan of the whole.

Functionality is the next criterion to be considered. Judgment about balance or proportion rests upon the relation of design to objective. A well-designed object is one that functions effectively as it was intended to do. An excellent chair is one that is good for sitting in. A fine musical composition effectively conveys the intended musical idea. Functionality refers here not to practical utility—though a functional object may well be useful—but to the achievement in concrete reality of the purposed form. A properly functioning thing is one that carries out the idea implicit in making it. The form or idea may be "practical" or "impractical" from the standpoint of personal or social needs; this distinction is not relevant esthetically. What matters is how effectively the ideal is achieved by the artifact—not in the sense of good craftsmanship, but in that of good design. Designing involves the imaginative exploration of possible ways of approaching a given objective; it is a task of experimentation and discovery.

While functionality refers to the performance of a design, another standard, *finesse*, refers to the execution of a design. Both of these aspects of esthetic excellence are closely akin in that in the absence of finesse even a well-designed thing cannot function in the manner appropriate to it. Finesse is refinement, finished-ness. It is produced by skilled craftsmanship, by the ability to control materials expertly. It depends upon long and intimate familiarity with the materials to be used and upon sustained practice in working with them. Finesse declines in a society where the demand for ease, pleasure, and quick results predominates. Skill in craftsmanship is attained only by arduous and protracted effort sustained by a concern for ideal values and dedication to the task of realizing them in material things—that is, by a zeal for incarnating excellence.

Esthetic effect is a matter of perception of *meaning*. Quality is not mere surge of feeling. It is feeling united with form. A quality is a significant form—that is, a form that signifies something. Esthetic meanings are not necessarily expressible in ordinary factual propositions. An object is esthetically meaningful when it has some deliberate plan or structure. It is meaningless when it has no discernible intelligible order. In a sense, of course, everything has some kind of order; even the most chaotic hodgepodge has a structure, albeit a very complicated and unusual one. Hence, meaningfulness must refer to the presence of certain reasonably simple patterns of organization. This consideration carries us back to the fundamental criteria of unity and diversity. The meaning of an object is the unity that relates the diverse parts within a complete whole. A meaningless array of things is a collection that has no perceptible system of coordination into one concrete entity.

Esthetic quality is said to have *depth* when the meaning of the perceived object is not immediately apparent to the unpracticed observer, and when the object is capable of yielding a succession of mutually enriching meanings. A painting has depth when it commands prolonged attention and rewards sustained, reflective scrutiny. A novel or a poem is deep when it bears frequent rereading, each time yielding insights not previously evident. The enduring treasures of civilization have this quality of depth. They remain from one generation to the next because they contain an abundance of meanings which give them freshness and vitality. By contrast, superficial objects are ones whose meaning is obvious and trivial, so that continued observation of them causes boredom. They demand no effort and evoke scant admiration or affection.

Though esthetic experience is not simply inchoate feeling, but structured perception, it still is founded in emotional response. Intensity is an essential quality of such a response. Clearly, esthetic worth is not simply proportionate to the degree of intensity; loud sounds are not necessarily better than soft ones, nor are bright colors preferable to pastels. Qualitative worth requires *measured intensity*—that is, feeling appropriate to the occasion. Sometimes the indicated effect is a breathless calm—a virtual suspension of animation; at other times a violent excitement is called for. The measure to be applied is the meaning of the perceived object. The observer's feeling-state should accord with the meaning of the thing. Esthetic discipline is required to insure such accord. Seasoned qualitative perception comes from long practice in channeling emotions to correspond to the significance of the occasion.

The realization of measured intensity of feeling depends not only upon the sensitivity and emotional discipline of the percipient, but also upon the *expressiveness* of the esthetic object. Expressiveness is the power of conveying meaning. A poorly constructed object interposes barriers or distractions in the way of the intended and implied significance; the words and images employed, the details of design, are not all marshaled to produce a clear and unequivocal impression. Expressiveness is actually implicit in the ideas of balance and finesse. The separate term is used here because of its connection with feeling-tone. An object that has been well designed and expertly constructed will express its meanings unambiguously and will evoke the appropriate feeling-response in the disciplined perceiver.

Art effects a transformation of nature. It has an *ideal* quality. The creative, constructive energies of the human spirit are employed in discovering and incarnating ideas not ordinarily found in things that have resulted from the nonhuman processes of nature. Even when natural things are observed, human imagination transforms them so as to emphasize certain ideal aspects. For esthetic imagination, the starry night sky is not simply a pattern of light spots on a dark background. It is a tapestry whose infinite varieties of meaning have been recited by poets, lovers, and scientists as long as men have turned their eyes upward and wondered. Thus, ideality appears in the esthetic interpretation of natural forms. But it is even more apparent in the humanly created forms—in the artifacts of culture. Here qualitative worth is measured not by precision in imitating nature, but in the construction of things that will express the ideal more effectively than natural objects can.

It is this property of ideality that justifies the nonutilitarian view of esthetic worth. Esthetically valuable things may be practically useful, but they need not be. In fact, esthetic worth tends to have an inverse relation to practicality, since forms are ideal in the degree to which they transcend the necessary limitations, confusions, and compromises of ordinary life. The greatness of a work of art consists to a large extent in its power of revealing possibilities that could scarcely be fully realized in actuality. This is not primarily a question of the ideal in the sense of nobility or beauty—though these are measures of worth, too. Ideality here refers to selection and simplification for expressive effect. Actual affairs are always muddied with irrelevancies and frustrating complications. A work of art aims at removing all of these, so that a clear, strong, consistent—in this sense, ideal—message is conveyed.

Another measure of esthetic value is honesty, integrity, or sincerity. A piece of work is sincere when there is agreement between what it appears to be and what it actually is; that is, when the meanings revealed through continued acquaintance with it are consistent with one another. A dishonest work is one that has a deceptive appearance, that leads one to a certain expectation and then yields something different. A building with a "false front" is insincere, because the appearance does not jibe with the inner form. A musical composition is dishonest when its meaning as a whole is incompatible with the meaning of certain parts. Honesty is integrity, or wholeness. Each part must contribute to the purpose of the whole. It will not do to say that a work of art may be intended to represent chaos and disorder. That would be similar to saying that a sentence may represent nonsense: it may do so, but it is of no worth in discourse. So, any artifact has worth only as it embodies a unified idea—as was pointed out in connection with the criteria of unity, variety, harmony, and balance. Sincerity is singleness of purpose, particularly as regards the concordance of external form with inner substance.

By the *purity* of an esthetic object one could mean its ideality, in the sense that no alien elements intrude into it, or one could mean its sincerity, in the sense that it reveals but one purpose. Neither of these entirely legitimate meanings is intended here. Purity is here synonymous with nobility or spiritual elevation. A pure or noble work evokes love and devotion in the beholder. An impure or ignoble thing stimulates greed and lust. There is doubtless some truth in the saying that to the pure all things are pure. Expectations do to some extent influence perceptions. Nevertheless, purity is not simply a subjective factor. There are things that feed the appetites and stimulate acquisitive activity, and these differ profoundly in kind from the things that evoke a self-giving response.

From the point of view here set forth, purity is the most important of all esthetic qualities, for it is the foundation of all value, including esthetic value. A drama or a painting that fosters unworthy desire undermines the very basis of whatever worth may be ascribed to it on other grounds (for example, unity, depth, or measured intensity), while a work of art that helps to release men from the bondage of self-interest serves to establish and confirm its value foundation. The most serious error in modern esthetics has been the general rejection of the ideal of purity or nobility on the ground of esthetic irrelevance. It has been held that the only *esthetically* relevant criteria are those of formal excellence, and not of spiritual quality. This position results from the failure to recognize the foundation of all value in the distinctive spiritual decision in favor of worth-serving instead of self-serving.

Sincerity is one kind of *truthfulness*—namely, that in which the object is true to itself, or in which its full actuality is consistent with its initial and external appearance. Another kind of truthfulness refers not to the internal consistency of the object, but to its external relationships. A true work of art is coherent with other instances and modes of apprehending what is and what ought to be; that is to say, it illuminates the meaning of life. A false work is contrary to other evidences of fact and worth, and therefore it causes doubt and confusion in the beholder. A tragic drama is true insofar as it throws light on man's basic predicament which springs from his freedom of choice. The more impressive and insightful the portrayal, the truer is the drama. It is more difficult to say what truthfulness in music means. Yet in this case, too, there may be an illumination of life. Music also has a message—carries a meaning—and this meaning either does or does not agree with corresponding meanings derived from other experiences.

The criterion of truthfulness may appear to deny the worth of fiction. It may also seem to contradict the notion of ideality, which makes a virtue out of departure from actuality. These negations would hold only if esthetic truth were limited to literal fact—as it is not. Factual propositions are themselves only partial abstractions from the whole truth; they never tell the whole story about the things to which they refer. Esthetic truth is another kind of revelation of what is so, through symbolic forms other than those of literal fact. Fictional works may be profoundly true, provided their literal untruths are employed as vehicles for a symbolic revelation of truth. Similarly, though the idealizations of art do not represent things as they actually and naturally are, they vividly portray the true forms of actual things, by the use of emphasis and simplification, or they may afford a true vision of excellence such as actual things do not exhibit. Thus, fiction and idealization in excellent art are means for achieving greater truthfulness than would be possible through fidelity to literal fact.

The final standard is *righteousness*. Since values are interdependent, esthetic worth is connected with ethical rightness. Esthetic value is not in an independent realm, where its own criteria bear no relation to other measures of worth. Art is not for art's sake, but for goodness' sake. Hence, when loyalty to values is affirmed, the stereotypes of the artist as free of moral restraints (and as a better artist because of the absence of such inhibitions) and of morality as contrary to esthetic enjoyment are repudiated, and the congruence of esthetic excellence with moral goodness is asserted. A morality that restricts or cripples creativity is in that respect defective, and an esthetic that denies or subverts ethical standards is therein faulty.

The foregoing criteria suggest some of the general standards defining esthetic excellence. They do not exhaust the possibilities of qualitative measures. To a certain extent these criteria overlap, and there are others that could be substituted for some of them. These may nonetheless serve to define the nature of qualitative worth.

Qualities such as these are universal in the sense that anyone may apprehend them, given the requisite personal discipline and conditions of observation. In this respect esthetic excellence, like truth, is public. The sense of beauty and depth of perceptual meaning are not private, untestable, and unsharable emotions. They are qualities of experience which result from the given forms of things in relation to the structures of properly habituated personality.

Not only are these qualities potentially universal in being thus public and sharable. They are also universal in their spheres of application, as was pointed out earlier in showing the meaning of esthetic democracy. The products of the so-called "fine arts" are exclusively devoted to esthetic purposes, but they are not the sole objects of esthetic concern. Still, they do have a special and distinctive importance, which to some extent justifies the custom of setting them apart as esthetic objects *par excellence*. Music, drama, painting, sculpture, poetry, architecture, and the dance fulfill a representative function in culture. They serve as standard-bearers for esthetic values, with a minimum of complication by concern for nonesthetic purposes. Creations in the fine arts especially excel in the quality of ideality, which must often be subordinated in ordinary affairs. The ideal character of the fine arts should not result in isolation from other spheres of life, but should enable them to be of greater service in lifting the esthetic level of all experience. Thus, their unique qualities may sustain, rather than negate, the pervasiveness of democratic concern for quality.

The many so-called "useful arts," such as carpentry, machining, and cooking, differ from the fine arts only in the predominance of the practical purposes for which the products are designed. These purposes define the idea or form of the esthetic object or act in a somewhat more restricted fashion than is the case where the artist is free to follow his own imagination without limit. The line between the fine arts and the useful arts is actually not clear; and there is good reason for it not to be drawn sharply, given the democratic principle of comprehensive esthetic relevance. Some fields, such as landscape gardening, interior decorating, and fashion designing, could quite appropriately be classed as either "fine" or "useful" arts. The artist, the artisan, the craftsman—all are concerned with embodying meanings in objects of sense.

Esthetic qualities are important even in scientific and technical fields, which are commonly regarded as the farthest removed from the arts. Good scientific theories are works of art. They harmonize a variety of facts within the compass of a unified conceptual structure. They, too, have meaning, depth, ideality, purity, and other attributes of qualitative worth. The common term "a beautiful theory" is thus quite apt. Applied science is an art, as the etymology of the word "technical" (from the Greek, *techne*, "an art") attests. The task of the engineer, for example, is to apply scientific knowledge to the creation of objects of use. In designing a material structure to perform most efficiently, the quality of functionality is especially important. In modern machine design, finesse—which in this field would more suitably be called precision—is also of crucial significance.

Among the scientific fields, mathematics has a particularly intimate connection with esthetic excellence. Mathematics is the science of form. It provides an exact and comprehensive treatment of such ideas as symmetry, rhythm, and function, which enter so largely into esthetic judgments. Moreover, mathematical systems, like scientific theories, are themselves esthetic creations of a high order.

Judgments of quality are pertinent also in the management of personal and corporate life. To be a civilized person is to conduct one's life in accord with such principles of excellence as consistency, balance, variety, and functional efficacy. A "wise" person is one whose deeds measure up to these and other esthetic standards. Emotional maturity is judged by such criteria as sense of proportion, correspondence of feelings with reality, unity of purpose, and flexibility—all of which are of an esthetic nature.

This range of esthetic concerns is emphasized because of what it means for education. Esthetic learning does not occur merely in the study of "art." It belongs prominently also in all of the so-called "academic" subjects, including science and mathematics, and in everything that is done in schools and homes for the development of manual, emotional, social, and civic grace, wisdom, and competence.

The study of the traditional arts ought to epitomize and vivify the general esthetic goals that apply to all the affairs of life. These specifically esthetic disciplines may thus be saved from the exclusiveness and fastidiousness that have so commonly reduced their power of elevating the whole level of culture.

Of particular significance for education is the application of esthetic criteria to human personality itself. Teachers and parents are to some extent fashioners of children's lives. Everything depends upon the models of worth that are used in the conduct of this work. The standards appropriate for education are precisely (though not exclusively) those that define esthetic excellence. Thus, the principles of esthetic value here discussed may serve not only as guides in creating and appreciating what are called "art objects" and as criteria of qualitative excellence in curricular matters outside of the arts, but as attributes of the good life and as a source of general educational aims.

The subject of manners is really a subdivision of the general subject of esthetics. Judgments about manners are made by applying the principles of esthetic excellence to the field of human relationships and personal conduct. Good manners are modes of behavior that are fitting and appropriate to a particular situation; bad manners are modes of behavior that are out of place in the same situation. The evaluation of fitness within a specific context is clearly an esthetic process.

At first it might seem that the study of manners is a matter of minor importance, hardly meriting treatment on a par with such major themes as intellectual life, work, and political organization. While there are books of etiquette which new brides and others may consult, manners are seldom the subject of serious social analysis by contemporary scholars. The study of manners is regarded not as a significant part of formal courses of instruction, but as entirely incidental to the program of most schools and colleges. What is there to study, it may be asked, when manners are nothing but arbitrary conventions, customs that have been developed largely as a result of historical accident? Surely there can be no truth or falsity, no right or wrong, about manners, no better or worse to call for analysis and to invite inquiry? Are not manners at the most a topic for anthropological description, and have not anthropologists shown that customs vary from society to society and from group to group in bewildering complexity, permitting no universal normative judgments?

Closer scrutiny suggests that manners are not as superficial as the viewpoint above would indicate, and that—rightly received—they are of great significance in democracy and education. Fundamentally manners are *symbolic forms*, which point to meanings beyond themselves. It is these meanings, not the forms of conduct in themselves, which are important, for they reflect the ideals and the spirit of a culture. Manners are a kind of language, a "language of the act," which often conveys meanings more effectively than can words. The crucial significance of linguistic skill is generally acknowledged. It clearly follows that the study of manners, one of the most powerful and commonly used kinds of language, is of considerable importance. Good manners express and help to conserve sound social values; bad manners manifest social decay and hasten the disintegration of civilization. No analysis of the good life and of the good society can be satisfactory without a consideration of the system of manners, which is an outward sign of inward spirit and purpose.

Manners ought, then, to be a subject of major concern in education. Instruction in manners and customs should be one of the essential parts of the curriculum. While homes are often particularly well fitted to provide such instruction, schools share in this responsibility, supplementing, correcting, and affording intellectual reinforcement for the teaching of manners in homes. In some cultures the principles of social conduct have been the chief subject of instruction in formal education. The best example is the long-enduring and highly stable classical Chinese civilization, where the Sages' writings, which were the source books for instruction, dealt for the most part and in great detail with the behavior appropriate to various persons, positions, and situations. Consideration of examples such as this may help to dispel the prejudice against the study of manners within the formal curriculum, by showing that people in other well-developed and successful cultures have considered the refinement of interpersonal relationships the central objective of education.

The present unhappy condition of mankind is not unrelated to the neglect of education in manners. The makers of modern industrial civilization have been preoccupied with the conquest of nature and with the advancement of knowledge and not with the patient and exacting inculcation of right habits in human relationships. Compared to the inhabitants of certain other cultures and times, most people today, with all their knowledge and power, are unskilled in the fine arts of personal and interpersonal conduct. Moderns have largely failed to see that technical mastery and intellectual opulence are a curse instead of a blessing in the absence of a system of mature social relationships mediated by a thoroughly learned code of manners. The relative neglect of manners in contemporary education is evidence of the dominant concern for understanding and control as compared with the patient weaving and preservation of the social fabric.

The world is, of course, not to be saved from its present discords and estrangements by the teaching of certain codes of conduct. Manners are all too often regarded in this fashion, simply as external acts to be learned and automatically performed. The important factors are the personal attitudes and social meanings of which the manners are the outward signs. Proper education in manners consists of teaching right relationships through the act-language by which these relationships are symbolized.

From a democratic standpoint, manners and education in manners are likely to appear suspect because of their usual association with aristocratic societies. The term "manners" is commonly thought to refer to the etiquette of the drawing room and hence to have pertinence only to the "upper classes." In aristocratic societies ordinary people tend to be thought of as unrefined and as needing manners only when they enter into relationships with "high-class" people. There is ample reason for democratic suspicion of manners, since customary codes of behavior are by nature traditional and conservative. In the long struggle for human freedom and equality the status quo had to be challenged, and with it the system of symbolic acts which helped to sustain it. The commoners who pressed their claims against kings and nobles could hardly be expected to regard with favor the ceremonials that expressed their own subordination. The French revolutionists were notoriously unmannerly in relation to their royal opponents, and the various communist revolutions have made a clean sweep of feudalistic and capitalistic patterns of behavior.

The rejection of aristocracy, whether by a democracy, by communism, or by some other collectivist system, does not, however, entail opposition to manners as such, but only to aristocratic manners. Every society needs symbols that embody its shared values. Every culture requires a reasonably stable set of customary acts to express its corporate spirit. The decline and the neglect of manners—

the absence of any clear code of conduct—are evidence of confusion about values and the loss of common ideals. When aristocracy gives way to some other stable social form, aristocratic manners are replaced by a system of symbolic acts that express the character of the new society. Fascists and communists have definite and striking ritual systems, which differ sharply from those of the older societies that they displaced.

Democracies, too, have behavior codes which express democratic intentions. The fact that there is relatively so little concern for manners in modern American society is not a consequence of democratic commitment but a sign of uncertainty and indecision concerning our values. Contemporary democratic culture is ceremonially impoverished. We do not possess a rich and secure tradition of symbolic acts which remind us of the faith we live by and which give body to the meanings we share.

What sort of manners do belong to a democratic society? What code of behavior should Americans teach their children? In answer, it should be granted at the outset that there is no one right pattern of manners for democracy. As indicated earlier, manners are a language. It is characteristic of language that many different symbolic systems can be used to express roughly the same world of meanings. To be sure, the meanings expressed by French, German, Japanese, Russian, and English are never identical; there is an inescapable element of untranslatability in every language. Still, this fact of linguistic singularity does not negate the general principle that there are many possible ways of symbolizing the same reality. In regard to the language of manners, it follows that there is no single code of customary conduct that expresses the democratic spirit. It is not the external act that should be the matter of concern, but the idea that it conveys.

Thus, there is room for endless invention and variation in the modes of behavior appropriate in a democracy. There is no fixed and inflexible code, deduced from democratic principles, which all who are faithful to democracy must observe and which should be taught in all homes and schools. Creative experimentation and individual or group variations in manners are in order, provided only that each pattern is designed to represent democratic meanings. Assuming that this proviso is satisfied, wide latitude in manner systems is desirable, because of the resulting greater interest and esthetic richness and the encouragement of freedom and individuality instead of sheer conformity.

Manners are not, then, simply arbitrary conventions, but are subject to normative judgments in the light of democratic ideals. If certain democratic values are presupposed, there will be corresponding appropriate ceremonial forms to express them. Furthermore, the manners characteristic of a democracy of desire will be quite different from those proper to a democracy of worth. In the former there is a constant tension between anarchistic individualism and collectivist pressures to conform, since the will and the wish are sovereign, and the basic problem is to effect a tolerable adjustment of competing wants. The two fundamental meanings to be represented in a democracy of desire are self-will and majority rule. The behavior appropriate to self-will is self-expression: doing what one wants to do, being emancipated from the restraints and represssions of old-fashioned times, acting the way one feels. The resulting "modern" manners appear to the adherents of more traditional views as "unmannerly" and the essence of rudeness.

Along with these manners of self-expression—and limiting them—are those that reflect majority rule. Their primary principle is "appearing to stay within the law," giving the impression of complying with the essential regulations for preserving public peace and order, looking innocent, not getting caught in an antisocial act. The function of such manners is opposite to the function of the manners of self-expression. They provide self-concealment instead of self-display. They signalize conformity to social demands—not, however, for the sake of common values, but in order that one may be left free to pursue his own ways. Such manners are a shield against criticism and interference by others. They are a "shell" or a "front," behind which one can live his own life undisturbed.

In such a democracy, manners are instruments of egocentricity. They constitute an ingenious and endlessly various complex of acts that enable a person to do and to get the most of what he wants without letting his avarice show and without getting a reputation that will close off or diminish his supply of gratifications. They enable one to cheat in marriage, or on examinations, or in business, or on income taxes, all the while appearing to be a decent, patriotic, even God-fearing person who, like all sensible people, wants only his share of the good things of life and would never do any harm to anybody.

Quite different is the rationale for manners in a democracy of worth, where customs and ceremonies are designed to express commitment to universal humane values. They are an outward sign of inward devotion to what is true, just, and appropriate to each occasion. The approved actions are calculated neither to express nor to conceal persons, but to celebrate and dramatize what is good. Such behavior lends grace to a person, and in a sense it serves as a mantle of honor to redeem his own dishonor, but these benefits are incidental and derivative rather than the primary objectives of conduct. Manners are thus modes of service, instead of ways of taking advantage. They reflect the intention of giving, not of getting. They are symbols and instruments not of power but of appreciation, compassion, and concern.

In a democracy of worth the destruction of traditional social symbols, which has taken place so widely in modern society, would be halted. Meaningful customs cannot be created overnight, nor can their symbolic power be assured by fiat. Well-tested codes of conduct provide an important living link with the past. Respect for such customs is a vital source of social continuity, security, and even productivity.

However, this respect is not for tradition as such, but only as a proven bearer of values. Authentic democracy therefore requires not only a principle of cultural conservation but also of criticism of customary behavior. Inherited codes of conduct often stand in the way of needed improvements. They may have been appropriate under earlier social circumstances which the tide of events has drastically changed. Hence, new codes adequate to the new occasions of modern life must be devised, and ways must be invented for improving the process of creating meaningful social symbols. As suggested earlier, the mass media can play a decisive part in this process. Given the rapidly changing character of modern industrial civilization, it is also necessary to shift the emphasis in manners away from the external forms (which may have to be modified as the conditions of life shift) to the democratic meanings that they express.

To sum up: Modern young people need to be taught manners: not the code of the emancipated ego, nor the pattern of conformity to the will of the majority, but the action-language of democracy, with due respect for worthy traditions from the past and determined criticism of unworthy ones. Their instruction should emphasize, not the overt acts in themselves, since these may soon become obsolete, but the fundamental democratic principles and ideals which the acts serve to dramatize.

It is not feasible to offer here a detailed and comprehensive analysis of a system of manners expressing the values of democracy. It must suffice to give several illustrations of situations to which the question of appropriate conduct in a democracy of worth is relevant.

Consider first manners of *speech.* These are governed by the fundamental principles of consideration for the word and for other people and the will to create community by reciprocal communication. These root principles may be developed more specifically in such corollary principles as the following:

The speaker should have respect—even reverence—for the language he is privileged to use. The most important rule of manners in speech is to use language with regard for its proper dignity and worth, and not thoughtlessly, carelessly, or cheaply. Language bears the personality of the speaker, and when inferior words are spoken, personality is degraded, both in the one who utters them and in those who hear them. Speaking is properly an art, and spoken words ought to be the loving handiwork of an artist. No true artist creates objects that do not command his admiration and affection. So, too, should a person's speaking be a creating and an offering of something worthy of high regard.

It is astonishing to hear even people of high achievement and excellent reputation use mean and foul language on many occasions, as though such effusions had no real significance, being mere sounds which are dispersed as soon as they are said. This habit actually reveals a basic disrespect for language and for the ideal values of which words are the vehicles. Human beings have a duty to respect words as bearers of life, and hence to use only words that symbolize what is true and right.

Speech should be ready but not continuous. It is desirable to be alert and sensitive to the need to engage in conversation. One should be able to talk freely and easily, without awkward pauses and agonized struggle for words. In general, silence is not golden—at least not the empty silence where two or more people confronting one another lack either the ability or the concern to employ language to create a shared experience. On the other hand, there are occasions when silence between companions is desirable, when the uttering of words would break an unspeakable communion. Readiness in speech simply means the ability to speak easily when appropriate, and otherwise to remain silent. Compulsive talkers are not well mannered. Some people have the habit and feel the obligation to maintain a steady stream of conversation whenever they are not alone. Proper speech has a rhythmic quality, a pattern of ebb and flow, of refreshing pauses to consolidate ideas, to reflect on what has been said, and to prepare well for the next utterances. Continuous talking in any event is ruled out on the grounds of respect for language, since a steady stream of utterances can hardly be carefully enough considered and artfully enough fashioned to make it worthy of high regard. Language, like money under inflationary conditions, loses its value as a medium of exchange when issued in excessive quantity and without regard for the real assets underlying it.

Speech should be appropriate to the occasion. It is bad form to have a "line" which one recites with minor variations to all and sundry. Such speech is fostered by those who believe in self-expression as a major use of language. Good speaking manners manifest sensitivity and flexibility, so that what is said may be true and relevant to circumstances. This does not mean that the content of speech should be compromised in the interest of expediency, but simply that it should serve truth and right as they pertain to the particular event.

Talking should be *with* others and not *to* them or *at* them. It should be in the mode of dialogue, not monologue. This is true even of public speaking, where audible response from the audience is not possible. Address should still be in such a manner as to invite and expect response and not only reception and acceptance. Those who use language to express themselves—rather than to communicate something of value to others—are not concerned with either the situation in which they speak or the persons to whom they speak.

If true communication is to take place, it is evident that speech must occur in proper order. Each speaker must wait his turn. The proper order is not always or even usually one of regular sequence and of "equal time." Proper order depends upon the inner logic of the conversation and the potential contributions of the participants.

To apprehend the right order is not easy. It requires awareness by each party of the developing pattern of the conversation as a whole and progressive evaluations of the place of each person in the common enterprise. Talking is an art, but not an art of the individual creator; it is a social art, requiring the ability to work with others in a cooperative creative venture.

Those for whom speech is a tool of desire can have scant concern for proper order. For them, the only propriety is that of adjusting to the strivings of others, so that each gets a reasonably satisfying share of self-assertion. Truly decorous conversation is founded on the assumption that the purpose of speaking is not to serve anyone's interests but to bring to light the good and the true, that all may better cherish and serve it. With such a goal no one competes with others for a place in the conversation, nor rudely interrupts, nor despairs of "getting a word in edgewise." Each awaits the right time to speak, speaks in the light of the whole and for the sake of all, and defers to others when he senses that a fitting moment for their contribution has come.

Well-mannered speaking conforms to accepted conventions of linguistic usage. There are rules of grammar, syntax, and pronunciation which govern correct speech in a given time and society. To follow these conventions faithfully is evidence of respect both for language and for those to whom it is directed. Grammar is, as it were, the skeletal structure of speech. To violate it is to destroy the integrity and articulation of the symbolic system. Hence, careful instruction in proper grammatical forms should be an important constituent of the educational program.

These principles suggest some of the criteria for judging manners of speaking. Americans are particularly in need of giving heed to such ideals. As compared with some other peoples—notably the English and the French—Americans are flagrantly careless with words. To remedy this condition the art of conversation needs to be more assiduously and thoughtfully cultivated in homes and in schools. A greater concern and respect for elegance of style and for power in the spoken word should be encouraged. Fascination and delight are the appropriate attitudes toward the incalculably rich treasury of linguistic forms. One of the most serious losses in the modern activity-centered education, which to a considerable extent has taken the place of the classical linguistic curriculum, has been the decline in concern for refined speech. Words are the most powerful bearers of life and thought. Only if young people learn to employ language gracefully and with discrimination can they hope to enter into the full measure of their humane patrimony.

Next consider manners in *eating*. One should eat so as to show mastery over appetite rather than subservience to appetite. Man is like the lower animals in having to eat to live; he should not be like them in his manner of eating. All animals eat and drink to satisfy hunger and thirst, but in man these activities may be transformed into bearers of meaning. Through the power of reason they are suffused with significance. They take on a symbolic character. Man does not *merely* eat; he eats significantly.

In accordance with this principle, eating should be done in an orderly, controlled manner. One should not eat ravenously, devouring food in response to the imperious urgings of hunger, but with a restraint that indicates that the person, not the food, is in command of the situation. Moreover, the physical evidences of eating should be minimized.

While enjoyment of good food is certainly commendable, it is not good manners to rivet one's attention upon the food, even when one is very hungry. The meal is ideally an occasion for communion with other people, and it is to this consummation that the activity of eating should be directed. Partaking of food provides signal opportunities to symbolize concern for the welfare of others, through offering food to one's companions, sensitivity to their needs and feelings, and mutual enjoyment of the fruits of the earth. Thus, interest and attention ought to be concentrated not on what is being eaten, no matter how attractive it may be, but upon the people with whom the occasion is shared. Even when a person eats alone, he should practice centering his thoughts upon the relationships of worth which the energies of life support and not upon the food and drink themselves. Fascinated absorption with the process of ingestion is appropriate for the dog with his bone or the infant on the mother's breast, but not for mature persons. Instruction in manners that sustain the habits of detachment, control, and social sensitivity in eating are part of the long and never-completed task of weaning.

One further application of the central principle is the rule that in general food should be handled by implements and not directly by hand or mouth. This practice is dictated in part by hygienic considerations, since the hands are used for many other purposes and may carry sources of infection. The more basic reason is that the use of tools—a unique human capability—helps to make eating a truly human activity. It lifts the human being from the animal level of direct contact with the objects of consumption. Knives, forks, and spoons permit greater finesse in the handling of food than is possible by tearing, grasping, or sucking. They also leave the hands free and clean for other distinctively human functions.

Good manners in play follow four main principles. Of first importance is fidelity to the rules of the game. Play is a mannered, disciplined human activity, in which success depends upon scrupulous adherence to various formal premises. Breaking the rules for one's own gain or making one's own rules is cause for exclusion from play. The first rule of the game is fair play, and the canons of fairness are predetermined by common agreement. The basic code of manners for any given game is thus contained in the definition or constitution of that game.

The second principle is enthusiasm, seriousness, wholeheartedness. It is bad manners to play perfunctorily, absentmindedly, or listlessly. If one cannot play with vigor and singlemindedness, he should not play at all. The whole point of a game is energetic pursuit of a short-range objective within the framework of a given set of rules. The spirit of play depends upon such concentration of effort. It is unfair to those with whom one plays to undertake the game in a distracted and divided frame of mind, for the spirit of the game is a consequence of the common dedication of the players to the pursuit at hand.

This enthusiasm for the playing should be coupled with an attitude of detachment about the results. One should play hard and with the aim of winning, but should also accept success and failure in competition with equally good grace. Good sportsmen take both gains and losses with equanimity, as part of the game. It is bad playing manners to react to losses with ill temper or dejection. For the true sportsman every contest is a new beginning: he carries no burdens of earlier defeat and wears no garlands of prior victory; he plays each game solely for itself, as if there were no other.

Good manners in play presuppose loyalty to partners and respect for opponents. In team play it is the effectiveness of the team, and not individual performance, that counts most. Thus, each player must learn to subordinate his personal ambition to the success of the organization of which he is a part. He must cultivate sensitivity to the reactions of the others and concern for the best utilization of their peculiar abilities. Respect for opponents is made manifest by evident appreciation of and admiration for their achievements and by scrupulous concern for fair play.

All of these principles of good manners in play comport best with a philosophy of life guided by devotion to worth, rather than with an acquisitive philosophy. The good player loses himself in the game. He is faithful to its rules and willingly submits to their yoke. While at play he is wholeheartedly dedicated to the activity in and for itself and for what it does for him. He is indifferent to success or failure, which so wholly dominate acquisitive pursuits, and he knows the secret of finding the good life through losing it in concern for comrades and in duly honoring competitors.

Finally, consider the manner of *teacher-pupil relationships*. In reaction against the authoritarian formalism of classical education, modern educational progressives have advocated a relationship of essential equality between teacher and student. They regard teachers as partners in inquiry with their students, the main difference being the greater experience of the former, because of which they can serve as "resource persons" in the learning process. The corresponding appropriate manners are those of friends and colleagues. This egalitarian position grows out of the view that knowledge is simply an instrument to serve human interests and that there are no criteria of value beyond those of human satisfaction. With such a view, the function of the teacher is to help the students solve their problems and meet their needs.

The manners appropriate for teachers and students in a democracy of worth are neither those of the classical authoritarian school, where it is presupposed that the schoolmaster knows the truth and is expected to inculcate it, nor those of the progressive school, which is built on the principle that truth is by definition what solves human problems. A school in a democracy of worth is founded on the premise that there are values of truth and right, not of human determination, to be sought and served, and that teachers, though never fully in possession of these values, are the appointed custodians and mediators of them to the young. The office of the teacher is therefore an exalted one, and the manners of teachers and students should fittingly symbolize that exaltation. The teacher should be regarded with honor and shown deference by his students, not because of any personal superiority or privilege, but as a mark of devotion to the matters of worth that he in his official capacity represents. The teacher should exercise authority and the students render obedience, never absolutely and unquestioningly, nor in the spirit of personal command and submission, but always with regard to evidence and for the sake of what is right.

The principles illustrated in the foregoing examples may be summarized and integrated by the statement of certain general ideals of character from which good manners spring. The most fundamental of these ideals is *respect for other persons*. The cardinal characteristic of a well-mannered person is respectfulness, to any and every other person under all circumstances. This respect cannot be based on what a person actually is or does, for many people are not really respectable most of the time, and nobody is really respectable all of the time. Democratic respect springs rather from devotion to the good of which every person is potentially capable. From this respect follows considerateness for the uniqueness and individuality of each person and concern that everyone be himself and not molded according to the will and desire of anyone else.

Good manners also depend on *self-respect*. Actually self-respect underlies respect for others, since one's own being is the source of knowledge of personal worth and of human potentiality. One who has no faith or hope in and for himself cannot have a positive outlook on other people. A well-mannered person has the sense of dignity, the poise, and the confidence born of a vivid consciousness of his privilege in participating in the human venture. Bad manners are symptoms of an inability to accept oneself, resulting in various attempts either to escape existence ("crawling into one's shell," getting lost in the crowd) or to prove one's power and importance (self-assertion, exhibitionism, aggressiveness).

Respect for self and for others produces *gentleness*. People with good manners are "gentlefolk." Their relationships are based on persuasion rather than on force. They live as reasonable people, who appeal to the understanding and consent of free agents rather than to the sanctions of superior power. In aristocratic societies the gentleman is defined as a person of high social position, one born into the "right" family. Gentility in a democracy has nothing to do with social status, but depends only on the considerate, patient, tender, and reasonable quality of character. Every person in a democracy can and ought to become a gentleman.

Proper manners are evidence of refinement of character. A refined person is no longer crude; that is, he is no longer in the state of nature. He is not barbarous, but civilized. He has achieved rational control of brute impulses. He has finesse, is trained, has become disciplined. In the broadest sense, refinement is the fundamental goal of all education.

Another character trait implicit in good manners is modesty, or humility. This quality comes from knowing one's own limitations and having a just appreciation of one's place in the whole scheme of human relationships. The modest person avoids extravagance in speech and action. He has a sense of proportion and balance. Above all, he has a lively awareness of the significance of other persons and the ability to articulate his activities constructively with theirs.

Refinement and humility beget patience. The ill-mannered person cannot endure delay and frustration in satisfying his demands. He is stimulated by success, but dejected and irritated by failure. The well-mannered person seeks to understand a situation, with due consideration for the conflicting interests of others, and then endeavors to act in accordance with what is possible and just. He can suffer the defeat of his private plans because the meaning of his life is contained not in them but in his commitment to the good, which is neither made nor justified by him.

Obedience is a further character trait needed for appropriate conduct. Proper human relationships rest not only on respect for persons but also on respect for the orders of authority which differentiated social existence requires. In a democracy these structures are quite different from those in nondemocratic societies, but they are nonetheless essential, and willing, intelligent observance of them is requisite to right behavior. Good manners are incompatible with the spirit of autonomy. They grow from due recognition of necessary functional differences in a complex society and from acceptance of the just requirements of membership in it. Manners are the symbols of allegiance to the approved principles of the social establishment.

Obedience is not to be construed as including compliance with unjust social orders. Good manners are usually defined in relation to the existing conventions of society. From the standpoint of a democracy of worth this conception is inadmissible. Signifying loyalty to an unjust system, conventionally regarded as good manners, from a more fundamental view is bad manners. Concern for manners should never undermine necessary social criticism.

Finally, right manners are an expression of *sincerity*. They reveal the person. Perhaps the most widespread abuse of manners is their use as a shield to hide behind. It is commonly supposed that one of the main functions of social customs is to give people an acceptable appearance, regardless of the real person behind the appearance. Education in manners is then tantamount to teaching techniques of deception. Conduct that is designed merely to put up a good front is ill-mannered, no matter how correct it may be by conventional standards, for it is in effect a lie. Good manners are a true report of intended loyalties. This does not exclude manners that make a person appear better than he is. There is nothing wrong with "putting one's best foot forward," provided it is really one's own foot, and provided taking the step is a sign of a genuine commitment to become the person thus represented. Sincerity of manner is honesty in the disclosure of personal aspirations.

Work is a third domain of creative activity. Broadly speaking, work is an art. The worker is an "artisan," a molder and maker of things. Good work requires skill in production, careful design, and excellence of form. It is criteria such as these that link the values of work with those of esthetic excellence and good manners within the general category of creative effort.

The evaluation of work in the economy of life is directly related to the general character of the social system. In particular, the development of democratic forms of social organization has profoundly affected the outlook on work. In the aristocratic society, labor is for slaves, not for free men. The mark of a gentleman is having leisure— not having to work. Labor is regarded as degrading, as beneath the dignity of a man, as a burden to be borne by those who live under the command of others. However, this aristocratic denigration of work applies chiefly to manual labor, for the intellectual tasks of management, of government, of scholarship, and of artistic creation are regarded as quite appropriate for free men.

Democratic society repudiates the contrast of slave and free and thereby universalizes the responsibility for work. In principle no one is exempt from work, and no fixed classes of persons are assigned to the labor of hand and brain, respectively. Society is not expected to be stratified with respect to labor and leisure, for work is accepted as an intrinsic and universal component of the human situation.

The climax of the democratization of work has come about through machine technology, under which machines are used to perform most of what was formerly done by slaves, and much more besides. Machines have radically altered the nature of work, largely by eliminating man as a source of animal power and by reducing to a minimum the routine and repetitive types of work that men must perform. With the continued development of automatic machines, the proportion of jobs requiring intellectual rather than sheer physical effort is rapidly increasing, with the prospect that before long virtually all labor will be technical, managerial, or creative. Even complex intellectual processes are more and more being performed by machines, thus moving the requirements of labor still further in the direction of imaginative planning and evaluative judgment.

Thus, modern inventions have reinforced the democratization of society by obliterating the duality of manual labor and intellectual labor and by making it possible—even necessary for the sake of efficiency—for everyone to engage in the kinds of work reserved in aristocratic societies for gentlemen.

The universalizing of work has been an important factor in the growth of democratic education. Since work is everyone's responsibility, means must be provided for preparing workers to do their jobs effectively. Furthermore, as the nature of the tasks needing to be done has become increasingly complex and as the intellectual factors in work have become dominant, the required duration and attainment level of education have sharply advanced. Hence, education in modern industrial society is strongly oriented toward occupational preparation. It follows that work and education are closely interrelated in contemporary culture. Prevailing attitudes toward work are reflected in educational programs and objectives, and educational ideals and practices have an influence on vocational life. The nature of democratic vocational values is accordingly of major importance to all who teach.

Contemporary vocational life mainly reflects the concerns of the acquisitive outlook characteristic of the democracy of desire, and education largely follows this pattern. According to this prevailing conception, work is regarded primarily as a means of getting what one wants. A person works in order to achieve, and achievement means reaching the goals one has set for himself, securing the goods and position he craves, fulfilling the ambitions he has entertained, satisfying the demands he has made on life. In short, the goal of work is success. The purpose of labor is to overcome obstacles to progress. One makes progress by "getting ahead" (of other people). According to this view, the harder a person works, the more he is likely to succeed. The more diligently and skillfully he does his job—and, hence, the better his educational preparation for it—the more he will be rewarded for his efforts.

Work is thus regarded as a price to be paid for subsequent satisfaction, beyond the work. The laborer "slaves" at his job in order to become "free" for enjoyment when the job is done. The goal is outside of and beyond the task, in the rewards that are due for accomplishment. Under undemocratic autocracies the workers labored by compulsion, without hope of real reward and hence without any opportunity for "success." In the democracy of desire, rewards are proportioned to productive achievement, so that the degree to which a person may satisfy his desires is directly related to his labor output.

The freedom-for-satisfaction which is secured by labor under this system is perfected by the money system. The worker is not rewarded by payment in specified goods and services but in money which can be exchanged for whatever is needed or desired. Money is the guarantee of liberty in the fulfillment of wants. It is the source of independence outside of work, the proof that beyond the job one is truly a free man and not a slave.

Money is the modern symbol of autonomy, of unrestrained self-determination. It is easy to understand, then, why the rewards sought for work are conceived in monetary terms. To labor for money is to secure the right to autonomy. Money is the assurance of having whatever the heart desires. In a democracy of desire, money is the absolute good, from which all blessings flow, precisely because it is neutral in respect to values: it contains no judgments of better or worse, no directions about right or wrong. It is the token of unconditional power, of unrestricted liberty. Money is the measure of success, for the meaning of success in such a society is having the power to command what one wants.

When want-satisfaction is thus dominant, work becomes of first importance, for it is the prime road to success. A person's whole destiny depends upon getting a job that pays well. The ideal of character is the "productive personality," one who "gets things done," the "go-getter." Such a person need not be overtly aggressive, like the rugged individualists who dominated the American business scene in the late nineteenth century. Instead, he may follow the way of the "organization man," who merges his life into the corporate pattern. In either case the goal is the same—namely, success in the job. The conditions of success may differ from one type of work to another or from era to era, but the achievement objectives are identical.

In the success-oriented society, education is completely vocationalized. All teaching and learning are justified in the light of their contribution to work. Education is the key to social mobility, via the ladder of occupational achievement. The prime motive for going to school, for doing well in studies, and for staying in school to the highest level possible is to secure a good job. This vocational emphasis affects not only the manifestly practical fields of study, such as the technical and professional disciplines, but even the "pure" liberal arts and sciences, which have commonly been represented as the studies appropriate for the nurture of the free man—studies whose justification and worth lie solely in themselves and not in any extrinsic purposes. In our acquisitive society it is now the fashion to insist that there is nothing so practical as theory (thus defending the study of "pure" and apparently useless subjects), and that a broad humanistic education is really the best preparation for ambitious young people today because their work as executives will require a deep understanding of human motives and the capacity, gained from a wide cultural perspective, to adapt readily to the new circumstances of a dynamic civilization. Though there is doubtless much truth in these claims, their validity is not the point of present interest, which is rather the further evidence they provide of the pervasiveness of vocational criteria and motives in contemporary education.

Under the desire-dominated philosophy of work the hunger for rewards stimulates a vast outpouring of human energy. Enterprise flourishes. Eager and ambitious men, women, and children vie with one another for pre-eminence in production in order to secure a larger share of the rewards that accrue from these efforts. Meanwhile, work takes on the aspect of an unbearable burden. Dominated as it is by the limitless demands for rewards, after which others too are grasping, work becomes an oppressive and destructive force in human life. Because of the strain and anxiety occasioned by it, the intrinsic satisfactions in labor are lost and the extrinsic satisfactions, which are supposed to be the reward of effort, are themselves spoiled by the ever-present consciousness of the human price being paid for them.

In order to justify the unpleasant and anxious exertions required in this competitive scheme, the worker searches for more intense kinds of satisfaction which will enable him to forget his burdens for a time and to prove to himself and to others that the struggle is worth while. He engages in acts of conspicuous consumption, of extravagant display, and of debauchery, which put even heavier pressure on him to earn enough to pay for them and at the same time drain him of the energy needed to compete successfully. The result is a vicious circle of alternating determined effort and frenetic grasping for enjoyment, both increasingly destructive of personal well-being.

Thus, man is reduced to the condition of slavery by the very work that is meant to liberate him. The harder he works for the liberty that is supposed to be its fruit, the more tightly the shackles are fastened upon him. This condition is a consequence of the unlimited nature of human wants. As long as the fulfillment of desire is the criterion of human good, mankind follows a path of certain futility, for each craving supplied leads only to a new and larger demand. Attainment of each goal opens up the vista of even more ambitious objectives to be reached. Success is an insatiable overlord. Linking work to want-satisfaction places an unbounded demand on the worker, thus committing him to abject servitude.

This overpowering compulsion to work under the desire philosophy is accompanied by a basic devaluation of labor. Work is regarded as the means to an end different and distinct from itself. One does the job for the sake of what comes after the day's work. The monetary rewards are what count, and for their sake the burdens of labor are endured. Of course, if desires can be satisfied and rewards can be obtained without work, so much the better. Hence, alongside the emphasis on work appears a pervasive rejection of labor. A person works in order to get out of work. For many people the whole meaning of a job is contained in the promise of vacation with pay. Stenographers will sit for fifty weeks at their typewriters sustained by the prospect of two weeks in Bermuda. Teachers will endure nine months of torture in the classroom and six weeks of drudgery in summer school for the sake of a month in Europe or at a resort. Similarly, many workers are buoyed up during their years of labor by the thought of a happy retirement, while still others are spurred to extraordinary effort or are willing to undertake unusually hazardous or unpleasant assignments so as to make enough money to retire early. Unfortunately the dehumanizing effects of protracted, intense labor without intrinsic meaning generally render the worker incapable of enjoying the retirement freedom which he so eagerly anticipated.

Further evidence of the rejection of work is the multiplication of labor-saving devices in our advanced industrial society. There can be no question about the value of machines that make it unnecessary for men to serve as beasts of burden, greatly increase the efficiency of the craftsman, and release human beings for higher forms of activity. However, a host of modern gadgets, of which electric can-openers and push-button automobile window lifts are typical, are not primarily functional but are toys for the amusement of people "who have everything," and are symbols of the repudiation of labor. Again, there is the curious self-contradiction of a society with ingenious and industrious people expending great productive efforts to avoid the necessity of expending efforts.

In still another direction the attitude toward work when the interest philosophy prevails is evident in the phenomena of criminality, particularly in the various forms of larceny. Graft, bribery, misappropriation of funds, forgery, and allied criminal acts are attempted short cuts to satisfaction. They are ways of getting what is desired without working for it. In recent years in the United States there has been a mounting number of thefts by "respectable" white-collar employees and officials as well as by the usual professional criminals. This is not surprising in a society so largely devoted as ours is to pecuniary gain and so ambivalent about work.

Less spectacular but safer are the many legitimate ways of getting something for little or nothing. Sinecures that pay well but make few demands are considered a great prize. Many a corporation or government official draws his salary but renders scarcely any services. Strong labor unions protect many men in positions that technical advances have rendered unnecessary and obsolete. Capping all these ways of winning without working are stock market and real estate speculation. For many people nothing better epitomizes the American Dream than the possibility of making a fortune simply by paper transactions without ever engaging in any *real* labor.

Phenomena such as those described above seem to require the following view of the relation between interest and effort: When the good is defined by reference to the pursuit of interests, work will be expended only when it is necessary to gain the desired ends. When desires can be attained without effort, no work will be done. Thus arises the attitude that the good life is a life without work, and that the measure of the value of existence is freedom from toil. This view is accompanied by the expectation that the benefits of civilization will continue to accrue, as gifts of nature, without any demand on the energies of men for their creation and maintenance. This is the situation so tellingly treated in Ortega y Gasset's *Revolt of the Masses*. Modern man takes the products of civilization for granted, as if they were dropped from trees in a tropical paradise. He rejects the demand placed upon him continually to make and remake culture. He denies the need for unremitting effort by each generation to re-create the forms of life that lift mankind above the beast.

The consequences of this devaluing of work are twofold. First, men are afflicted with an oppressive feeling of boredom. The freshness and vigor of life are replaced by dispirited lassitude. The capacity for keen enjoyment departs, and one is beset by a sense of meaninglessness. One no longer feels needed or wanted. The stimulus of high purposes and exciting goals is gone, and one comes to regard himself as a worthless parasite.

The subjective woes are accompanied by objective ones. In the work-despising society, culture is imperiled. The hard-won institutions of civilization decay and disintegrate. Refinement lapses into grossness, and profundity fades into triviality. Standards deteriorate, and qualitative discriminations disappear. A pall of dull mediocrity hangs over the land.

Homes and schools are necessarily implicated in these conditions. Education cannot escape the ultimate effects of the acquisitive philosophy. With the growth of American industrial society in the nineteenth century, it became apparent that education was an important road to success. If young people were to rise above the level of their parents, they clearly needed the knowledge and skill that education could supply. Schools and colleges were established in great numbers, and more and more young people took advantage of this great new opportunity for upward movement on the ladder of success. It was hard work, but the rewards of educational achievement were great and worthy of the effort.

As education to ever higher levels became a general obligation, it assumed more and more the aspect of a burden rather than an opportunity. Students increasingly occupied themselves with finding ways of avoiding the tasks set for them, and teachers spent more and more energy in the disciplinary role of trying to keep the students on the job.

Partly to meet this unsatisfactory condition, a progressive movement in education was inaugurated. Its proponents sought to re-establish the vital connection between the student and the curriculum and thus to make the effort of learning meaningful, by relating studies to the student's own actual life situations. This was in some respects an admirable and well-conceived direct attack on the problem of work devaluation. In the hands of skillful teachers the new methods of instruction, appealing to the active or latent concerns of the students, were the basis for outstanding educational achievement. The new philosophy above all provided a foundation for the continual reconstruction of the curriculum by removing it from its traditional position of static detachment and setting it into direct relationship with the changing interests and problems of human life.

Despite its merits, the new education proved to be corruptible. Why? The corruption came from emphasizing the child and forgetting the curriculum. The new theories provided no sufficient foundation for knowledge and values. The focus was on man as an intelligent social organism seeking to solve his problems and satisfy his wants. The true and the good were dislodged from their positions of independence, priority, and permanence and were subordinated to considerations of human interest and satisfaction. Success-oriented education in the long run leads to enslavement by work and to a countermove to reject work. This explains the curious phenomenon of "soft pedagogy" arising out of an educational philosophy aimed at stimulating serious effort by students. The concern for making studies interesting, useful, and relevant degenerated into the attempt to make students comfortable. The rigors of academic discipline were supplanted by painless studies which everyone could enjoy—but which few were able to respect.

The widespread practice of academic dishonesty is a further reflection of the prevailing view of work. If results can be obtained without labor, no effort will be expended. If the desired grades and certificates can be secured by the short-cut route of cheating on papers and examinations, why undergo the pain of doing the work honestly? Recent surveys indicate that most students do not regard cheating as a serious offense, and that many accept it without difficulty as one of the tools of academic success.

It is instructive to reflect on the fact that the main challenge to the softness and triviality in the modern American curriculum has come as a result of communist successes. We have been frightened into re-examining our educational system by the spectacle of Soviet achievement in science and technology. The frenzy of our reaction is a symptom of our involvement in precisely the same success system that underlies the communists' zeal. Despite its rejection of private property, communism is the extreme case of a gain-motivated social system. Ambition to succeed, the will to compete, and the pursuit of power are central to communist ideology. The autonomy of man (through collective organization) is the central article of communist faith. Communist will to work will eventually be dissolved in a sea of meaninglessness. Successors to the present generation of revolutionists will enjoy the affluence of the people's paradise, they, too, will look upon work as something to be avoided, and they will at length also suffer the oppression of boredom in a world without values. Thus, though Americans may indeed need to reconstruct their educational system, it should not be done in the light of the communist model, whose central success principle is already at work undermining our own civilization.

Thus far our analysis of the democracy of desire as it bears upon work has concentrated on the resulting alternation between slavish effort and avoidance of labor. Two further consequences of this philosophy merit consideration: the obliteration of qualitative distinctions between kinds of work, and the atomization of the occupational structure. When the only important concern is the rewards of work, and when labor is regarded simply as a means to monetary gain, the nature of the occupation is of secondary importance. Work is work, and what one does is determined by the rewards offered. The choice of occupation is then governed largely by marketplace considerations. The fundamental questions are not: What will I contribute? What is the value of the service I will render?—but: What inducements and privileges are provided? What are the salary and fringe benefits? What opportunities for advancement are offered?

When this system prevails, education is commandeered into the service of the work market. Curriculums are arranged in response to occupational demands. Schooling is regarded mainly as job preparation. If the biggest rewards are offered in business, then business schools and prebusiness courses thrive. If the current demand is for scientists and engineers, institutions and studies designed to equip them for this work are created. Consistent with the general pattern, qualitative distinctions and independent evaluations even in education are subordinated to criteria of demand.

The other consequence of the acquisitive philosophy is the atomizing of the occupational structure in modern industrial society. If gain is the criterion of value in work, efficiency—maximum results from minimum effort—is the major consideration. This efficiency requires a high degree of occupational specialization. Each worker performs one kind of task, which he learns to accomplish with great speed and accuracy. The specialists must be directed and coordinated by managers whose job it is to maintain effective organization of the parts. In this kind of society essential qualities of human nature are sacrificed to productive efficiency (and to the consequent consumptive abundance). Human beings lose their full, many-sided humanity when they specialize too narrowly. They become things rather than persons when they are trained only to do a particular limited set of tasks according to a standard formula. They fail to rise to their stature as creative individuals when they are treated as interchangeable and replaceable parts in the social machine. By concentrating on one activity they miss the sense of the whole, which is a major source of the sense of meaning and purpose in work. Moreover, the development of a managerial hierarchy powerful enough to weld the specialist workers into an effective unity presents a threat to democratic freedom and engenders habits of mind that undermine the individual's sense of civic responsibility.

The dominance of specialism is clearly evident in modern education. Success in scholarly production, like success in other kinds of work, requires high concentration of effort. Furthermore, the various occupational specialties depend upon training programs of a correspondingly narrow and intense character. Specialized scholars stand at the summit of academic prestige, and subject-matter compartmentalization characterizes the curriculum, even to some extent in the elementary schools. Academic generalists are regarded with pity, condescension, or contempt and usually find it possible to survive in the academic scramble only by redeeming their generality through affiliation with one of the specialized disciplines. Broadly humanistic studies suffer, while technical disciplines thrive.

In a democracy of worth, work is not a means to achieve desired benefits, but a response to the call of duty and a channel for devoted service. It is a way of fulfilling responsibilities and of creating and sustaining things of value. The obligation to work is universal, since responsibility for the right belongs to everyone alike. This universality of duty is the ground of the democratic character of work. Responsibility for the right is no respecter of persons, groups, or classes; none are exempt from its claims.

The measure of goodness is neither productivity nor the satisfaction of wants. It is qualitative, not quantitative. Since work measured by such standards is no longer subject to the command of boundless desires, the furious striving of the success-oriented society is absent. Instead, work is regarded as creative activity performed in obedience to the ideal of goodness. It is accepted in proper relation to other activities of life. It is not alternately grasped and rejected, as it is when desire governs. It is regarded in perspective and with a sense of proportion in the total economy of life. With this attitude, work is not a burden, but a creative opportunity. One is not a slave, subject to the tyranny of the drive for success, but a willing servant of the good.

More important still, labor done out of devotion to the good is justified not by extrinsic rewards but by the quality of the work itself. Thus it is a source of meaning. It has intrinsic value. It is accepted and welcomed as a significant and essential feature of life—as a necessary ingredient of the human situation. When work is valued in itself and is seen as a means of expressing one's loyalty to the good, it is welcomed rather than avoided. It is an occasion for rejoicing, for enthusiastic endeavor different in spirit from the feverish, anxious striving of the ambitious. There is no thought of resort to dishonest means to escape effort, no subterfuge, and no bypassing aimed at getting something for nothing, since the whole motive for work is not getting but giving, making, serving, creating.

In the democracy of worth a person works because he sees an opportunity to advance a good cause, to meet a real need. Life without work is viewed with aversion, and the right kind of work is embraced with thankfulness as a source of personal and social well-being. Constructive activity is essential to health of mind and body. Human beings are endowed with capacities that need to be employed; if they are not used, they atrophy, and personality deteriorates. The elemental necessity for work and its fundamental standard of rightness stem from this basic human requirement for the active exercise of native capabilities. Besides this personal need for life-giving activity, work is necessary for the preservation and advancement of civilization. Under the philosophy of worth each generation accepts its responsibility for making and remaking the culture. It is understood that the benefits of civilization do not come automatically from the cornucopia of nature but must be continually created and renewed by human effort.

While education in such a society contributes to the preparation of workers, the whole educational effort is not vocationalized. Preparation for an occupation is only one among several major objectives of the schools, and this goal is always pursued with due regard for the basic needs of human nature and of the good society. When the universal obligation to work is an unquestioned assumption, teachers and parents can require and expect serious work by children. Sustained labor is regarded not as an imposition to be avoided but as a normal and just component of human existence. Teachers and pupils do not judge the desirability of various studies and learning activities by the pleasure, comfort, or satisfaction they yield; their sole concern is for the contribution made to the development of right habits of thought and conduct. Young people readily learn to respect parents and teachers who respect them enough to make demands upon them commensurate with their ability and inspired by concern for truth and right. They cannot respect parents and teachers who either exercise arbitrary power over them or are guided primarily by their wants and wishes.

Human beings are made for hard work; they grow and thrive on its challenge and find zest in submitting faithfully to its yoke. Yet young people will not normally discover this without the sustained and patient insistence by adults that they expend effort in significant work. This is the obligation of home and school. The key to effectiveness in such adult leadership is the sincere appreciation by those who teach of the intrinsic worth of the work they ask their students to do. And this appreciation grows out of the teachers' own loyalty and enthusiasm for the work to which they are called.

When values, instead of interests, are the governing consideration, discrimination among different kinds of work becomes important. People do not choose their jobs simply on the basis of money return; their first concern is the worth of the work, the contribution it makes to a significant life. Furthermore, the distribution of occupations within society is not determined simply by the pressures of the market. Instead, workers are apportioned to various jobs with due regard for both individual competences and the needs of the good society. Ideally the desirable distribution should be achieved through choice by individual workers, with maximum freedom to change from one position to another. To accomplish the ideal, this freedom must be accompanied by adequate information about personal capabilities and the needs of society, together with a widespread sense of individual responsibility for the good of all.

In attaining this goal, education plays an important part. One of the main tasks of the school is competent vocational guidance, which is governed primarily not by the principle of helping the student prepare for and get the position he wants, but by the objective of teaching students to know their own abilities and the nature of their society and persuading and inspiring them to devote their energies to the tasks that most urgently need to be done.

An obviously crucial question is: Which work is good, significant, and right, and which is not? No simple and direct answer to this question is possible. The response can only be an indirect one, to the effect that the goodness of work is measured by its contribution to personal and social excellence, the standards of which cover the whole range of human concerns. Thus, an occupation that makes use of intellectual powers consistently with the canons of true knowledge and dedicated inquiry is in that respect valuable, as compared with one that neglects, degrades, or misuses the gift of intelligence. Employment in the mass media is worthy if it is devoted to the publication of true, significant, and elevating materials; otherwise, it is not. Jobs that promote refined tastes and richness of esthetic life for the community are in that respect good. Similarly, work that conserves the resources of the earth, advances mental and physical health, sustains love and fidelity in family relations, minimizes arbitrary class and race distinctions, subserves the principles of economic and political justice and the cause of international cooperation, and as a true vocation becomes a service of worship: such work is, in these several respects, good.

Hence, proper vocational guidance requires a comprehensive set of value standards. It is not sufficient merely to appraise personal abilities and social demands and to find the best balance between the two. Human beings are capable of both good and evil conduct, and societies make both right and wrong demands. Occupational counseling is both a technical and an ethical enterprise, but the ethical aspect is the more fundamental of the two and the one more neglected in contemporary practice. Probably no other step a young person takes is as crucial for the total significance of his life as the choice of work, including the educational preparation necessary for it. In this decision the primary orientation toward giving or getting comes to the fore, and with it a host of consequences and applications in a great variety of more specific human concerns, as indicated in the preceding paragraph. Vocational advisement, if it is to be of real educational value, should consist not in one or a few interviews on entering or leaving school, but in a continuing dialogue between the student and his parents and teachers in all fields as well as with professional guidance officers. This dialogue should be regarded as the primary opportunity for teaching true democratic values, for in it the issues of what is really worthful and whether one shall live for satisfaction or for service become "existential"—personally decisive—rather than merely theoretical and speculative. In the continuing discussion of vocation the student must face the questions: Who am I? Who shall I become? What shall I make of my life? A counselor can help a student to answer these questions if he believes there are values worthy of loyalty and if he has reflected long enough and deeply enough to arrive at some conviction as to what some of those values are.

One further consequence of orientation around values instead of around success is the moderation of specialization. Concern shifts from productive efficiency alone to the requirements of the good life. Specialization is regarded as a means for increasing the individual's qualitative excellence of achievement and for making possible higher forms of cultural life through the organization of differentiated skills. The gains from differentiation are balanced against the need for wholeness and variety in the development of personality. Furthermore, while specialists in organization and management may properly be used, the whole responsibility for the coordination of work does not rest upon them. Every person needs to be conscious of his place within the social complex and aware of the relation between his special contribution and the services performed by others. He must then assume responsibility for the welfare of his organization and of the human commonwealth as a whole. This he can do only if he has both specialized skills and breadth of understanding.

In education this value orientation with respect to work results in emphasis on *general* studies—that is, studies that are devoted to the growth of humane values and not simply to technical competence. General education is concerned with what a person needs to know and to become as a human being, not merely as a cog in the corporate mechanism. Generality does not preclude high concentration. It does preclude the narrow pursuit of knowledge and skill without concern for their relevance to the whole pattern of truth and right. Properly speaking, general education is not superficial, despite the contrary testimony of some efforts bearing that name. True generality is necessarily profound, because it involves a consideration of complex relationships, the discernment of fundamental relevancies, and the exhibition of value premises. Nor is general study, rightly conceived, only elementary and introductory in nature. It is by nature more advanced and reflects a higher level of cultural attainment than specialized disciplines, because it presupposes and goes beyond the particular competences to an analysis of their larger bearings and grounds for justification. Thus, in a democracy of worth the program of education is conceived not solely or mainly as preparation for successful pursuit of an occupation but as the gateway to a worthy life, in which work has its proper place within the larger vocation of being a civilized human being in a humane society.

Ideally recreation is a bulwark of democracy, because in leisure-time pursuits it is possible for a person to choose his activity as a free individual. Work is generally more regulated and less subject to personal preference than recreation. Certainly it cannot be so readily discontinued or exchanged for another kind as can recreation. Generally one can engage in many different sorts of leisure activities, according to inclination and occasion. In this realm the individual is his own master; he is free to determine the use of his time as he will.

The values to be realized in recreation are not the same as in other forms of conduct. The usual contrast is made between work and recreation. The differences here are mainly twofold. First, work is more to be evaluated by reference to social purposes than is recreation; recreation is more purely individual in its relevance. Thus, the values of personal uniqueness and individual variability are particularly central in the life of leisure. It is in this domain that uniformity, conformity, repetition, and standardization are most effectively overcome and the true fruits of creativity are realized. Second, work and recreation differ in the duration of their respective purposes. Work is devoted to more enduring purposes than is play. Leisure-time activity is more frequently consummated within a brief span of time as compared with the years-long cumulative character of most work. A game is played, a picture is painted, or a garden is cultivated, and each activity is regarded by the amateur as a complete experience, rounded out within minutes, hours, or months, as the case may be, while for the worker—in the parallel cases of professional player, artist, or farmer—these achievements are but incidents within a continuous career. Recreation serves the special values of short-term consummation. These are the values that were analyzed in our discussion of esthetic excellence in Chapter 5. Recreation thus provides unique opportunities for both individual differentiation and esthetic creativity.

The development of modern machine technology in industrial society has wrought profound changes in the relationship between work and leisure, with correspondingly far-reaching effects on the values of civilization. Now that machines have taken so much of the burden of work off men's shoulders, the time each person must devote to labor has dramatically decreased. Leisure time has moved from its former peripheral position in the economy of life to become a major fact of existence. Until recently, recreation for the ordinary person was relegated to the few marginal hours remaining after the long and heavy week's work had been done, and to the occasional holiday. Because of machine power this condition no longer obtains. Of the 168 hours of the week, fewer than 40—less than 25 per cent—are ordinarily claimed by a job. Leisure is thus no longer the privilege of a select few; science and invention have been a great support to democracy.

The average worker has been so far released from wearing toil that the privileges of "aristocrats" and "ordinary people" have been exchanged. Contemporary aristocrats—the people with the best education and the greatest ability—labor harder than ever at their increasingly complex tasks, while people with lesser endowments of energy and intelligence now have time to spare. The leisured gentlemen of former times are now too busy to cultivate their recreation properly, and those who have been relieved from toil and given the liberty of children of abundance do not usually have the traditions of civility and the habits of discrimination to enable them to use their free time wisely.

In this way recreation in advanced industrial societies has become a dominant mass phenomenon. Leisure-time pursuits are no longer marginal, nor is their style any longer set by a relatively small group of privileged people. Since recreation is a major preoccupation of the great majority of people, the nature of leisure-time activities profoundly affects the whole tone of cultural life. By and large that tone has been set by the pleasure principle. The average person associates recreation with freedom from responsibility, with having fun, with doing what one wants to do.

In view of the transformations in the human situation effected by technology, we may expect the role of leisure to be increasingly influential in modern society. Does this mean that civilization will be more and more dominated by the pleasure principle? Not necessarily. Recreation is not inevitably tied to the pursuit of satisfaction; there is no inherent conflict between recreation and loyalty to the good. Given the importance of recreation in modern culture, the central imperative is to cultivate forms of recreation that are in accord with standards of qualitative excellence. Only by so doing will leisure activities contribute to the strengthening of democracy.

We are now in a position to discuss the place of recreation in democratic education. Every person needs to be prepared not only for an occupation and for assuming the responsibilities of participation in civic life, but also for using his leisure time well. Hence, recreation is a proper educational concern, and the nurture of recreational capacities is a part of the teaching task.

This educational responsibility is by no means universally recognized. It is widely assumed that children do not need to be taught how to play, and that education should deal only with preparation for such long-term pursuits as vocation, family life, and citizenship. According to this assumption, recreation is what a child does on his own at those times when he is not being educated. Play time is "free time," to do with as one wishes, unconstrained by parents and teachers and without the directives and judgments of explicit education.

Conscientious parents and teachers are much concerned with how a child uses his play time. They know that he does not cease to learn when he is not being formally instructed. In fact, they are aware that he often learns much more from the experiences of play time than from classroom disciplines. Wise parents accordingly take pains to provide their young with healthful opportunities for recreation and to live in a physical and social environment that will afford a constructive play life.

The educative effect of recreation holds for adults as well as for children. Every person continues to learn throughout life, both in his occupation and in his leisure pursuits. The special educational significance of the latter lies in the freedom they afford for self-direction, experimentation, and broadening of personal perspective and competence.

Granted that recreation is of educational import, the question remains of where it should be taught. In particular, should the schools leave the teaching of recreation to parents and to other social agencies specifically designed for that function, or should instruction for the right use of leisure be a part of the school curriculum? The position taken here is that both schools and other institutions and agencies should assume this responsibility. Opponents of this view point to the overburdening of school curriculums with the most diverse conglomeration of subjects, to the detriment of the "basic" intellectual studies. They point also to the rapid expansion of knowledge and technical skill required for effective living in the modern age, and they ask how the schools, with their limited share of the student's time, can afford to spend any of it on instruction in recreation, which they believe he either does not need or can get outside of school.

These critics err in their estimate of the contemporary cultural situation, in their understanding of what recreation is, and in their appraisal of the relation between work and play. Recreation is no longer on the margins of life; it is a major factor, if not the major one, in determining the tone and temper of mass culture. Properly conceived, recreation is as serious and demanding as any work, and preparation for it calls for the highest level of intellectual discipline. Furthermore, recreation cannot without serious distortion of personality be compartmentalized as the advocates of "work only" schools recommend. Work and play are intimately intertwined, and the school in educating for one educates for the other also. Schools are for the education of integral persons, and while some specialization of responsibilities among social institutions is desirable, no such vital and inseparable aspect of learning as recreation should be eliminated from the program of the schools.

Recreation education is the common responsibility of many different agencies—homes, schools, community service groups, clubs and other voluntary organizations, the mass media, adult education agencies, libraries, and even business organizations. This plurality of responsible agencies removes from the schools the necessity for actually providing the major share of recreational facilities. It does not, however, make any less imperative the inclusion of recreational concerns within the school curriculum, for it is in the program of formal education that meaning, perspective, and direction in leisure activity may best be taught.

The pleasure principle, which is commonly taken for granted as appropriate in recreation, has influenced the whole of educational practice. Many teachers believe that all learning should be "fun." They have adopted the "happiness" approach to teaching, avoiding anything unpleasant or painful either to themselves or to the students. The children are treated as playmates and pals; conflicts are minimized; and discipline, the exercise of authority, and, above all, punishment are shunned. The same principles have taken hold in many families, where sweetness and light and good times have been the primary objectives of family living.

The consequences of this primary pursuit of pleasure are a general lowering of standards, disrespect for authority, disorderliness, and loss of morale by teachers (or parents) and students alike. Enjoyment turns out in experience not to be a viable foundation for educational practice. It is a delusion that learning can be improved by making it pleasant. While such an approach may engage the interests of the students temporarily, it does them a long-term disservice by encouraging them in attitudes and habits that are ultimately life-destroying. Education cannot be securely founded on any such superficial and deceptive play philosophy. Whether it be pleasant or painful, it needs to rest on the enduring foundation of loyalty to the good. Even learning to play well is not always pleasant. The good player accepts the bitter with the sweet as ingredients in a good game. The disciplines of high recreation are as exacting as those of any vocation. Learning how to use leisure time well is a rigorous process demanding the highest level of devotion by teachers and students alike.

The increasing importance of leisure in modern society makes it appropriate that recreational considerations should assume major significance in education. There is every reason why the spirit of recreation should pervade the schools. But to affirm this is not to endorse the "fun" philosophy. A sound concept of recreation is rooted in value rather than in enjoyment. Education ought to be "creative" and "re-creative" throughout. It ought to be suffused with the joy, exhilaration, expectation, and excitement which accompany a hard-fought contest for worthy ends. If modern man can learn to use his free time well, he will live well generally, for the employment of leisure is the measure of selfhood. Thus, when recreation is rightly conceived, it is a suitable major guiding concern for education as a whole.

These considerations constitute the justification for what is commonly called a "liberal education." A liberal education, literally and historically, means education for men of leisure—men who are free to choose what they will do with their lives, men who are not slaves. Before the machine age liberal education was necessarily aristocratic, because only a few could enjoy sufficient leisure to make education for it necessary or desirable. With the general emancipation effected by technology, liberal education has become a democratic possibility. All persons are now entitled to leisure, and all are in need of education for the wise use of their freedom. To assert that modern education should be infused with the ideals of recreation is to affirm the centrality of liberal studies in the curriculum.

Traditional liberal education centered around classical literature. It required the mastery of the Greek and Latin languages and the study of the great works of Hellenic and Roman antiquity. Mathematics, which is actually another kind of language, was included among the subjects carried over from ancient times. Philosophy, history, poetry, and drama were also taught not as specialized departments of knowledge, but as components of the classical literary tradition. This study of the classics, which for generations had comprised the ideal of liberal education in Europe and America at least until the beginning of the twentieth century, provided men of leisure with a common body of language and thought and a set of symbols of distinction which set them apart from ordinary people. Furthermore, it furnished approved models of excellence, which served to inspire and direct successive generations of students toward the peaks of civilized achievement.

Within the present century this traditional concept of liberal education has been under heavy attack. Although some educators still cling to it with fervent tenacity, most regard it as out of keeping with the conditions and needs of modern industrial democracy. It is hardly cause for wonder that a curriculum designed for the privileged few in a largely agrarian society should prove unsuited to the needs of the new era of universal leisure in an industrialized society. The attack has frequently been directed at the idea of liberal education itself, apart from its classical form. The "useless" education for leisure, best represented by the traditional studies, has been despised because it supposedly does not increase one's occupational efficiency. In the busy, striving age of progress, the study of the classics has seemed a luxury few could and none should afford. It has also been supposed that leisure would take care of itself, since it was regarded as requiring no positive attainment, but only the natural capacity for relaxation and pleasure.

This rejection of liberal education of any kind is unwarranted. Hopefully, we are not yet willing to write off the ideals of human freedom for the sake of productive efficiency. Nor can we ignore the urgent need for educating modern man to employ his leisure well. If classical liberal education will not suffice for today's needs, what kind will? This is the question to which an answer is required if the authentic re-creative character of education is to be attained.

Liberal education for modern democracy should be developed in accord with the following six principles. First, it should remain true to the nature of recreation as devoted to intrinsic consummatory values. Liberal studies are to be prized in and for themselves and not for the sake of other purposes to which they may contribute. True humane learning—the learning that sets men free—is justified mainly by the intrinsic value of what is learned, not by its usefulness. It is not a tool for better adjustment, of whatever kind, but an opportunity for love and loyalty to what is recognized as excellent. In this respect ideal modern liberal education agrees with the allegedly useless classical education. Both are dedicated to intrinsic worth. This principle of value in and for itself is violated when what are termed liberal studies (and what may be so for other students) are pursued for the purpose of becoming a professional in liberal learning (as scholar and teacher). Many a student of the traditional liberal arts approaches them in just as utilitarian a fashion as the usual student in pharmacy or engineering approaches his studies, and much of the instruction in the liberal arts is in fact technical and occupational in character. True liberal learning requires no ulterior justification. It is to be loved first and used secondarily.

The second principle that should govern modern liberal education is the primacy of qualitative excellence. Like the first, this ideal is also shared with classical liberal learning. The new liberal education should remain classical in the sense that its materials are to be drawn from the high points of civilized achievement. What a person does as a free man—in his leisure—ought to be a source of elevation and inspiration, a means of re-creation, not an occasion for stagnation or degradation. Recreation should be measured by rigorous standards, not marked by a relaxation of standards, and the same rule applies to the liberal education by which a person is prepared for such activities. Thus, the curriculum of liberal studies is to be guided primarily by concern for high quality, not by considerations of student popularity and interest—though these may be welcome by-products.

The following three principles distinguish the desirable new liberal education from the traditional liberal arts. The third ideal is that of progress. The old liberal education made use of a relatively fixed corpus of standard materials. It was assumed that these were of permanent worth and that no changes or improvements were necessary. The result was the neglect of important recent products of civilization and the loss of a sense of contemporary relevance. Liberal education should not be based upon a circumscribed canonical body of literature. It should be open to new developments and subject to continuous appraisal and revision in the light of the criteria of excellence. This is not to be taken as implying an automatic preference for the new over the old. Since the persistent civilizing power of a work is one of the signs of its worth, well-tested traditions have an edge over innovations. Liberal studies should not be antitraditional; they should not be partial to novelty and obvious contemporary relevance. The principle of progress simply means that the education of a free man should draw upon the resources of civilized excellence from all periods of history and should be fashioned with due regard to the profound changes taking place in the modern world.

Fourth, modern liberal studies ought to reflect the differences among human beings. Not only should there be progress; there should also be variety. Traditional liberal studies were the same for everybody. They provided a kind of lingua franca for the educated elite. In today's pluralistic democracy no such uniformity is appropriate. People cannot be forced into a single common mold. There is no one uniform way of excellence. Differences in temperament and in native capacities make persons respond in different ways to the same situations, and indicate the need for educational provisions of considerable latitude. Particularly in an age where leisure is nearly everybody's privilege, it is not to be expected that each will use his freedom in the same manner. If a standard course of liberal studies is provided under these conditions, many people will fail to find therein their own pathway to excellence and will lose the recreational preparation that a more varied program would have offered.

This need for variety can be met by a good modern liberal education because of a fifth principle which it satisfies—namely, breadth of scope. In this respect modern liberal education differs most markedly from the traditional classical education. The older studies, as already suggested, were linguistic, literary, and mathematical. Modern liberal education is far broader. It includes the natural sciences, the social studies, and the fine arts, too. In fact, it has at length become evident that the content of a study is not what makes it "liberal" or otherwise, and that any subject of study can be included in a liberal education, provided it is treated in a liberal fashion. What does it mean to treat it in such a way? It means to deal with it in relation to its universal humane relevance; that is, as it pertains to the loyalties of men unconstrained by physical and social necessities.

From this point of view, liberal education may appropriately be concerned with anything in the whole range of human experience. Clearly the sciences are admirably suited for the growth of loyalty to truth as an intrinsic value and to the human communities that truth in its many formulations brings into being. Studies in such fields as law, education, and theology, which are commonly (and properly) thought of as vocational in orientation, may also be approached from the liberal standpoint as vehicles for devotion to civilized values. Even obviously practical skills like carpentry and welding can be taught liberally by exhibiting their manifold relationships within the fabric of civilization and by employing them as occasions for the deliberate celebration and embodiment of inherent excellence.

Classical liberal learning was more exclusively bookish than the modern type proposed here. It was more obviously "intellectual." But this should not be construed as approval for nonintellectual practical or manual activity within the scope of liberal education. Liberal learning must include intellectual apprehension, or it is not an activity befitting a free man—that is, a person who guides his life in accordance with the inward persuasion of the good. Thus, an unlimited range of subjects are appropriate to liberal education, provided they are taught in a liberal manner. This breadth of scope is the basis for a program of liberal studies in a pluralistic democracy in which all the citizens are expected to participate.

The last of the six principles has to do with the organization of the curriculum. Classical liberal education was essentially general, because of its reliance upon literary works of broad human pertinence. Modern scholarship has become increasingly specialized along narrow departmental lines, and instruction has tended to follow the same pattern. At the present time much of what is called liberal education in the arts and sciences is organized as a collection of specialized studies. The requisite breadth of learning is supposed to be insured by the requirement for "distribution" of courses, to prevent a poorly balanced program. This type of curricular organization does not in fact usually achieve the aims of liberal learning. Specialized courses, which are conducted within the strict limits of a technical discipline, may be excellent preparation for the professional worker in that field; they are not likely to provide for the best use of leisure by the liberated modern man. The latter needs "general education" studies of a high order. These do not refer to those sterile and boring courses which teach many things in general and nothing in particular, nor to broad surveys which never go deeply into anything. "General education" here means studies that are carried out with primary concern for their universal human relevance and with due attention to those ideas of fundamental importance which span the gulfs between the specialized disciplines.

If modern liberal education is to provide for the nurture of free men, it must regain the ideal of generality which characterized the traditional liberal arts, but it must do so without sacrificing the variety and scope made possible by modern advances in knowledge. The curriculum should be organized in response to the need for integrity and depth of outlook rather than primarily to serve the purposes of professional academic scholars. Even specialized subjects that are not themselves interdisciplinary should, for purposes of general education, be related with other fields. Many—if not most—studies—such as literature, philosophy, history, religion, geography, and anthropology (to name only some of them)—by their very nature draw upon a variety of other fields of study and thus are particularly suited to general education, provided they are not ruined for that purpose by professional zeal to make them into precise, technical, exclusive disciplines—as occurs even in such a naturally general field as literature, when its promoters restrict it to technical textual analysis.

Liberal studies ought not, of course, to comprise the whole of education. Provision should be made at all ages and levels for both vocational and recreational preparation. Even in the play-school activities of the very young, matters of vocational import, such as correct speech, are learned. At the other extreme, college and university education, even in the graduate and professional schools, should never completely exclude liberal-recreational studies. Furthermore, the two varieties of study can never—and ought never—be sharply separated from one another. They should interfuse with one another in a mutually supportive fashion. With skillful teaching it is often possible for the same course of study to be vocational for those students who need it to be and a liberal study for those who do not.

In fact, when concern for worth governs, the distinction largely vanishes between labor and leisure, occupation and recreation, and the respective kinds of education which prepare for each. Work that issues from devotion is no longer a slave's burden, and play is no longer the pseudo liberty of one who seeks escape from himself and his condition. Both are forms of a free man's service. Labor is performed in the same freedom of spirit as play is, and leisure is occupied in fulfilling the vocation to be a man.

In education for true liberty, whether in work or play, it thus appears that the spirit of liberal learning should prevail. Liberal education—in contrast to vocational education, in the usual sense of that term—is fundamental in that it is concerned with the ends of all living, toward which both labor and leisure are aimed. It opens the way to consummatory values, which contain the meanings and sustain the purposes of life. It provides for the understanding and perspective that yield the sense of wholeness, balance, and proportion to human existence. Under modern conditions, with changes occurring so rapidly that most specific occupational preparation becomes quickly out of date, it even appears that a fundamental liberal education is the best vocational education, for it develops the powers of imagination needed to meet new situations and the understanding of interrelationships required by life in an increasingly interdependent civilization. Hence, the recreative spirit may and should infuse and transform occupational effort, and the ideals of liberal learning become the measure of fundamental vocational study.

This view of recreation in a democracy of worth entails a transformation of our whole educational philosophy and practice. In the ultimate view education is re-creation. It is the process of reproducing high civilization in human personality. The fundamental presupposition in this view is that the activities by which persons are brought to true freedom issue from loyalty to what is true and right, which is the only sure and enduring source of creative energy. The home or the school that is founded on the re-creative idea is not partial to the easy and the pleasant path. It is profound and serious in spirit and purpose; it is exacting and disciplined in method and program. Its motive is not the desire for efficiency or for social control, but rather a glad response to the lure of perfection, from which true liberty springs.

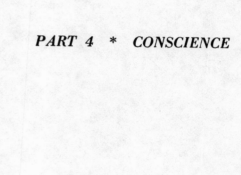

*PART 4 * CONSCIENCE*

From the values of intelligence and creativity we turn to a consideration of conscience. This classification of values is somewhat arbitrary, to be sure. Our discussions of intelligence and creativity have repeatedly had reference to matters of conscience. Intellectual responsibility is a moral obligation. So also are the right use of the mass media of communication, the elevation of taste and manners, and the right choice of work and play. The several realms of value are interconnected and overlapping. The division into kinds merely emphasizes dominant features. Intelligence centers around the ideal of truth, creativity around qualitative excellence, and conscience around right conduct. In chapters 9 to 16 our attention will be focused on problems of ethical responsibility—that is, on decisions concerning human relationships to the nonhuman world, to self, and to other persons. Consideration is now directed to the problem of the right uses of nature. What is man's responsibility with respect to the natural world? What are the standards by which his relation to his physical and biological environment should be measured?

In no other respect have the changes in the human situation been more striking than in this matter of man's relationship to the natural world. Until recent times human beings were forced to live a precarious existence in the face of the largely unpredictable and uncontrollable forces of nature. Wind, water, fire, wild beasts, insects, and disease kept man constantly on the defensive. Although he could to some degree carve out islands of security, he was always surrounded by the threat of destruction and faced with the certainty of frustration by the unruly elements. Through his understanding of natural processes, man has now learned how to use the forces of nature for his own purposes and how to protect himself against their destructive effects. Nature is regarded no longer as something merely to be accepted but as a world of resources to be discovered, understood, transformed, and put to use.

While this reversal in power position has had profound effects on the outward conditions of life, even more important for mankind is the revolution that has occurred in the human outlook. Man has risen from the position of nature's slave to that of potential master. This change has appeared to be a most striking confirmation of man's essential autonomy. No longer need mankind cower before its ancient enemies in the natural world. No more must men supplicate and propitiate the gods, the supposed custodians of the forces of nature. The new powers of prediction and control prove that man can determine his own destiny.

In one respect this growth in the power available to man has supported the democratic movement. The feeling of helplessness in the face of superior powers has been dispelled. Men do not now make a virtue of resignation to the circumstances of life. This sense of power is widely shared, for everyone in the new industrial society participates in the domination of nature. Even some who stand relatively low in the prestige ladder now lord it over nature, as they drive great machines which coerce the earth to do their bidding, or shape and twist tough metal as if it were putty, or with explosives obliterate any obstacle in the wink of an eye. Today "miracles" are performed by ordinary people, not just by a special class of men on special occasions.

At the same time the growth in human power has introduced some grave perils for democracy. The danger is that the new powers over nature will also be used to put men into subjection. The control of the natural environment carries with it the control of the human beings who depend upon that environment for their health and sustenance. The ability of men to order nature has increased the violence of tyranny and made the winning and preserving of democracy both more necessary and more difficult. Accordingly, the major problems of contemporary man are not how to understand and control physical nature, but how to maintain a just and stable social order and how to achieve self-understanding and personal integrity.

With respect to the latter problems, modern civilization has lost ground. People now seem, on the whole, less sure of the meaning of their lives and less skillful in their relationships to one another than people of many earlier times. Classical literature is rich and illuminating in its treatment of the inner life but is generally of little value for the understanding of the external world. The situation is just the opposite at the present day. By comparison with our brilliant knowledge of the world about us, our insight into ourselves seems paltry. We have become confident of our ability to deal effectively with nature and are impatient and discouraged at the meagerness of our success with ourselves. Today natural sciences and engineering ride high, attracting the largest funds and the most able personnel.

Not only has the successful management of nature diverted attention and effort from human problems and diminished man's confidence in his ability to come to terms with himself and his neighbor. It has also exerted a profound influence on the way in which human affairs are approached. Before the modern age, self-mastery and social maturity were regarded as goals for free men struggling individually to win their souls. Now that the secrets of effectively dealing with the physical world have been discovered, it is widely assumed that man must be dealt with in the same manner as the world of nature. If invariant natural law, classification, and regulation have proved so successful in mastering nature, why not use the same tools on man? But to treat human beings as natural objects is to deny their essential characteristic of freedom. Under the technical approach to human problems people are regarded as things to be pushed and molded into conformity with the blueprint of the social planners. The current concept of "social engineering" reflects this mechanistic attitude toward human beings. Such an outlook is clearly antidemocratic.

The scientific study of man is neither futile nor immoral. We cannot hope to cure the ills of mankind without persistent and devoted scientific study of human beings. Such inquiry is not in itself undemocratic. On the contrary, it is one of the best hopes for democracy. What *is* undemocratic is the direct transfer of concepts and methods from the nonhuman world to the human world—the reduction of the sciences of man to the sciences of nature. The success of the natural sciences in comparison with the study of man makes this transfer tempting. It is nonetheless mistaken. Men can be analyzed and managed as natural objects, but only at the cost of their essential humanity. The true sciences of man are based upon concepts and methods appropriate to their human subject matter. The crucial categories include ideas of freedom, intelligence, meaning, commitment, and obligation which have no parallel in the natural sciences. Appropriate to the human realm are the methods of democratic education, grounded in the ideal of persuasion of free persons in the light of an assumed commitment to truth and right. Man can gain more and more reliable knowledge about himself and his kind. This understanding ought not, however, to be applied mainly to control other persons, but to develop powers of self-control for the sake of the good. This is the goal of education in a moral democracy.

The growth of modern scientific civilization has brought both opportunities and perils for democracy: opportunities in the vast new resources made available to mankind, and perils in the increased power men can use against and over one another. These developments are all a consequence of education. The technical marvels of the modern age are dependent upon scientific knowledge, which has been gained by educated people. It is educated men and women who have unlocked the secrets of nature and enabled mankind to master its environment. The success of these efforts has in turn led to a transformation in education. In classical education the chief aim was the transmission of a valued cultural heritage. In the contemporary world this aim has been subordinated to that of managing, exploiting, and transforming the environment. The spirit of the old education was receptive, respectful, backward-looking; the spirit of the new is active, dominating, progressive.

Accordingly, the educational system makes far greater provision than ever before for scientific and technical studies. Given the complexity of our machine civilization, broad and thorough preparation is necessary in these fields. The control of natural forces is a continuing—even a growing—challenge; to meet it an increasing company of trained natural scientists and engineers will be required. Furthermore, the technical revolution has stimulated the growth of universal education. The new artificial environment belongs to everybody, and everybody needs to be taught to understand it and to use it well. The vast complex of man-made things among which and by which we live do not take care of themselves. They require maintenance, repair, and skillful management. Since all or nearly all members of society share in these responsibilities, universal education to a high level is essential for the security and progress of modern industrial civilization.

There is a correspondingly urgent need for more education in the social studies and in the humanistic disciplines. The social studies can provide the understanding requisite for creating a social system in which the abuse of the power released by machine technology may be minimized and in which these forces may be constructively employed for the general welfare. The special office of the humane studies in the present day is to sustain the sense of meaning in a dehumanized machine world. The humane studies are also of crucial importance for suggesting guiding ideals in a time of rapid cultural transformation resulting from new inventions. Scientific knowledge and technique are neutral with respect to values. Only disciplines in which attention is directed to the intrinsic goods of existence, rather than to facts and instrumentalities alone, can re-create the sense of direction lost in the dissolution of traditional culture.

In these times of need for both technical and humanistic education, the effectiveness of each is impaired by the divorce of the two from one another. In the atmosphere of competitiveness and defensiveness which accompanies a success-oriented philosophy of life, the several components of education have become separated into specialized disciplines. The result is a fragmentation of culture which is mirrored in the self-alienation and dis-integration of persons.

The office of modern education is to nurture humaneness within the new world generated by the progress of invention. It is not to produce two hostile camps—of engineers and of men of letters—who neither understand one another nor care to. The required unification of learning can be effected in four principal ways. First, the arts, literature, philosophy, and religious studies should address themselves to the world that now is, in all its technical complexity, and not only to the simpler world of the past. Machine culture is the context in which human beings now think and act. Painting and architecture, novels and plays, epistemological and theological systems, should take full account of the new things and ideas that scientific theory and engineering skill have brought into being. Humanists should acknowledge their membership in the contemporary world, seek to understand it in its own terms (which means making a serious effort to gain authentic scientific insight), assimilate its ideas into their world of composing, building, and analyzing, and assume responsibility for guiding the course of its further development.

Second, scientific specialists should recognize, celebrate, and try to communicate the humane values implicit in their own disciplines. Scientific investigation is motivated by ethical principles of a high order. The universal ideals of scientific truth manifest an advanced level of spiritual development. The history of science is a drama of faith, patience, devotion, and heroism comparable to what are usually accounted the great religious and moral movements of mankind. Technology and pure science are humanly significant, in themselves and not just in their tangible products.

Third, scientific research and education should be conducted with full consciousness of the broad consequences of discovery and invention—for good and for ill. In view of the grave dangers that accompany the irresponsible use of power, the people who best understand the sources and uses of the forces they help to unlock have an obligation to work for the right employment and social control of natural energies. Science and engineering should never be taught as isolated specialties, wholly neutral to human welfare, but always with deep concern for their potential effect on the well-being of mankind.

The fourth means of effecting a union of scientific and humanistic learning is through the development of the social sciences. By definition the sciences of man combine the human with the scientific. Until recently those sciences have been marred by a slavish imitation of the methods and concepts of the physical sciences (as, for example, in behavioristic psychology). It is now being recognized that such reductive procedures yield a superficial understanding of man, and that new approaches are required, which take account of what is uniquely human. There is evidence of increasing dialogue between social scientists and workers in literature, the arts, philosophy, theology, and history. In due course mature social sciences will emerge as perhaps our most powerful link between the natural sciences and the humane disciplines.

The modern mastery of nature brings into high relief the central ethical problem of democracy, which is the theme of this book—namely, the contrast between the democracy of desire and the democracy of worth. Control of natural forces as a result of scientific knowledge has greatly enhanced modern man's sense of power. Since men now possess powers formerly ascribed to the gods, men have come to regard themselves as lords of creation. The drive for power—individual or collective—emerges as the basic human tendency. Anyone—or almost anyone—can have what he wants if he has enough "know-how." Contemporary man has great faith in technical progress; there are no human interests that he does not feel can eventually be satisfactorily provided for. In short, an assumption of many moderns is the potential omnipotence of mankind.

Implicit in this faith is confidence in education as a means to the desired consummation. For modern man, as Bacon said, knowledge is power—not virtue or illumination. The more knowledge one acquires, the larger is his share in the command of natural forces to fulfill human wants. Hence, the striving for autonomy in this age of control is accompanied by pressures for more and more education, to supply the knowledge that enables man to subdue the earth.

Nor is human ambition satiated by the subjection of the earth. The new horizon, which first opened fully to view in 1957 with the launching of a man-made space satellite, is the mastery of the whole universe! Man now knows that he is not limited by the confines of this planet. He has not only inherited the earth; he has possessed it and is fast consuming it. Now his grasp reaches out toward the heavens. Quite literally he seeks new worlds to conquer. To be sure, the problems are enormous, and the progress to date is slight—no man has yet traveled beyond the earth's effective gravitational field. Still, plans are under way for creating the necessary vehicles and artificial environments for space travel and residence, vast resources of intelligence and materials are being expended on research and development in the field of space technology, and increasing numbers of able young people are being educated for future work in this field.

The magnificence of scientific achievements is beyond question, and the prospects for the future are no less brilliant. Nevertheless, the assumption of human autonomy and of man's absolute sovereignty over earthly and cosmic nature is not warranted. Nature has not surrendered to man. The basis for modern technical progress is the knowledge built on the patient watching and listening for nature's ways. Modern science came into being when men renounced their preconceptions, preferences, and prejudices and adopted the practice of painstaking and systematic observation and experiment.

Contemporary man's power is thus a consequence of his willingness to follow and obey. The disciplines of science are rigorous. No person is fit for scientific work if he is interested only in commanding. The good scientist or engineer has a first loyalty to fact, and to that loyalty all considerations of power and interest are subordinate. The so-called mastery of nature in reality is nature's victory over human ignorance and self-will. Man's power is nature's power released to him in consequence of his obedience to truth. Under these circumstances the fitting attitude is not arrogance, but a profound sense of humility and gratitude for the knowledge revealed and the powers entrusted to mankind.

Another aspect of nature's check on unrestrained human demands is the fact of limitation in natural resources. For our brilliant exploitation of the earth the price exacted is present or eventual exhaustion and devastation of the natural estate. Human acquisitiveness invites nature's eloquent rebuke.

In the democracy of worth, therefore, human dependence upon nature is duly acknowledged. Technical progress is not regarded as proof of human autonomy, but it is a reward for attending to the truth. Furthermore, care is taken to understand not only the sources of power but also the conditions for its continuing availability. Since earth is gratefully recognized as mankind's home, it is important to give serious consideration to the natural conditions for human well-being and survival.

One requirement is the maintenance of a healthful physical environment. Industrial processes and motor vehicles have filled the atmosphere with noxious fumes. There is some evidence connecting the steep rise in lung cancer with this pollution of the air. Recently radioactive fallout from nuclear testing has introduced another and far more dangerous type of air poisoning. Ways must be found for ending this contamination of the atmosphere, even at the cost, if need be, of curtailing technical progress. Similar observations hold for water and soil. Industrial wastes, which are now dumped into rivers and seas or buried in the earth, make water and earth unfit for human use. Air, water, and soil are essential to human well-being and must not be used as receptacles for the excrescences of the industrial organism.

In addition to the healthfulness of the environment, attention should be given to its esthetic qualities. In our heedless lust for power we have disgracefully disfigured the earth. The landscape has been defaced by ugly buildings, both industrial and residential. The pleasant land has been overlaid with great swaths of concrete to accommodate vehicular traffic. Forests have been chopped down or burned, and wild animals hunted to extinction. To halt and reverse this destruction of natural beauty, not only must standards of individual taste be raised, but much stricter social controls must be exercised. Architectural planning should have regard for the preservation of natural beauty and not only for utility and economy in the structures themselves. Tight regulation of roadside signs and establishments should be instituted to remove the offenses to good taste and the barriers to the enjoyment of nature which present policies permit, with the happy exception of some of the newer expressways. The expansion of the highway system should be checked by the restoration (under government support) of efficient rapid transit systems. City planning should make ample provision for parks and trees, and federal and state parks and forests should be steadfastly maintained against all encroachments by commerical and utilitarian interests.

A considerable part of the esthetic interest of nature comes from the various forms of wild life. To save the birds, beasts, and fish from complete destruction, hunting and fishing have to be controlled by a system of limits and licenses. Aside from this requirement, there remains a question of conscience with regard to the killing of animals for sport. These activities feed the impulses toward autonomy and dominance which undermine true humanity. The death of the animals is loss enough, but it is not half so serious as the injury to personality that occurs in one who kills his own sense of reverence for life and his sense of kinship with living things below him in the order of creation.

A third requirement for the conscientious use of nature is to take due account of the limitations of natural resources. Up to now the people of the industrial nations of the world have lived as though the material bounty of the earth were inexhaustible. We have been profligate with our natural capital, squandering it with no concern for its limits. In this respect we have been guilty of a "plutocracy of the present," through grasping material privileges without taking account of the needs of future generations. Such a way of life is just as undemocratic as the forcible subjugation of the poor by the wealthy at any given epoch. Democratic justice as between generations requires the employment of the earth's resources in such a way that they shall be conserved, restored, and replenished for continued use by our children and our children's children.

To this end, the soil—from which our nourishment comes—must be carefully husbanded by the use of the many techniques now well understood by scientific farmers, such as proper drainage and irrigation, contour plowing, crop rotation, fertilization, and preservation of forests and grassland. The alarming drop in the water table must be arrested, by restricting the amounts of water available for industrial processes and pressing forward on the development of processes for removing salt from sea water and for the control of rainfall. Particular care must be given to the problem of mineral resources, which are rapidly being depleted, with no possibility of replenishment. Our present and expected rate of consumption of these materials spells the doom, in the not distant future, of industrial civilization as we know it. The only hope for continued existence is in the development of new processes that require little metal or in the discovery of means for artificially transmuting abundant elements into the scarcer ones. Finally, major consideration will have to be given to the limitations of the energy supply. Wood, water power, coal, oil, and gas are insufficient to provide for the world's energy needs over any extended period. Uranium and other substances used in atomic fission processes are not in great abundance and are irreplaceable. The major hopes for continued energy abundance are in the invention of controlled atomic fusion processes and in the harnessing of solar power.

This brief review of what must be done to establish right relationships between man and nature suggests something of the educational task. Young people must be acquainted with the facts about the earth, its resources, and the consequences of using them in various ways. This is primarily the function of the study of geography—not mainly as a learning of place names, populations, and products and a drawing and reading of maps and charts, but as a responsible consideration of the earth as mankind's home. The all-important problem of geography, properly taught, is how human beings can build and maintain just and enduring relationships with their natural environment. This is an ethical problem—a question of conscience—as well as a problem of fact and technique. Up to now the moral considerations have been absent or subordinate. Education in modern industrial society has been organized for maximum material production and consumption, on the premises that labor is scarce and that natural resources are boundless. Education for a just and enduring future civilization needs to be radically reconceived. Training for the heedless and profligate exploitation of materials, without regard to problems of waste, depletion, and contamination, must give way to teaching the responsible and circumspect use of man's estate. In such education scientific knowledge and engineering skill will be taught not as means of making good the claims of the autonomous human will against nature, but as resources for the informed pursuit of the good.

The most crucial of all the problems connected with the uses of nature still remains—namely, the question of population. The development of modern machine civilization is in part a consequence of the growth of population. Large-scale industry and the accumulation of wealth presuppose an abundant supply of labor and ample markets. The notable advances in invention in recent decades have been stimulated by the presence of a large and apparently insatiable mass of consumers. At the same time as the growing population, by creating demands for more of nature's products, gives impetus to industry and commerce, it creates the problem of shortages and throws into clear relief the limitations of the earth.

The spectacular increase in population in modern times is itself a result of scientific and technical discovery. Through medical research the death rate has been dramatically reduced, and the average duration of life in industrialized nations has been greatly extended. Advances in machine power, applied to agriculture, manufacture, and transportation, have raised the general standard of living and made possible the support of a much larger total population than in earlier epochs.

Thus population and material progress have been mutually supportive. But now the swarming multitudes which cover the face of the earth and eagerly strive and compete for its bounty threaten to destroy man's estate. They already tax it to near exhaustion, and yet the pressures and the demands increase without any sign of reversal.

With respect to this problem the issues of democracy are squarely joined. The individual will to procreate ought not to be the ruling factor. If it is, and population continues to mount, universal anguish and strife will result. War and starvation will reduce or altogether eliminate the human species. As the competition for a share of the world's limited goods becomes more bitter, justice will vanish in the desperate struggle for survival, and tyrants and bureaucracies will arise to establish some order among the needy and fearful people.

The solution to the population problem lies in the assumption of ethical responsibility for the voluntary limitation of family size, for the sake of the welfare of all persons now living and yet to be born. Because the resources of the earth are finite, there will necessarily be population control of some kind. The human species cannot make demands on the world that are beyond its capacity to supply. Earth's material limits stand as the final negation of all demands for total human sovereignty. The question is whether the control will be by the force of physical circumstance, by the violence of human strife, by the power of absolute rulers, or by the persuasions of dedicated intelligence.

The question of the use of contraceptive measures for birth control is relevant here, but comments on it will be reserved for Chapter 11. Suffice it to say at this point only that the ideal mode of population control in a democracy of worth is determined not by the maximizing of pleasure and the minimizing of burdensome consequences, but by positive consideration and concern for the well-being of other persons within and beyond the immediate family and even beyond the present generation.

The central role in the development of ethical democratic controls for population rests with education. The young must learn enough about man's natural home and about his utilization of its resources to understand the conditions for permanent, secure, and healthful residence in it. They must also be taught the lesson of conscience that with respect to the uses of nature each person is his brother's—and his children's and his children's children's—keeper.

We turn next to a second matter of conscience—namely, the relation of persons to their own nature, to the concerns of health. Health is one of the fundamental human values, and the promotion of good health is one of the basic moral obligations. Health is wholeness, as the common etymology of the two words suggests. To be healed is to be made whole, to become a well-functioning unity of life. The moral obligation for the advancement of health thus rests upon the duty of becoming integral persons, with the human powers fully operating and cooperating in accord with their proper natures.

Health is an elemental good upon which all other goods depend. The pursuit of truth presupposes sound intelligence. The creative arts cannot thrive on illness. Work and play demand vigor of body and mind. Justice in families, in nations, and in the world as a whole can thrive only when the persons to be related to one another are soundly constituted. Just as mankind cannot continue civilized existence without regard for the resources of external nature, so are all the benefits and achievements of life grounded in personal health.

There are complex problems regarding standards of health and methods of treatment which belong within the province of professional medicine and are beyond the scope of lay inquiry and of ordinary education. One of the objectives of health education should be to develop confidence in the medical profession and reliance upon it rather than upon superstition, hearsay, hunches, or private experimentation for the treatment of illness. Well-informed people know the limits of their knowledge and are acquainted with the expert resources available for dealing with what is beyond their scope.

Nevertheless, it is also a proper aim of health education to advance the layman's understanding of medicine. A person who comprehends the principles of medical treatment is able to cooperate with the physician more intelligently in carrying out curative measures. He is also likely to be able to identify significant symptoms and thereby to assist the doctor in making an early and correct diagnosis of illness. Knowledgeable laymen further act as a check on medical malpractice. When the curative arts are regarded as secret skills, to be jealously guarded from public scrutiny and communicated in esoteric language only to other members of the guild, the lay public has no protection against fraudulent or misinformed professional activities which the medical associations may fail to detect and control. While professional standards must be set and enforced largely by the profession itself, educated laymen can be of great assistance in keeping the quality of practice high.

From a democratic perspective, medical treatment should be given with the informed consent of the patient. Doctors ought not to render their services with a "take it or leave it" attitude but should assume the role of teachers in relation to their patients, instructing and persuading them in the ways and means to health. Professionals in medicine should be accorded high respect and should be granted status and rewards commensurate with their special contribution to human welfare. But in a democracy of worth they should not become an autonomous ruling body, a powerful new class of medical technocrats, subject to no limits in their self-determination. Medical practice ought to be guided solely by considerations of truth and right. When the motive of service yields to that of prestige and power, the fundamental security of people dependent upon the high quality of medical treatment is jeopardized.

What are some of the conditions and habits of life which engender personal wholeness? There are ten factors which may be regarded as appropriate in a program of general health education in a democracy of worth.

First, the healthful life manifests a *proper balance between work and recreation.* Relaxation should be harmoniously alternated with effort. The good life exhibits a rhythmic pattern. Gainful occupation and play are mutually supportive components in a unified life. A person whose occupation is sedentary needs active recreations. One whose job requires constant association with people may require contrasting times of quiet solitude. Those who labor with intellectual abstractions often benefit most from leisure-time activity in the field of arts and crafts.

The nature of both work and recreation should further be governed by the age, experience, and native capacities of the individual person. What is healthful to one person may be injurious to another or to the same person at a different period in life. Good health is a consequence of engaging in activities for which one is sufficiently mature, well-endowed by nature, and prepared by education. Constructive work and play provide a focus and an outlet for personal energies. A person is healthy when he is functioning according to his capacities. People disintegrate when they are idle or aimless, badly adapted to their occupations, or perfunctory at play.

The problem of proper balance between work and recreation is of special importance to young people and to elderly people. Persons in the middle years for the most part have established places in the occupational scheme. They feel useful, and their abilities are fully engaged, particularly when they have combined their work with complementary play activities. In youth and age, on the other hand, the feeling of not being wanted, of being superfluous and at loose ends, is common.

For the good health of all citizens, well-organized opportunities for both work and recreation should be provided for people of all ages. In a democracy no person should ever be considered unimportant, unprepared for living, or obsolete. The human career must no longer be segmented into successive life phases devoted to play, study, work, and leisure (retirement); instead, work and recreation must be permanent components in the balanced life, while study is a continual and life-long concomitant and an inspiration and resource for these activities.

Healthful living, secondly, depends upon *safety*. The good life from which wholeness results is one in which proper precautions against injury are habitually taken. Concern for safety is essential for the preservation of life itself, upon which the good life must rest. Safety education begins in the earliest days of the infant's life, in the continual watchfulness of parents against any danger to the helpless child. As the child grows and his powers of action increase, he must be saved from an increasingly wide range of perils, of which he is at first unaware. He cannot be permitted to discover most of them for himself, for in many cases the learning experience would result in serious injury or death. Hence, there must be strong prohibitions and taboos in relation to water, fire, highways, electrical equipment, poisons, high places, and the like. Firm direction, and even physical punishment if necessary, are required to enforce the elemental lessons of safety. Still, parents and teachers should keep the teaching of safety realistic, avoiding the creation of fears and inhibitions that are out of proportion to the actual dangers.

One of the features of good vocational and recreational preparation is instruction in safety factors at work and play. Hazardous occupations should as far as possible be avoided. Insofar as they must be carried on by someone—for example, mining and radiological work—every available safeguard should be insisted on—such as proper ventilation, lighting, and shielding. Even jobs that are not intrinsically dangerous may become so if safety devices are not conscientiously used. In the recreation field, expertness in sports reduces the likelihood of injury. One of the objectives of physical education is to develop skills that make it possible to play hard yet safely. Another goal is to develop the habit of scrupulously observing the rules of the game, since one of the main functions of rules is to keep play within the bounds of safety. More important than these matters of safety through skill and rule keeping is the ethical question of promoting and participating in forms of recreation that are unavoidably dangerous—for example, football for very young boys or motorcycle racing at any age. It is always possible to choose sports that call forth all the courage and skill one possesses without exposure to needless risk of injury.

Because accidents still occur under even favorable safety conditions, a part of everyone's education should be mastery of the essentials of first aid. Through an understanding of the elemental rules of treatment for the injured, damage may be minimized and subsequent medical care may be made more effective. A layman's knowledge of such techniques as artificial respiration and bandaging wounds may make the difference between death and survival for an injured person.

Following upon the matter of safety is a contemporary health problem of the first magnitude—namely, the *proper use of motor vehicles.* The automobile is a major hazard to life and limb in the modern world. Our whole way of life, including our patterns of working and residence, have been revolutionized by it. By their numbers, speed, and power, automobiles constitute an ominous environmental influence, an ever-present threat of violence. Under these circumstances the will and pleasure of the individual may not safely govern the use of motor vehicles; strict social regulations are necessary. Minimum standards of age, health, and skill for all drivers must be set and enforced. Juveniles who look upon driving as a sport must be kept off the road. People who are infirm by reason of illness or age and who do not have the alertness and reaction speed requisite to good driving should also not be licensed. Periodic tests of knowledge and skill ought to be required of all drivers. Automobile makers should be made legally responsible for the mechanical safety of their product, and all automobiles in use should be inspected regularly.

Provision should be made for driver training—possibly as an adjunct to the school program—to insure that every person has an opportunity to learn the right use of the automobile. Enforcement of traffic regulations should be managed by a sufficiently large and adequately compensated corps of traffic policemen, and penalties for the more serious offenses should be substantial—including permanent revocation of licenses of drivers who appear to be a persistent menace to the public safety.

A fourth health consideration is the practice of bodily exercise. As machines have lifted more and more of the burden of labor from men's backs and hands, demands upon the human body have greatly declined. Transportation, too, no longer calls for physical effort. Walking and climbing have almost universally been replaced by riding. Many Americans will not even walk a few blocks when they have an automobile at their disposal. This multiplication of effort-saving mechanisms has ushered in a new era of physical ease. Freedom from necessary physical exertion has become a cardinal objective of the good life.

But man cannot with impunity ignore the claims of his body. During the eons of evolutionary development his physical structures came into being in response to the challenge of the environment. To remain healthy a person needs to make use of these bodily capacities.

Since such efforts are generally no longer physically required, they have to be voluntarily assumed. It is the primary function of physical education to build habits of exercise that will serve throughout life to supply the need for healthful bodily exertion. Since health is wholeness, this goal cannot be reached by concentrating solely on *physical* activity. A human being always acts as a whole, never simply as a body or a mind. Hence, physical education should be devoted to the development of coordinated intellectual-social-physical activities which meaningfully engage the energies of the total person.

It is a symptom of our contemporary cultural disintegration that the "intellectual" phases of education have been so sharply separated from the "physical" ones, and that physical education has been so largely relegated by academic people to the "all brawn but no brains" category. In principle, physical education provides the best opportunity for the harmonious development of the entire person, through contests of skill in which intelligence, esthetic imagination, social sensitivity, and moral purpose are channeled through significant physical activity. The highest task for health education in a society devoted to excellence is to discover and introduce into the cultural stream modes of living that will fully employ bodily energies in ways that are at the same time consonant with the ideals of reason, qualitative judgment, and ethical concern.

Habits of *cleanliness* are a further goal for health education. The basic principles of personal hygiene should be taught by parents, and schools should reinforce this home instruction, especially by supplying the physiological and psychological grounds upon which the practice of cleanliness rests. It may be shown that by having due regard for cleanness of the body and of clothing one both helps guard against disease and does honor to other persons and to oneself. Being clean is not simply a physical good; acts of purification have a symbolic significance, too—as many religious rites testify. But apart from the formal ceremonial aspect, being clean has an elevating effect on the entire person. It is an overt manifestation of devotion to the ideal of purity, a recognition of human transcendence of simple biological existence.

In teaching children to be clean, it is important not to inculcate attitudes of fear and disgust regarding bodily processes. There is evidence, for example, that toilet training based on repugnance for excretory products may result in psychological damage. Likewise, table training that is too early, too rigid, and too negative may induce permanently disabling attitudes. Being clean should not be a means of assuaging irrational guilt feelings. Compulsive, automatic scrupulousness is a sign of illness, not of health. A child should be encouraged by adult attitudes to accept himself and everything related to his body and issuing from it from whatever channel. Then in his own good time (which is usually not long) he will be able to reorganize his bodily activities so as to conform to established social customs.

The last point may be made in another way—by asserting that a healthy concept of cleanliness is primarily positive rather than negative. Modern sanitation has emphasized the elimination of dirt and the killing of germs. We live in a sterilized civilization. The sanitized culture may also be a sterile culture. The ideal of personal purity is positive in emphasis. It is directed toward the disposition of material things (none of which are evil in themselves) so as to serve goodness most fully. It is aimed not at the total negation of a part of creation, but at the right ordering of created things within the whole economy of life.

A sixth factor contributing to good health is proper *dietary habits.* The relevant matters here are the kinds of food eaten, their quality and quantity, and the manner of eating them. As to kinds, one principle is that of balance. We possess considerable well-tested knowledge of nutrition, from which it is possible to plan meals so as to supply the substances needed for abundant health. This basic nutritional information should be regularly included in health instruction. Another principle is that of avoiding foods that impose special organic strains—for example, fats for people whose bodies accumulate rather than use them or salted foods for people with certain circulatory maldispositions. A proper diet is not assured by following one's fancy, responding to the inclinations of appetite and the momentary leadings of taste. The desire principle may be quite deceptive in decisions about food. It is usually the case that in the long run plain and superficially less appetizing foods are more healthful than rich and fancy ones. While food should be attractively prepared and appealing to the taste, the proper criterion for selection is not immediate hunger satisfaction but reliable knowledge of what is healthful.

Concerning the quality of food, the problem is to a large degree one of social organization and control. The pressures for efficient collection and distribution of foods in urban society and the demand for short cuts in food preparation in high-speed civilization have brought into being a vast food-processing industry. In the interests of efficiency and convenience the quality of many foods has been sacrificed. They have been excessively refined, with resulting loss of nutrient values. They have been mixed with preservatives, dyes, and softeners to make them keep longer, look better, and cook more quickly, but again with possible loss of nourishing quality and perhaps serious long-term detriment to health through the addition of toxic substances. Individuals should be educated to these dangers and encouraged to use foods that have not been ruined by processing. Consumers should organize and support cooperatives devoted to the production and distribution of high-quality foods, scientifically tested for nutritional value and for freedom from adulterants. In addition, citizens must be taught how to secure strong, well-staffed, and amply financed government agencies which are dedicated to the health of the people and serve them through a well-enforced body of pure food laws, a well-organized inspection and grading system, and a continuing broad program of research in nutrition and in food production and processing. As in so many other areas of life, prime concern for ease and profit in the matter of food supply has destructive consequences. The health of all the people requires the restoration of a principle of qualitative excellence as the controlling ideal of the food industry.

Regarding the quantity of food consumed, appetite considerations again ought not to govern. People in an economy of abundance have a special difficulty in that their wants are not disciplined by the scarcity of food. Most Americans eat too much. Overeating in many cases is a consequence of personal frustration and loss of meaning. People try to fill the void in their lives by consuming food. Failing to discover claims of enduring worth upon them, they seek refuge in immediate sense gratification. Excessive eating may also be an expression of the power urge in people who inwardly feel powerless, for nothing more clearly demonstrates mastery over things than does the act of devouring them. The healthy person—one who is whole— gratefully receives food (rather than grasps for it) as a welcome energy source for performing the acts of devotion in which his life is centered. He regards his body as an agency for the channeling of the materials of nourishment into the service of worthy ends. Such a person is not controlled by appetite; he harnesses appetite for the sake of high purposes. As a symbol of this subordination of desire, the ancient practice of periodic fasting has special value. That most well-fed moderns tend to feel deprived and anxious if circumstances force them to miss a meal is evidence of how subject they are to desire and how largely their feeding habits are governed by psychological craving. When the act of fasting is united with deliberate re-dedication to the good, it provides a clear reminder that goodness of life does not consist in obedience to the compulsions of organic existence.

Finally, in the manner of eating, the healthful way includes the avoidance of excessive haste, of much irregularity, and of emotionally tense situations. Food should be partaken with due respect for the functional characteristics of the human organism. The integral person accords the act of eating its rightful place in the whole scheme of life; he does not cheat it of its fair share of time, of its regular place in the ordering of existence, and of its portion in the gift of serenity. Here health and etiquette impinge on one another. Instruction in good table manners serves more than esthetic purposes, for good table etiquette preserves the sense of leisure and order and the relaxed atmosphere which are requisite to good health.

A seventh matter of considerable importance to health is the use of *alcoholic beverages.* A consideration of the marked effects alcohol consumption has on human behavior makes it evident that questions of conscience are at stake. Alcohol acts as a narcotic—first, in suppressing the higher mental functions and then, as larger doses are taken, in reducing a person to the animal level and finally to unconscious vegetative immobility.

It can be argued that, ideally, alcoholic beverages should not be used at all, that any substance that renders a person less capable of functioning at the highest human level is not appropriate for human consumption. The contrary argument, in favor of some form of drinking, takes one or more of the following three lines: the religious, the social, or the psychological. Deep in the religious tradition is the custom of using alcohol as a symbol and a vehicle for divine inspiration. Drinking induces a transformation of feeling which removes one from the ordinary and everyday realm into a different world, in which the tensions and anxieties of living are dissolved and a sense of release is enjoyed. Such a total change in outlook is regarded as a glimpse into the life of ecstasy and bliss which is the consummation of the religious quest. Religious drinking generally takes place within the strict discipline of established ritual and hence usually does not go to the harmful excess of deep intoxication. Social drinking is also ritualistic in character, but without the other-worldly overtones of the religious act. The purpose of social drinking is to facilitate interpersonal association by releasing the inhibitions and defenses that commonly separate people from one another.

Both the religious and the secular-social uses of alcohol depend on its psychological effects, but they differ from purely psychological drinking in their emphasis on the objective forms and shared purposes of corporate life. Psychological drinking is a reflection of individual craving for satisfaction. A person who feels lonely, lost, and insecure may find temporary relief and release through the transfigured state of consciousness produced by alcohol. Such psychological drinking is a symptom of personal ill health and is at best not a cure but only a means of escape.

The prevalance of alcohol consumption may be connected with the pervasiveness of the pleasure principle in a democracy of desire. When wanting things is the motivation for conduct, persons are in a permanent state of frustration, because it is in the nature of things that all wants cannot be fulfilled. Alcohol provides a temporary refuge in a world where the barriers, hostilities, and denials of reality are dissolved. Such use of alcohol thus merely serves to render more tolerable a system of life that is unhealthy at the core.

Beverage alcohol is an important topic for health education in homes, schools, churches, and other social agencies. Basic information about the physiology and the psychology of drinking should be widely disseminated. Furthermore, the following five specific problems should be covered in education at the secondary level and beyond. First, the nature and treatment of alcoholism as an illness should be presented. The symptoms, diagnosis, and prognosis of the disease, as far as they are known, should be made clear, and its genetic, physiological, psychological, and moral factors should be analyzed. Second, the fatal connection between drinking and driving needs to be accented. In the automotive age public safety is incompatible with the general practice of alcohol consumption. The importance of heavy penalties and speedy judgment on those who drive while intoxicated must be made clear. Third, the economic aspects of drinking should be considered. Alcoholic beverages are expensive. They impose a heavy drain upon individual resources and family budgets and constitute an unproductive drag on the national economy. Reflection on the relative amounts spent for alcoholic beverages and for such items as education and medical care provides a sobering lesson in relative values. A fourth problem is liquor advertising, whose misleading and value-subverting nature should be made clear by viewing its claims in the light of established facts.

A fifth and most difficult set of problems is the social control of alcohol production and consumption. Even if one holds that the goal toward which society ought to move is the complete elimination of alcoholic beverages, the imposition of prohibition by law does not appear appropriate, as it subordinates values of freedom which take precedence over those of abstinence. Drinking that is a symptom of social and personal malady cannot be effectively eliminated directly; it can be eliminated only by the healing of personality through the exchange of the life of satisfaction for that of devotion. In the absence of this fundamental conversion, other means of control must be employed and should be taught to all citizens. These include licensing and inspection of all liquor producers and distributors, the curbing of the corruption, vice, and crime which tend to cluster about the liquor traffic, and restriction on the sale of alcoholic beverages to minors. Perhaps most important of all is the development of social customs and pressures against individual and solitary drinking for psychological relief and in favor of community rituals in which the need to belong and to celebrate the goodness of life can be constructively satisfied.

Concerning the next matter of health—the use of *tobacco*—relatively little need be said. The problems associated with it are in some ways similar to those of alcohol use, but are as much less serious for immediate behavior as the psychophysical effects of smoking are less marked than those of drinking. For the long run, there is considerable evidence of a high correlation between the amount of smoking (chiefly of cigarettes) and the incidence of certain diseases, notably lung cancer and circulatory failures. In health education the injurious medical consequences of smoking should be made explicit, and the various problems of personal hygiene, fire safety, economic waste, and advertising deception connected with tobacco use should be discussed.

A ninth health concern of increasing gravity relates to the use of drugs. The medical profession is the primary guardian of the people's health in the matter of drugs, for the questions at issue are generally technical and cannot be properly assessed by laymen. Nevertheless, there are broad ethical concerns which are beyond the range of technical competence alone to settle. Medicines are meant to be aids to healing, but there are dangers to health in relying too heavily upon them. No question arises in connection with medicines such as insulin, which supply a vital deficiency without which life cannot go on at all. But serious issue may be taken with the frequent and somewhat indiscriminate use of such drugs as antibiotics. At this point medical practitioners are not in full agreement. Since the body must marshal its own natural defenses if it is to fend off diseases effectively, antibiotics should perhaps be reserved for emergency situations in which the natural defenses are insufficient.

Everyone needs to be taught the right use of other drugs such as digestion aids, cathartics, reducing pills, stimulants, pain relievers, and tranquilizers. In general, our satisfaction-dominated philosophy of life has led to the overuse of these remedies. When a person has an unpleasant symptom, his impulse is to take a drug to make him comfortable. The proper course is to regard the symptom as a welcome warning signal and then to discover and set right the condition that caused it. More often than not the discomfort is a result of unhealthful ways of thinking and acting which need to be rectified. Thus, it is usually wise to avoid palliative drugs, which obscure the true state of health and delay the rectification of life that dis-ease should prompt.

Certain drugs are so dangerous that their use must be rigidly confined to authorized medical treatment. Included are such habit-forming narcotics as opium, morphine, cocaine, heroin, and marijuana. Like alcohol, these drugs afford temporary escape into a transformed psychic world, in which the stresses and pains of ordinary life are obliterated. But unlike alcohol (except for alcoholics), these narcotics cannot be used regularly without progressive addiction and ultimately fatal consequences. The rise in narcotics addiction in recent years, particularly among young people, is in large measure a result of the prevalent decay of purpose, the loss of stable values, and the feelings of personal estrangement, loneliness, hopelessness, and meaninglessness which characterize the present age. Drugs admit one to a haven of light and life, the momentary grasp of which is preferred by the addict to the boredom of ordinary self-centered existence, despite the darkness and death which are the price of the fleeting ecstasy.

It is essential that young people be carefully instructed in the nature and effects of narcotics. They must also be helped to understand the measures required to maintain strict control of drug production and distribution, particularly in view of the incentives to delinquency, violence, and crime which unfortunately accompany general prohibition. There should, further, be diffusion of knowledge about possible ways of rehabilitating drug addicts and open discussion of the moral and social issues that must be settled when decisions as to treatment have to be made.

The tenth and last aspect of health education to be considered concerns *mental health*. As mentioned before, health is wholeness. Well-being of the body is not separate from that of the mind. A well person is unified, integral, organized for the full and free exercise of all his capacities. Organic disorders often have emotional and intellectual consequences, and many diseases of the body have their origins primarily in psychological disturbances. Many physicians state that a substantial proportion of the bodily complaints they are asked to cure are psychogenic in nature. Furthermore, recent discoveries have demonstrated the close relation between blood chemistry and endocrine balance on the one hand and emotional health on the other.

It follows that sickness is not to be overcome by piecemeal doctoring of separate parts or functions. Medical specialization is essential for the development and exercise of high technical skill, but it must be supplemented by the understanding of the person as a whole and comprehended within a unitary pattern of treatment. Good health is a by-product of complete, integral right living.

Mental health is peculiarly the province of education. In a sense this is its ultimate aim, for all of the other rightnesses of life are caught up in the sanity of sovereign mentality. Mental health means personal integrity—the unification of bodily functions and emotional impulses through the power of true ideas and worthy purposes. Emotional well-being is not, as the advocates of a satisfaction philosophy suggest, a liberation of impulse for the uninhibited fulfillment of desires. It is the condition of disciplined security in the release of self for responsible dedication to the right. Whatever is done to educate a person to respond to excellence and to abandon futile and self-defeating self-seeking is a contribution to mental health and thus to the welfare of the person as a whole.

Turning now from questions of conscience in relationships with nature and with self, the present chapter and the next five will be concerned with conduct in relation to persons, beginning with the private face-to-face associations within the family, broadening out to the larger, more impersonal connections within the community and the nation, and concluding with problems of world responsibility.

The family is the fundamental social unit, and for its establishment sexual life exists. The importance of the family is in proportion to the dignity and worth accorded the individual person, for in the family new persons come into being and are cared for with unbounded concern for their well-being. In this activity of procreation and care for children the self-regarding and self-serving ways of the parents are to a large degree transformed into acts of self-giving and self-sacrifice. Thus, the family may be a source not only of human generation but also of regeneration, in which the usual gain-seeking attitudes are replaced by ones of self-forgetful dedication and joyful responsibility.

The family is the source and bulwark of democracy. The very idea of the boundless worth of the individual person can be truly and inwardly understood largely through the experience of the parent-child relationship. In the larger social community, in the affairs of business, and in civic life the notion of the infinite value of personality is a noble abstraction more than a living reality. Yet in the ordinary family the assurance of unconditional concern is an everyday actuality. Democracy as a comprehensive ideal of life is the extension beyond the family of the devoted care that good parents provide for their offspring. Any weakening of the family will accordingly be reflected in the decline of democracy generally, and a widespread belief in the importance and the stability of families will help to sustain democratic ideals in other spheres of life. Furthermore, the democracy that grows out of family experience is a democracy of worth, since it stems from loyalty to the good of the person and not from acquisitive impulses. It is based on willingness to sacrifice for the sake of others rather than only on satisfaction of one's personal desires.

This natural democracy of worth in the family is the ground for the concern to educate the young. Parents are not content merely with begetting children and supplying them with the means of physical existence. Parents want to open the way for their children to grow in wisdom, grace, and honor through nourishment by the best fruits of civilization. Education is the attempt to fulfill the high hopes and fervent expectations which center around a child at his birth; it is the effort to make good the promise of a new life in its boundless potentiality.

These family-grounded ideals for the nurture of children are also the proper basis for education outside the family. Schools and other educational institutions should be regarded as extensions of the family and as instruments for accomplishing what parents intend for their children but for practical reasons cannot themselves perform. It is an error to regard the state as the primary agency of education and the family as simply the agency of procreation and support. The primacy of the family in education rests upon the spontaneous devotion of parents to their children—a devotion that supplies a model for the relation between teacher and pupil and that is undermined when education is regarded as a direct responsibility of the state. It is for this reason that parents should be given the right to send their children to schools of their choice, provided certain minimal standards of safety and competency are satisfied, and should not be required to utilize state educational facilities.

The fundamental source of family degeneration is the insinuation of the way of desire into the pattern of family relationships. The parents may regard the child as a means to fulfill their own ends. Through their progeny they may seek to overcome a feeling of loneliness, emptiness, or uselessness. In return, they may try as far as possible to supply the child with what he desires. This reciprocity is in effect a commercial one: the parties to the transaction exchange benefits with one another on a *quid pro quo* basis.

Ideally, the parents' devotion to their child should be unconditional in character. All traces of bargaining should be excluded. The child is not to be welcomed, accepted, and appropriately rewarded when he yields satisfaction to his parents, and rejected when he fails to produce as desired. He is to be accepted and cared for as a person, without regard to how well or how poorly he may live up to his parents' expectations and hopes for him. He is not a marketable commodity, to be bought up or written off, and measured by price. He is a unique person to be loved for himself, without measure or calculation of benefits.

In its unconditional quality the love of parents for the child is to be like their love for one another. But the parent-child relationship differs from the parents' relation to each other in this respect: while the parents entered into a joint covenant of mutual dedication, the parent-child relationship was established by the parents' intention and action without any possibility of the child's knowledge or consent. From this basic inequality in the establishment of the relationship stems the demand for a unilaterally unconditioned love of the parents for the child.

From this statement of the ideal of family love it should by no means be inferred that wants and satisfactions have no place in family life, nor that parents ought to make no demands upon their children. The fulfilling of desires is a happy consequence of good family life. Parents properly give innumerable satisfactions to each other and to their children, and children likewise please their parents. That this is so is a matter for gratitude. But to rejoice in the benefits of familial association is quite different from affirming a prudential basis for family life. Husband and wife enter into a covenant of loyalty from which it is hoped joy and happiness will continually spring, but which maintains whether or not these benefits actually accrue. Similarly, parents who take upon themselves responsibility for children may reasonably hope for the joys of affection returned and pride in healthy growth and worthy achievement, but the obligation to love and care for their young holds whether or not these legitimate desires are fulfilled.

In like manner, while it is right that parents should supply a child with things he wants, his wanting them ought not to be the reason for providing them. The parents' prior consideration should always be the child's need. If he desires what is right and good for him, that is cause for rejoicing; if he does not want it, then ways should be sought to lead him to a change of affection. This is the prime objective of the family's educative effort: by loving persuasion and by example to engender habits of commitment to what is of worth, instead of living for self-gratification. Granted that no parents can claim full and true knowledge of what is for the benefit of the child, the obligation still rests with them to govern their action with respect to him in the light of their best understanding of his real needs. Since the child's wants often provide clues to his needs, they should be hospitably considered and never discounted or rejected simply because they are objects of desire. The parents' responsibility is always to evaluate the child's requests and then to respond in the light of what appears to be right. Furthermore, as far as the child's maturity permits, he should be included in the process of evaluation, so that decisions are not simply imposed arbitrarily from above, but can be recognized by him as issuing from intelligent love and as such may be accepted even in cases where they are not welcome. Such occasions of mutual engagement in the making and weighing of requests constitute the most decisive of all educative opportunities, whether within or beyond the family. For it is in these encounters of the parent with the child that the values by which one lives are most tellingly communicated, and that the most crucial of all lessons—that of the primacy of loyalty to the good—may most impressively be taught. It is through these events that the child can learn to distinguish between rejection and affectionate discipline and to prefer mature love to easy indulgence.

Even though the unconditional reciprocity which belongs to the relation between the parents because they have covenanted with one another does not pertain to the parent-child relationship, the child does owe full obedience to his parents during the time of his dependence upon them. This obligation is qualified only by the principle that parents may not make grossly unjust demands upon the child, on pain of interference by the state as guardian of basic human rights. The child's obedience is not to be regarded as payment for benefits received from the parents; such an interpretation is ruled out by the unconditional nature of the parents' commitment. The duty to obey is simply an ingredient in the concern for the well-being of the child and for his proper education. It is not in any way for the satisfaction or profit of the parents, to make life easier for them (though that may be a welcome by-product), or to gratify their appetite for command. A child can experience the meaning of secure love only through being dependent on persons who supply authoritative direction for his life.

Few doctrines in recent decades have been more injurious than the one that opposes the exercise of parental authority in the name of liberty and democracy. The eroding of the parents' authority and the repudiation of the children's obligation to obey has seriously contributed to the disintegration of the family and has undermined the education of the young in crucial respects. The trouble has come from a failure to distinguish between kinds of authority. Absolute, arbitrary, manipulative authority—power over others—is an evil thing; it belongs neither in the state nor in the family. But responsible authority, which derives from devotion to the good, is right and necessary, especially in the family. It is just this distinction that provides the basis for understanding why children owe obedience to their parents.

The foregoing principles of parent-child relationships—concern by the parents for the needs of the child and the obligation of the child to obey the parents, within the context of intelligent and benevolent authority—are the foundation for the right kind of education not only in homes but also in schools, which are established to aid and complete the family in its educative task. Teachers have a primary duty to serve their pupils and not to gratify themselves, whether by a sense of power over the lives of others, by the enjoyment of their students' affection and respect, or by the intrinsic stimulus of interesting studies. Students, on the other hand, have the duty to render obedience to teachers within the limits of their recognized authority. Teachers ought to be given clear and unequivocal authority to conduct the work of education, and they should be afforded all necessary support, by parents and by school and civic officials, in making their authority effective. Finally, every effort must be made to insure that persons entrusted with the office of teacher will be selected with regard to their dedication to the authority of truth and right and not of arbitrary command.

Considerations of the nature of the family underlie the analysis of sex relationships generally. The basic principle of the position argued here is that the bearing and the rearing of children are the end and aim of sexuality, in the light of which all sexual activities should be appraised. Because parent-child relationships most naturally exemplify the way of devotion and obedience as opposed to that of self-gratification, the sexual relations that eventuate in procreation ought also to be founded in self-giving love and not in desire. Sex provides the crucial case of desire at odds with devotion.

The widely prevailing satisfaction philosophy has accorded sexual gratification a high place among the good things of life. To be regularly and fully satisfied in sexual experience is commonly accepted as an important human objective. The old-fashioned repression of sex is repudiated, and a new era of liberation is hailed. The stimulation of sexual appetite is a major aim of contemporary literary, dramatic, and pictorial productions, and the mass media are suffused with eroticism.

From this standpoint, the task of intelligence in relation to sex is not to master it or to control it in the way of earlier restrictive patterns of life, but to discover means of securing maximum sexual satisfaction for all people. In this new democracy of sexual desire the invention of efficient and inexpensive contraceptive devices and of improved drugs for the cure of venereal diseases is regarded as a signal advance toward the goal of the good life, for now it is possible to engage freely and widely in sexual intercourse with little fear of unwanted consequences, in the form of either offspring or infection.

When satisfaction is the criterion of good, the family is regarded essentially as a convenience and marriage as a means for sexual, economic, and social advantage. When the interests of the parties are no longer served by the marriage, the couple should be divorced, subject only to the requirement that due consideration be given to the care of any children resulting from the marriage. Even when the marriage is maintained, it is urged, extramarital sex relations ought to be countenanced, if discreetly engaged in, either in cases where for some reason the mate does not provide satisfaction or in any event for the added variety and richness of sexual enjoyments thereby provided.

The demand for full and free sexual satisfaction has been reinforced by certain reputedly scientific findings. From popular interpretations of Freud (in many respects incautious and one-sided) it has come to be widely believed that sexual impulses are the central factor in human existence, that social restraints on sex are the source of unhappiness and illness, and that uninhibited sexual experience is the basis for human felicity. Accordingly, sexual emancipation has assumed the character of a moral demand, and the imperatives of conventional sex morality have been condemned as contrary to human well-being.

More recently the studies of Alfred Kinsey and his associates on the sexual habits of contemporary Americans have shown how wide the gulf is between the persisting puritanic professions of respectable people and their average actual sexual behavior. The lesson usually drawn from these studies is that the outmoded pruderies of conventional middle-class sex ethics should be abandoned, and the liberties of sexual expression should be frankly, openly, and unashamedly accepted and enjoyed.

While it may readily be granted that certain hostile, fearful, and punitive attitudes toward sexual impulses will be harmful to personality, it does not follow that inhibition of sexual activity is intrinsically undesirable, or that a general relaxation of standards for sexual behavior is indicated. There is no evidence, scientific or otherwise, that personal and social well-being is proportionate to the degree of sexual gratification enjoyed. In fact, it may be closer to the truth to say that the refinement and ennoblement of personality and the advancement of civilization are in proportion to the degree of discipline and control of sexual appetite. From this perspective, the modern assault on sex standards in the name of freedom (more properly called license) presents a major threat to individual and social welfare, for it justifies and confirms sensual satisfaction as the regulating principle of life.

Sexual appetite, powerful as it may be, is unlike the craving for food and drink, which must be satisfied if life is to continue. Satisfaction of sex urges can be denied temporarily or permanently without any impairment of the person, provided the purposes of restraint are understood and accepted. Given sufficiently significant purposes, renunciation of sexual satisfaction will, in fact, tend to heighten energies and intensify the zest for living. Restraint is not good simply in itself. It is not beneficial when it is externally imposed simply as a denial of desire. But when a person comes to see the ordering of sex impulse as a necessary means to serving a high good, the sacrifice of gratification can become a source of well-being. It is difficult for a person to sustain that vision in isolation. The practice of continence in a concupiscent society imposes great strain on the individual. We need to work out a set of social expectations and conventions in which the proper regulation of sexual activity will be assisted rather than made more difficult by being thrust largely on the individual, as it is at present.

It is possible that the re-establishment of loyalty to the right in every aspect of life could be greatly fostered by a fresh acceptance of the ideal of sexual purity. Perhaps sexual discipline is the test case for dedication to standards of worth in every domain of existence. Furthermore, since sex has to do with the creation of persons, whose individual worth is the basic principle of democracy, the health and vitality of democracy may be directly related to the prevailing state of conscience with regard to sex.

Some of the principles of sex and family life which follow for a democracy of worth may now be stated. These principles also indicate the standards to be used in sex education—the basic ideals to be inculcated by explicit instruction in homes and at appropriate levels in schools, and even more essentially by the complex of accepted acts built into social and cultural patterns.

First, sexual activity should always be judged in relation to family ideals. The family is the end to which sexual relationships are a means. Sexuality is not an independent sphere, and sexual experience is not rightly regarded as an end in itself. The test of conscience for any sexual act is whether or not it is in accord with the central purpose of the family, which is to embody the ideal of individual worth through an unconditional covenant between husband and wife and unconditional commitment to children.

It follows, second, that sexual intercourse should take place only between husband and wife, and not outside of marriage. Extramarital sexual relationships undermine the family and betray the covenant of fidelity which ought to be established between marriage partners. The justification of premarital sex experimentation as a means of preparation for marriage and as a test of sexual compatibility for prospective mates is a rationalization for license and self-indulgence. Devoted couples can and should work out their sexual adjustments as a task of married life. Marriage should be a state of learning and growing together, in which the partners come together not in ignorance but in innocence, and participate in sexual discovery as a fresh and unique experience.

The limitation on sexual relationships to married couples extends beyond the complete act of intercourse to those forms of mutual sex stimulation that are a preparation for intercourse. The widespread practice of petting by persons who have no intention of marriage to each other is a consequence of the common acceptance of sexual relations as a means of satisfaction quite apart from family considerations. Since all physical intimacies between the sexes have sexual union as an implicit hope, intention, or inclination, they should be reserved solely for persons who have made a covenant of engagement to marry one another. Morally, petting is the equivalent of intercourse. It also contains an inherent psychological contradiction, in being at once an invitation to pleasure and a frustration of desire. Thus, it not only poisons the spring of sexual purity but also creates habits of sexual response which later make full surrender to a marriage partner more difficult to achieve. It is difficult for young people to refrain from petting in a society where this is generally accepted and practiced. To help them, the support and loving discipline of families is essential, and more especially of groups of families with similar standards, and of churches, schools, and other institutions with well-developed programs for more worthy modes of mutual association.

Fourth, within marriage sexual intercourse should be a means of procreation and of expressing the mutual devotion of husband and wife. It is no true and right marriage in which husband and wife consider themselves licensed to use each other for sexual purposes. Possession and use are subpersonal and wholly alien to the spirit of dedication upon which marriage should be founded. This does not mean that pleasure in sex has no place in marriage. Mutual enjoyment is important and legitimate, but only and always as a welcome concomitant of a relation established on sensitivity and consideration by each for the needs of the other.

One of the most serious of all contemporary problems is the limitation of population growth in order to establish a proper balance between human requirements and natural resources. The responsibility for population control rests with individual families, who should deliberately restrict their procreative activity. Family planning is important not only to help meet the general problem of natural resources but also to make it possible for each child born into the family to have the material and personal benefits he needs. In fact, as this latter concern is in most cases the only effective motive for limiting births, it is the best approach to the larger social problem.

Within the family, then, the question arises of how the number of children shall be controlled. There are three fundamentally different possible ways. The first way is to destroy what has been produced by conception, either by infanticide or by abortion. Infanticide is a form of murder and, as such, has been outlawed in all modern civilized societies. Since a fetus is a human being, deliberate abortion is also an unwarranted taking of life. Parents are in conscience bound to accept, protect, and nurture each life given to them, beginning with the moment of conception, at which time that life comes into being.

The second way of limiting family size is for husband and wife to refrain from sexual intercourse except for the express purpose of having children. By reserving the act of sexual union solely for procreation, intercourse gains extraordinary symbolic power. While those who wholeheartedly agree to live by this ideal do great honor to human personality and to the creative sources from which persons spring, the level of spiritual attainment and of personal discipline required to live in this manner is most unusual and probably beyond the capability of the average couple.

The third way of limiting offspring is to prevent conception from taking place. This approach permits the mutual enrichment of life through sexual union without each time assuming the responsibility for another child. Its justification is in the conviction that intercourse may rightly serve not only for procreation, but also *independently* as a means for husband and wife to express their love for each other.

There is no reason why contraception should not be humanely and sensitively practiced for the high purposes of family planning, social responsibility, and freedom for full and frequent sexual union. This does not mean that contraceptives make it unnecessary to discipline sexual desire. The governing principle of devotion to the marriage partner still holds, and full mutuality in the sexual relationship is still the aim. The value of contraception is simply that it enables the husband and wife to exercise parental and societal responsibility in controlling procreation without renouncing one of the most powerful means of communicating love.

A fifth basic principle is that all perversion and immaturity of sexual expression are to be avoided. The chief perversion is homosexuality, and the major form of immature sexuality is masturbation. These sexual practices are undesirable because they contradict the fundamental purpose of sexuality, which is the establishment of families and the raising of children. It is important that relationships within the family be such as to prevent the inversion of sexuality through fear or hatred of the opposite sex. Homosexual tendencies are chiefly a consequence of miseducation by parents who have failed to establish secure and loving associations with their children. Continued auto-erotic practices also reflect both inability to give oneself in a complementary way to others and a habit of seeking compensation in one's own bodily feelings for the frustrations of interpersonal associations.

Sixth, marriage should be a singular and permanent relationship. Polygamy is excluded by the democratic ideal of uniqueness, of which sexual union is the consummatory symbol. Families with multiple wives or husbands render impossible the unconditional devotion which is the ideal in marriage. Law and custom have sustained this ideal in advanced civilized societies by prohibiting multiple mating. While it is thus not lawful to have more than one husband or wife at a time, divorce makes possible a kind of serial polygamy. Such serial mating is probably even more damaging to family life—particularly to children—than ordinary polygamy. The prevalence of divorce is directly related to the prevalence of the desire philosophy. When interest and satisfaction are taken as the standards for conduct, mates who cease to interest or satisfy each other seek to dissolve their relationship. By contrast, when marriage is founded upon unconditional commitment to the other person, the desires and pleasures of the partners are secondary considerations, which have nothing what-soever to do with the objective reality of the abiding marriage cov-enant.

Marriage ought to be regarded as an opportunity for the making of a shared life, as a task to be undertaken with full acceptance of the inevitable pains and sorrows as well as the pleasures and joys. Many modern marriages run a downhill course from the high romance and ecstatic satisfaction of newly-weds, through the progressive frustra-tions and disappointments of people who measure one another by benefits received, to the divorce court. Marriage ought rather to begin with nothing except the promise of loyal devotion and then move through patient, constructive effort to progressively higher levels of mutual understanding and service.

To affirm the ideal of permanence in marriage is not the same as to argue the legal prohibition of divorce. It may frequently be better for a marriage to be dissolved than for mates to be forced by law or the pressure of custom to live together in a state of unholy hostility. Children in such households may suffer less from the insecurities incidental to breaking up the home than from the poisons of their parents' mutual antagonism. The point of the present analysis is that divorce ought not to be accepted as a normal and proper practice, for the benefit of couples who no longer satisfy each other. It should be seen instead as a lamentable consequence of establishing marriages on the deceptive and ultimately disastrous basis of want satisfaction.

Seventh, if marriages are to be permanent and productive of hu-mane values, marriage partners need to select one another not on the basis of romantic attraction and immediate sexual satisfaction, but out of regard for the long-term potentialities in the relationship for the creation of a worth-full shared life. The question prospective mates should ask is not: Can I find happiness with this other per-son?—but: Can we learn together and do things for and with each other in such a way as to bring into being new lives through our union nurtured in mature love based on dedication to what is true and excellent?

The eighth and final point is that in a democracy of worth not everyone need feel obliged to marry. Some people do not have the vocation to establish a family. For certain persons other channels of devotion may be more important than marriage and incompatible with an unconditional commitment to husband or wife. For those who have a mission to teach, to serve the poor and sick, to engage in exacting research, or to undertake dangerous and lonely assignments, family responsibilities may be an impediment. Persons who shun marriage simply to remain free to please themselves are not to be honored, but those are to be honored who have adopted other forms of dedication in place of marriage, whether by deliberate intention, by force of circumstance, or because no person has appeared with whom they could wholeheartedly make an enduring covenant. In fact, those who remain unmarried in the service of the right have the special opportunity to manifest loving concern for others without the natural impetus provided by matrimonial or parental relationships.

The subject of social class takes us as close as any other to the very core of democratic values. Nondemocratic societies essentially are ones in which people are separated into distinct strata, and the classical conception of democracy emerges from the attempt to organize a society of equals, free from the privileges or stigmas of "superior" and "inferior" rank. The American Dream has centered about the creation of this commonwealth of equals, without the levels of prestige that divided men from one another in the older and more traditional societies. Foreign observers of the American experiment, such as de Tocqueville in the mid-nineteenth century, as well as more recent ones, have been particularly impressed by the degree to which this dream has been realized in American life. In no other respect does our society seem to have succeeded so well in demonstrating the possibilities of respecting the dignity of all men.

On the other hand, there are many evidences in American life that rank and privilege are still with us, and that the pure vision of democratic equality has not been fully realized. Moreover, the idea of equality, on reflection, turns out not to be a simple one, so that the meaning of the democratic social ideal needs to be examined and defined. Are we a classless society, and if so, in what sense or senses? If we are not, ought we to work for the elimination of classes? What does it mean to say that people in a democracy are equal or should be equal? Can status and rank be abandoned, and should they be? These are questions that can be approached only through a careful analysis of the nature and uses of classification.

We begin with a look at the general meaning of classification. A "class" is any collection of things sharing some common property or set of properties. Classifying has two main purposes. First, it is the basis for all understanding of the world. Our experience becomes intelligible only through the formation of concepts, and concepts are kinds or classes of things. All cognition and recognition take place against the background of earlier experience organized conceptually. By means of classification we avoid the frustrating confusion of experience as a mass of disparate and separate items.

The second chief purpose of classifying is to facilitate control of things. When similar items are grouped together, they may be handled alike, within the sphere of relevance of the qualities defining the class. Thus, the classification of books by subject and by author in a library makes it possible to manage even a very large collection without confusion. Without such organization one could scarcely ever find any desired volume. Again, the classification of rocks according to certain types enables engineers to carry out mining or building operations with maximum safety and efficiency. Similarly, knowledge of kinds of foods is the basis for dietary control.

Of particular interest for our present discussion of social class are the ways in which the activity of classifying applies to people. First, it is possible to distinguish an inclusive class of entities called "persons." This is the species man. To be a person is to possess certain essential qualities and capacities which do not belong to any things in the nonhuman world. Persons share with some nonpersons such qualities as being mammals, animals, and living things. On the other hand, they are a special group in respect to such features as rational capacity, imagination, memory, foresight, language, and the ability to create and transmit culture.

This unity of all persons within the bounds of a single inclusive class is a fundamental fact for democracy. It is one basis for human equality. All persons are at least equal with respect to those qualities by which they are distinguished from all nonpersons. The special capacities of man—the glory of his knowledge, art, and invention, the wonder of his powers for sympathy, love, and reverence, as well as the tragedy of their perversion for selfish ends—have for centuries been faithfully acknowledged and appropriately celebrated through arts, letters, philosophy, and religion. In the past century, however, under the influence of evolutionary theory, the kinship of man with the animals has been more strongly emphasized. Nevertheless, the classical humanistic tradition, with its emphasis on the common distinctive qualities of man, provides stronger support for the democratic ideal of human equality than does evolutionary naturalism, with its concern for the continuity of man with the lower forms of life.

The problems of social class derive not from this classifying of men with the animals but from dividing the inclusive class of persons into subclasses. Human beings may be grouped according to any number of indices of similarity. Some of the features commonly used for classifying people are as follows: (1) Physical characteristics—sex, age, height, weight, color (of hair, eyes, or skin), blood type, body build, medical history. (2) Intellectual factors—"Intelligence Quotient," aptitude (mathematical, verbal, manual, etc.), achievement level in various special fields of study, area of specialization, academic grades and ranks, educational level reached, memory, imagination, abstractive and logical ability. (3) Emotional, social, and moral traits— degree of aggressiveness, initiative, maturity, self-understanding and self-acceptance, extraversion or introversion, neurotic or psychotic conditions, confidence, poise, friendliness, adaptability, selfishness or unselfishness. (4) Occupation—owner, executive, professional, clerical, manual, unemployed, plus various individual occupational classes and subclasses. (5) Residence—nation, state, city or town, district, or street, whether presently or by origin. (6) Affiliations—religious, political, civic, professional, social. (7) Economic—income, assets, and sources of each. (8) Marital status. (9) Ancestry. (10) Citizenship.

Why do we classify people? For the same reason that we group together other entities: for intellectual simplification and greater efficiency in management and control. It is more economical of thought and effort to deal with many people in the same manner than to devise a new scheme of idea and action for each person separately. When people are classified, they are necessarily regarded as things rather than as persons. A person is a unique individual. As a member of a collection he loses his concrete wholeness and is dealt with as an abstraction. Classification is a way of considering people impersonally and partially rather than in their singular completeness.

Class designations are a prime instrument of social regulation. In stratified societies each person is tagged with a class designation which fixes his place in the social structure. This allocation process serves to maintain social stability. Everyone is expected to know his proper place and to stay in it. Complex systems of ritual and symbol are evolved to make visible and vivid the class lines which separate one group from another.

The extreme form of tight and exclusive class structure is the system of caste, in which each person is permanently fixed from birth in a particular group. Various bases may be used for determining class characteristics—for example, color or occupation. The essential point is that each person must assume the caste to which his parents belong. He cannot by any decision or act of his own change his caste, and his activities in every department of life—particularly in such matters as marriage, eating, and education—are governed by caste regulations. The caste system is the ultimate form of undemocratic use of classification, throwing into sharp relief the relation of class to the preservation of social order.

A society organized along sharp class lines tends to be static. Its members are concerned more with maintaining it as it is than with risking experiment or modification. The social structure is closed, and the pattern of organization is regarded as complete and sacrosanct. It is generally believed that the laws, customs, and rituals by which the particular system is defined are written into the nature of things, and that the social structure is but a true reflection of the innate qualities of human nature in its several kinds.

Systems of human classification tend to be self-perpetuating and self-confirming. Persons who are initially grouped together according to some particular feature come to be treated as interchangeable units and thus are driven into identification with each other and into similar patterns of life which extend the range of likenesses. Class distinctions are converted in this manner into real divisions between people, with far more comprehensive significance than the particular differences in traits or functions by which they are defined. Aspects of persons that should have relatively superficial descriptive meaning are at length interpreted as basic qualities defining exclusive subspecies of humanity. "Executive," "laborer," "Catholic," "Southern Baptist," "Jew," "Democrat," "Republican," "Socialist," for example, are proper designations of occupational, religious, or political affiliation, but may under undemocratic pressures become class symbols which divide people into comprehensive separate groups for *other than* occupational, religious, or political purposes.

In this self-confirming propensity of the class structure, education plays a major part. Each new generation is instructed in the ways of the group. The young are initiated into the customs that have come to characterize the particular classes into which they are born. In this manner it comes to appear as though group characteristics are part of the very substance of personality. By their powerful educative effect class divisions are perpetuated and class lines are hardened, unless deliberate countervailing democratic influences are brought to bear. It is in this regard that universal free public education is so essential. It was pointed out in the last chapter that schooling is an extension of the educative function of the family and that parents should be at liberty to send their children to nonpublic schools. Such schools often develop along class lines, thus accentuating the existing cleavages among people. For this reason it is important for a democracy to have a strong public school system, and parents who cherish democratic ideals do well to send their children to schools, either public or independent, in which traditional class distinctions are minimized.

Regardless of whether a school is public or nonpublic, there are ever-present pressures for education to be conducted along class lines. Education is costly, and one of the ways of keeping expenses down is to put students into classes and to treat them as far as possible alike. Large classes and standardized lessons are much more economical than individual instruction. Furthermore, it is easy for teachers to fall into the attitude that their task is to fashion young people after the pattern of some ideal model. The idea of a standard set of virtues and accomplishments by which all should be measured is a class idea. Teaching in accordance with it presupposes manipulation and control of persons to shape them for membership in a collection of some particular character.

Class assignment in education may be determined in any of a number of ways. The most common determinant is chronological age. According to this method of classification, all students of a given age or age range are treated alike educationally, even though they may differ widely in the characteristics that are relevant to learning—as age is not. Another common mode of grouping is by some measure of intellectual aptitude or achievement. Such homogeneous ability grouping in schools is urged on behalf of increased learning efficiency. It has the defect of emphasizing only one kind of learning and of tending to create broad prestige rankings along intellectual lines. Pupils may further be put into classes on the basis of prospective occupation or occupation type, as in the European multiple-track system, in which at a certain age—say, twelve—pupils are separated into "industrial" or "vocational," "business" or "commercial," and "academic" or "college preparatory" segments. In some schools, chiefly nonpublic ones, the sexes are segregated, and in other schools racial and religious factors are crucial in deciding which students will be taught together.

Regardless of the criteria used for class placement, the purpose of such grouping is either to enable the teacher to manage the students more effectively or to use the school to sustain class distinctions recognized in the society of which the school is an agency. Whenever pupils are organized into classes and treated as classes, the tendency is always toward uniformity and conformity, toward externally imposed and defined discipline and order. Freedom and individuality, experimentation and creativity are not fostered by education in which class membership is regarded as important.

How do democratic commitments modify these undemocratic structures and tendencies in a class society? One answer has been that of revolutionary transformation, in which established orders of society are challenged and overthrown, and traditional modes of grouping people are discarded. The feudal aristocracies of the Middle Ages were one by one overturned by the forces of modern political, economic, and religious life. In communism and the new nationalisms of the present century established orders are being upset at an unparalleled rate, in the name of democracy. Whenever such revolutionary overturning of the traditional classes occurs, arbitrary traditional restrictions on individual human activity are removed, and great new resources of personal energy are released.

Despite the apparent gains for democracy through such revolutionary movements, the concomitant or eventual losses may be substantial. Anarchy and chaos may follow the destruction of the traditional social orders. Civilization is a balanced design of customs, principles, and expectations woven into the fabric of social institutions. When these established orders are all at once demolished, the injury to civilized values may be fatal. Furthermore, since no society can endure or make progress without some determinate structure and graded authority, new class distinctions quickly arise to take the place of those abolished by the revolution. They may be as rigid and exclusive as the ones they displace—though the relative rankings and the membership are usually quite different. The communist movement is a dramatic illustration of the present point. Although Marxist theory teaches the establishment of a classless society through the expropriation of the bourgeoisie and the dictatorship of the proletariat, in actual practice the self-styled "Peoples' Democracies" contain well-defined new classes.

The revolutionary approach to the democratization of the social order is characteristic of the democracy of desire. Attention is focused on the disparities in rank and privilege among various classes in traditional societies and upon the changes necessary to secure a larger share for the disadvantaged. Antagonism, conflict, and social tension and disorder are increased, and new class divisions are generated to counteract the destructive conflict. Manipulatory techniques are used in order to force people into the patterns that the new dominant groups prescribe. The manipulators represent themselves as true friends of the people, as "liberal" and "democratic," and as opposed to "authoritarian reactionaries," but all the while they are destroying the people and denying their freedom. Finally, the interest philosophy entails a general destruction of qualitative standards. Distinctions are obliterated in the name of democratic criticism of traditional classes, and a pall of mediocrity descends over the whole culture.

The democracy of desire cannot provide a satisfactory basis for the criticism of undemocratic forms of social class, for it is infected by the same subpersonal assumptions which render these modes of human classification offensive. For a true perspective on social class we must turn to the democracy of worth. Here the criterion for judgment is right instead of interest. Qualitative distinctions are recognized, and the value of classification as a means of embodying them is acknowledged. Orders of rank, of authority, and even of honor are necessary to social well-being. All civilized life depends on the process of ordering, and wherever there are designations of position or office within society there will inevitably be classes.

To admit the principle of classification is not to deny the need for democratic criticism of actual social class arrangements. Social classes are often unjust, and the order of society is in need of reconstruction, according to principles of right and not of class interest. The fundamental democratic principle for social class is that the orders and distinctions of society should be based upon the contribution made by a person to the good of society and not upon personal privilege. Status should be determined by function rather than by accident of birth or fortune or by success in the struggle for prestige. If one's personal capabilities and accomplishments fit him for important positions of leadership, he should be accorded the rank and the honor that symbolize the high value of his service. Classifying and ranking people is not inconsistent with democratic justice. Equity depends on a status system organized to objectify ideals of the social good. Ranking people is not in itself unjust. Injustice consists in ranking people incorrectly—in according honor and status for the wrong reasons, that is, for causes other than contribution to the common weal.

But what of the fact earlier pointed out that classifying is an impersonal process and, hence, in tension with democratic ideals? How does that square with the foregoing affirmation of class in a democracy of worth? While classifying is socially necessary and can be just, in a democracy each person is regarded as a unique individual, valuable in himself and not on account of any class or rank labels attached to him for social purposes. The status of a person ought, then, to be regarded as belonging to the position he occupies in the social structure and not as inhering in him personally. There is a fundamental truth in the idea of democratic equality. As persons all men are absolutely equal, in the sense that each is a singular, incomparable, irreducible self. To this unique, free personhood any and all status and class designations, rankings, and groupings are irrelevant. All are moral equals, answerable only to the claims of conscience with respect to their faithfulness in their individual callings.

Classification is essential to manage the different functions that must be performed in a community of persons with different capabilities. It becomes a source of injustice only when employed beyond the sphere of functional relevance. For example, classifications by age, sex, occupation, and income are relevant to such practical matters as insurance rates, clothing, hours of work, and taxes, respectively. They do not warrant separating people into exclusive classes such as old and young, male and female, workers and managers, rich and poor, and dealing with the members of each class in the same fashion over a broad range of relationships. The key to democracy in classification is found in the twin principles of *specificity* and relative *independence* of descriptive designations. Specificity means that a particular label applied to a person is to be used solely to refer to the limited and specific functions to which it is pertinent; it is not to be spread out to become an umbrella concept coloring everything he is and does. Independence refers to the fact that most qualities and capacities are not dependent on one another. Place of residence, intelligence, and political affiliation, for example, have no necessary connection; from the nature of any one it is not possible to deduce what the others must be.

Democracy, in short, is consistent with functional classifications but not with social classes. For practical social purposes people may be grouped according to the relevant characteristics. This grouping applies not to persons as such but solely to the abstracted qualities concerned. Social classes segregate persons into groups. In contrast, classification is an intellectual device which facilitates the effective interdependence of persons. As such, it unites people instead of dividing them.

The democracy of worth makes for an open society. Its openness is a consequence of the way in which classification is used. In a closed society social classes are static and inflexible. In the open society classification is dynamic and fluid. As circumstances change and new social needs are presented, fresh analytical and administrative tools are invented and applied; people are classified and reclassified in ever new ways in response to the needs of the social situation. Furthermore, a closed society tends toward a unitary hierarchical system of classification, in that to each person one basic class designation is applied, and this designation fixes the person's place in the rank order of society. An open society, on the other hand, is organized on the basis of functional pluralism, in which every person is classified in many different ways, each for a particular purpose, and in which no single *general* rank order is recognized. There are many orders of precedence and status with respect to the many types of relationships subsisting within the community, and each person is *independently* placed in each type in the relative position to which he is fitted. Finally, in the closed society a person cannot move from one class to another at all or only with great difficulty. In the open society, if a person's qualities change, the classes to which he descriptively belongs also change.

These ideals of the democracy of worth in the field of social class have direct application to education. Not only should democratic class principles be taught as rational ideals, but by being put into practice in the conduct of education, their concrete meaning should be visibly demonstrated. While the need for economy dictates the use of classes for school instruction, the uniformist tendency of class instruction can be moderated by deliberately taking account of individual differences within classes. The class should as far as possible be treated as a unit only for certain purposes of administrative efficiency, such as the keeping of attendance and the assignment of space and facilities. In the most significant aspects of instruction the unique capacities and attainments of each pupil should be recognized. The democratic teacher also does not seek to fashion his students according to some preconceived pattern, stamping them with the mark of his class, but serves as a mediator and helper of each student along the path that seems right for him.

Tests and measurements should be used with great circumspection and not to mark off students into separate groups for all purposes. Every test (for example, of verbal aptitude, reading speed, arithmetical skill) should be understood as a measure of a particular set of competences and should not be employed beyond its field of pertinence. Above all, no single score (such as the "I.Q.") should be accepted as a basis for setting up a rank order of students. Competences are of many kinds and cannot be assessed by any one test. Studies have also shown that most of the common intelligence tests have a social class bias; the vocabulary and thought patterns used in them generally follow a middle class pattern, thus putting the socially and economically more privileged in a preferential position. From a democratic standpoint it is important to devise and use tests that do not have this class bias, and to compensate as far as possible for the distortion introduced by existing measures.

Academic grading systems, as generally used, have two major defects. First, they force the translation of quality into a numerical measure. But personal achievement cannot be judged quantitatively. There are judgments of style, of logical cogency, and of ethical purpose, for example, which cannot possibly be summed up in a single grade. Second, the grading system usually leads to comparisons between students and, thus, to competition for status rather than concern for learning as such. Ideally, in a democratic school, marks would be eliminated altogether. No attempt would be made to classify students or their productions by a single number or letter symbol. Evaluation rather would consist in as full and rounded a description as possible of the students' abilities and accomplishments—a discursive critical judgment such as would be made by a competent observer of a work of art, a sensitive and sympathetic biographer, or a seasoned and humane critic. Moreover, the standard of comparison would be not the performance of other students but the best available models of what is true and excellent. In this way the students would be invited to serve the good rather than compete for status, and they would be encouraged to be individuals and not conformists, since their work would be judged by a process of qualitative discrimination and not by simple ranking.

Since relative rankings do have a permanent and necessary place in every social system, some numerical measures of school accomplishment may still be desirable. When an employer is faced with the task of hiring a worker and must choose one person from among several candidates, he is forced to establish an order of preference—that is, to sum up the many relevant competences in some sort of single numerical index of excellence. Since all social organization requires grades of authority and precedence, and since classification has a place in democratic society for functional discriminations, there is room also in democratic education for comparative grading of the type now common, insofar as the schools are called upon to supply some indices of competence for placement in the functional status system of society. The democratic ideal of unique qualitative judgment is in tension with the ranking requirements of organized society. Both kinds of evaluation have their place. However, it is desirable in schools to shift the weight strongly in the direction of individual discursive qualitative judgments and to reserve the numerical ranking solely for situations where competitive ratings are of the essence, as in scholarship allocation, honors citations, and certain job placement recommendations.

The undemocratic class bias in education extends even farther than the tests that automatically discriminate against students from the lower social and economic strata of society. Students from high status families are usually made to feel comfortable and welcome in school, by teachers and fellow students alike, simply because they are from families of good standing, while students from low status families are usually not shown such acceptance and approval. It is the proper business of the democratic school to serve as an influence against general social class stratification. Education has been and ought to continue to be the major agency for social mobility. Teachers should seek by every means to compensate for status factors imported by children from their families. Boys and girls from the less privileged homes should be given special attention and encouragement to make certain that their individual capabilities are brought to light and are not obscured by feelings of class inferiority. Children from high status families should be treated on their personal merits and should not be accorded special privileges because of their parents' position in the community.

It is not easy for schoolteachers and administrators to swim against the stream of social custom by such measures, since they have their personal reputations, ambitions, and social status to consider, and since these are closely linked to the manner in which they treat the young people committed to their instruction. Nonetheless, educators who are true to their democratic mission must take deliberate means to counteract social class pressures and must learn to be self-critical in order that their own unconscious class prejudices may be brought to light and as far as possible eliminated. The ability of teachers to resist external social class demands is greatly enhanced by their own success in becoming professionally competent and organized along professional lines. As long as teachers are regarded (and regard themselves) as lay people who make their living by teaching, they cannot readily transcend the class structure in the conduct of their work.

On the other hand, when teachers possess the authority of qualified experts in learning and in the guidance of learning, and when they are organized into strong professional bodies which faithfully exercise responsibility for high professional standards, they can freely teach with sole regard to individual aptitude and need and without fear or favor in respect to social class. Parents, too, can help to counteract undemocratic social class attitudes by supporting the schools in their efforts in this respect, by acknowledging the professional independence and authority of teachers, and by arranging the external social relations of the family on the basis of worth and function without reference to social status.

Several features of the American school system reflect the struggle against social class without denying the need for functional classification. First, we have repudiated the principle of the fixed multiple-track system, according to which pupils are divided at a specified age into mutually exclusive groups with different educational and occupational destinations. We may classify secondary school students for functional purposes into such groups as "practical arts," "commercial," "general," and "college preparatory," but there is nothing to prevent students from later changing to another group which appears to fit better their abilities and occupational plans.

Second, the comprehensive high school has been devised to enable students with different curricular needs to study within the same educational community. Separate schools established along ostensibly functional lines (for example, "technical" and "academic") may turn out really to be social class schools which by totally segregating one group from the other accentuate social class cleavages. The comprehensive schools (and their counterparts in higher education, the comprehensive universities) recognize the necessity for educational differentiation but, by keeping the students together in some classes and in the student activities program, minimize social class divisions.

The tension between class and classification is nowhere more evident than in the continuing discussions over ability grouping versus mixed grouping in the schools. Placing students of similar ability together certainly makes for easier and more efficient instruction; the more able students do not need to wait for the slow ones to catch up, and the slow ones are not made to feel inadequate in comparison with the fast ones. But ability grouping also tends to separate students into self-conscious status groups. Furthermore, as pointed out earlier, there are many kinds of ability; no single measure of general competence suffices for the ranking of students. From a democratic standpoint, then, ability grouping should be used with care and restraint. Students with similar aptitudes and attainments *in a specific subject* may properly be grouped together for instruction in that subject, but general divisions into inferior and superior should be avoided.

Furthermore, just as comprehensive schools are desirable as a solvent of social class lines, so classes with students of differing abilities are valuable, provided the classes can be internally organized so as to let students proceed at their own pace, with enrichment through greater depth and scope of materials independently mastered by the most able students, and with special assistance by the teacher for the less able. It is also possible in mixed grouping for some of the brightest students to help instruct the less competent. Some schools are now experimenting at the elementary levels with an ungraded school, thus returning in some measure to the teaching patterns of the old-fashioned one-room school. With intelligent management it is possible for pupils of different capabilities to be taught together and to learn values in associated living not available from a stratified educational program.

A fourth feature of American schools aimed at the minimizing of social stratification is the system of guidance counseling. The purpose of this program is to make deliberate provision for the individual needs of the student in ways not possible in ordinary class instruction. In guidance, the student is ideally considered as a unique person, without reference to membership in any group or class. The counselor is in an unusually favorable position to be sensitive to class injustices of which individual students are victims and to open up opportunities for overcoming these inequities.

Finally, the provision of universal free public education is the most dramatic evidence of the American rejection of a class ideology. While freedom for private education is (and should be) recognized, the system of strong common schools has provided a major symbol of the essential unity of the American people and the most important means of insuring the social mobility which is the hallmark of an open society.

Questions of racial justice belong to the general subject of social class and may be understood in the light of the analysis of classes and classification just presented. Some of the basic principles about class already developed will now be applied to the important special case of racial grouping. Problems of race deserve emphasis for two main reasons. One is the world-wide revolutionary situation, in which subject peoples of Asia and Africa are rising to claim their independence and their right to a fair share in the opportunities of life, and in which nonwhite peoples are challenging the exclusive privilege and world dominance of the white man. If democracy is to have any relevance and influence in such a time, the people of the United States and other democratic nations must demonstrate their understanding and practice of democratic ideals in the field of race relations. The second reason is the critical significance of the race question in American civic affairs at the present time, particularly in the field of public education. The historic Supreme Court decision of 1954 outlawing racial segregation in public schools and the subsequent, cautious, painful steps taken toward compliance with this ruling have forced a searching re-examination of conscience in the matter of racial justice in democratic education.

We begin by inquiring what is meant by race. In answering this question a distinction has to be made between popular lay conceptions of race and scientifically defined ideas on the subject. It is the former, non-scientific views which are socially influential and which must therefore constitute the starting point for our inquiry. Race is a mode of classifying people on the basis of certain features that are assumed to be biologically inherited and thus present from birth. It is also assumed that they cannot be changed by education or by any other act or experience of life. Racial divisions thus constitute a *caste* organization of society, with no possibility of mobility from one race to another.

The most common nonscientific basis for racial classification is skin color. People are sorted into "black," "brown," "red," "white," and "yellow." Skin color is the favorite distinguishing feature because it is so easy to identify. When an entire social system is permeated with racial distinctions, it is important to be able to recognize at a glance the race to which a person belongs, so as to leave no doubt about the behavior appropriate in relation to him. Two other popular types of racial designation are based on religious affiliation and national origin —for example, "Jewish," "Italian," or "Armenian."

Whatever the primary index of race may be—skin color, religion, or nationality—this unscientific view of race presupposes certain inherited characteristics that all members of a given racial group have in common. These characteristics include at least the following three kinds—physical features, psychological or personality traits, and cultural patterns—and they combine to make a *racial stereotype*, a standardized picture of the typical member of a particular racial group. For example, as to physical features, black-skinned people are often stereotyped as having short, kinky hair and thick lips, Jews as having hooked noses, and Scandinavians as being blond and blue-eyed. Psychological or personality stereotypes may represent black people as happy-go-lucky, Jews as highly competitive, and Germans as domineering. In the cultural sphere, blacks may be stereotyped as musical, Jews as financially astute, and the French as good cooks and expert lovers.

Racial stereotypes are invented in order to make possible standard responses to members of supposed races, and thus to help maintain established social traditions and distinctions. They authorize one to deduce a wide range of conclusions, without argument or evidence, from the single premise that a person is a member of a particular race. With stereotype reactions it does not matter if the presumed racial qualities do not in fact exist in specific individuals. The discrepancies are overlooked, and the atypical individuals are treated exactly as if they fulfilled the a priori judgments about them. Action in relation to all members of a so-called race is determined wholly by expectations and not by actualities. In this fashion, racial designation forces its victims into the stereotype role and makes their life the same as if they possessed the stereotype traits, whether or not they really do.

Racist attitudes of this kind are not instinctive, automatic responses to human differences. They are learned. They are taught by the older members of each self-conscious human group to its younger members. They are not generalizations from observation, inductions from the experiences of associating with other people. Popular race perspectives are part of the cultural pattern of a society; they are one of the products of "civilized" existence.

Clearly, such racist views are undemocratic, and the education that perpetuates them is undemocratic. Race stereotyping denies the universal qualities of humanity by separating them into distinct breeds. It imposes unnatural barriers to personal freedom, and it inhibits the development of individuality by standardizing expectations and responses. Racial divisions narrow the range of each person's permissible activities, condemning him to patterns of life prescribed by race customs.

One of the key objectives of democratic education should be to counteract racist education, thus liberating persons to be and become themselves instead of living in bondage to racial stereotypes. In effecting this it makes a great difference whether the guiding principles are those of desire or of worth. In the democracy of desire, in which the emphasis is on securing benefits, the less privileged races use education as one means of gaining power to challenge the more privileged groups. The result is the intensification of intergroup conflict and, paradoxically, the hardening of the prejudice that needs to be dispelled. The dominant races feel threatened by the attempt of the subordinate ones to gain equality, and hence are driven to seek still further grounds for discriminating against them.

The other basis for a democratic attack on racism is through concern for right, rather than for interests. This approach tends to dissolve racial distinctions through the growth of dispassionate understanding and serves to diminish racial conflict through appeal to what is universal. As in the democracy of desire, education may be used in the democracy of worth to gain social, economic, and political power for the sake of challenging the privileged position of the dominant races. But the primary intent of such challenge is for the sake of justice and to redress injustice, and not to secure benefits for the disadvantaged groups. The appeal is to principles of right that transcend intergroup rivalries and provide an objective standard of reference for the disinterested adjudication of competing claims.

The foundation of racial justice is a deep conviction of the unity of humanity and respect for the worth of every person. It is not enough to affirm these as abstract general principles; they must be controlling directives. Education for democratic race relations must go beyond factual instruction; it requires a change of motive, from that of promoting the prerogatives of one's own group to that of serving the right without calculation of personal advantage. This calls for a comprehensive reorientation, a total reversal of outlook which affects one's entire system of values. In effecting such a change of motives, factual understanding can be of considerable help. This is particularly true in teaching ethical conduct in regard to race. If one has a commitment to know the truth and to live by it, knowledge of the facts about race can help in the cure of nonrational race prejudices. While we cannot expect rational persuasion alone to eliminate race bias, it may be of considerable assistance in the following ways: it can expose the falsehoods upon which most racial prejudice rests, it can demonstrate the evil social and psychological consequences of racial discrimination, it can show the incompatibility of discriminatory policies with the known facts of human inheritance and development, and it can suggest means for eliminating the sources and effects of racial bias.

A number of rational considerations upon which democratic race attitudes should be founded will now be set forth. These are facts that must be taken into account in determining what constitutes racial justice. They should be included in the instruction of all young people in a democratic society.

First, no person can reliably or fairly be characterized simply by membership in a group, including a racial group. In whatever manner they are made, race classifications are, like all other modes of classification, abstractions, which cannot faithfully represent persons in their wholeness. Race designations at the most could have limited practical utility, by indicating certain common properties with specified functional significance. It is not right to put a race tag on a person and to consider it a meaningful indication of his personality. The complexity of the individual self, the infinite variety of personal differences, forbid any such categorizing of human beings.

Second, the race stereotypes actually used are for the most part built on false assumptions about the correlation of traits. Thus, it is not true that all Scandinavians are blond and blue-eyed, that all Germans are domineering, and that all Frenchmen are great lovers. Skin color has no necessary relation to other physical features nor to psychological and cultural characteristics. For any given shade of skin, persons may be found who have any of a wide range of other traits. The same trait variability applies to any other index of race, such as religion or nationality. Type patterns are maintained against the patent evidence because they permit the easy standardization of reactions and keep up the pressure for the preservation of separate racial subcultures which justify discriminatory practices.

Third, the usual racial indicators are inconstant, indefinite, and unreliable as means of classifying people. Skin color is not an enduring distinctive mark. It may change substantially as a result of exposure to the elements or because of health conditions. Yet no racist would claim that sunbathing or jaundice could bring about a change of race. A person born into a Christian or a Buddhist family may become a Jew, and a Jew may become a full-fledged Christian or Muslim. Furthermore, a whole spectrum of Jewishness may be found, all the way from complete and explicit identification with the people of Israel to the most remote and attenuated connection with Hebrew life and tradition. Similarly, while a person cannot change the country of his birth, he can adopt a new country and become so thoroughly identified with its people and ways that no one could possibly detect his foreign origin.

The most serious trouble with racial specification comes in connection with the offspring of mixed marriages. In the first generation the product is a "halfbreed," but further marriages complicate the picture. Generally the children bear the racial designation of the less favored of the parents' races, in order that the dominance of the "superior" group may not be threatened by those who cross race lines in sex relations. The point here is that the mixing of races, which has always taken place, makes nonsense out of racist theories, which presuppose the possibility of some simple racial identification. Consideration of the way in which people have actually come into being makes it clear that there are no "pure" races, that every person and the members of every group derive from a great variety of earlier peoples. Hence, it is not possible to assign people to sharply defined racial groups.

Fourth, the most common racial mark, skin color, is superficial and insignificant. It is superficial in that it refers to surface appearances only and not to anything pertinent to the person as such. It is insignificant in that nothing is signified by it, except the meanings that have been read into it by the prejudiced imagination and intention. From the fact that a person has a given shade of skin pigmentation no other fact of any consequence can be inferred, except that he will be accorded a certain kind of treatment by people in a race-conscious society. It is not possible, in general, to infer anything important about other physical qualities, character, emotional traits, personal habits, knowledge, or skills. Reflection on the obvious irrationality of continuing race prejudice may help to make clear our central theme that the first aim of education should be the awakening of devotion to what is good, in order that growth in knowledge and skill may serve some valuable purpose. Prejudiced people are not necessarily unintelligent; they have simply been prevented by self-interest from using their reason as a guide to just behavior.

It would be possible to define races by reference to traits that have some functional significance. For example, an important physical feature for medical purposes is the blood type. It is essential to discriminate between blood-type groups in giving and receiving blood for transfusions. Any inherited trait that actually makes a difference in what a person can do is significant within, but not beyond, the scope of the functions it affects. Such functional differentiation of people, however, is far removed from arbitrary racial separation based on nonfunctional traits.

Fifth, racism rests upon a confusion between inherited and acquired characteristics. Personal qualities that are due to environmental influences are wrongly ascribed to inherited racial patterns. For example, white supremacists have argued that Negroes are intellectually inferior to whites, and have submitted as evidence the lower average achievement of American Negro children in intelligence tests. What such comparisons fail to take into consideration is the effect of the Negroes' inferior average social, economic, and educational position upon their intellectual development. There is no evidence that skin color by itself has any correlation with intelligence. Intellectual ability does seem to be in part dependent upon inherited factors, but it is also greatly influenced by environment. It is a demonstrated fact, plain for anyone who is willing to see, that a person's knowledge, character, and skill are largely determined by his education in home, school, and community. Given the right conditions for growth, people of any shade of skin, any religion, or any nationality can develop into capable, cultivated, and civilized human beings. Racists have to deceive themselves about the significance of education in the fashioning of personality. By the same token, concern for education and recognition of its power to effect changes in human personality are incompatible with racial prejudice and help to diminish bias. The efficacy of education in the fashioning of character and the clear evidence of the plasticity of human nature through directed learning demonstrate the untenability of racial stereotypes, which presuppose the inheritance of fixed modes of conduct.

A sixth fact, already stated in reference to social classification generally, is that racial stereotyping tends to be self-confirming. People are forced by social arrangements and expectations based on prejudice into situations that make the intrinsically irrational and arbitrary racial distinctions to some degree justified. What inheritance cannot in fact bring to pass in regard to race characteristics, social influences may. While white supremacists who hold that Negroes by nature are incapable of exercising responsible political leadership cannot empirically defend that position, they can make it appear plausible by creating a society where Negroes are by custom excluded from public office and hence cannot by practice learn the arts of governing. Similarly, Jews have sometimes been forced by majority prejudice into defensive reactions that appear to confirm such anti-Semitic stereotypes as Jewish competitiveness and clannishness. Again, a prejudiced society which expects American Indians to be lazy and dishonest, Mexicans or Puerto Ricans to be vicious and delinquent, and Orientals to be subversive—in every case as a natural racial trait—is likely to adopt attitudes and policies toward these people which will lead them to some extent to respond accordingly.

People tend to live up (or down) to what others expect of them, because the image of oneself is developed in large part from the appraisals of others. The educative (or mis-educative) effect of a racially biased social order is to help actualize the images of man found in the prejudiced minds of its members. So powerful is the force of social influence that unjust racial appraisals infect the consciousness both of those who are discriminated against and of those who discriminate. Even in the bitterness and violence of their protests against racism, its victims sometimes betray their own fear that what the others believe about them might be true. Race discrimination is a vicious circle, the only means of deliverance from which is a steadfast devotion to truth and right.

Finally, racist attitudes are built upon a fundamental misunderstanding of the process of inheritance. The usual racist conception is that the blood is the carrier of inherited traits, and that a person's race is a function of the species of blood which he possesses. This theory of racial blood kinds makes it plausible to impute a common cluster of traits to all members of a given race. As every schoolchild who has been instructed in the rudiments of science now knows, or should know, modern genetics has provided a completely different account of the mechanism of inheritance, making untenable the blood theory upon which traditional race lore rested. It is now known that biological inheritance takes place through the genes. Each inherited trait is determined by one or more genes and is not a feature of a single type-pattern as required by the blood theory. Skin color is determined by certain genes, facial features by others, intellectual potentialities by still others. Moreover, in the reproductive process the various genes are to a considerable degree independently assorted. Skin color genes pursue a genetic history of their own, without reference to the path taken by genes that have charge of facial features and intellectual potentialities. This independence can be directly demonstrated by an analysis of the mechanism of cell division and combination in sexual reproduction. The law of independent assortment constitutes the scientific basis for refuting the idea of racial stereotypes. The standardized trait patterns of racist belief do not and can not exist because the genetic factors that determine inherited traits are in most cases physically separate from each other and thus can be arranged in a wide variety of different combinations.

Moreover, the science of biology also affords better understanding of the relation between heredity and environment in the determination of personality. Study of how organisms develop reveals that no trait is wholly fixed by either heredity or environment, but that every feature of a person is a product of a long series of interactions between the growing individual and his surrounding world. Every quality of a person is what it is by virtue of a genetic potential operating within appropriate environmental conditions. Some traits are affected relatively little by environmental changes. Eye color is one example. Other traits, such as intellectual competence, are greatly influenced by the conditions of life. Racist theories put the emphasis almost exclusively on inheritance (which is incorrectly interpreted), neglecting the essential role of environment. The modern sciences of genetics and ecology have clearly provided empirical grounds for rejecting these traditional race concepts and for recognizing the fundamental role of education in the creation of human personality—especially in respect to qualities that are so manifestly reflections of cultural patterns.

A factual analysis of race along the foregoing lines indicates the strong support that scientific inquiry can give to democracy. At the very least it shows the irrational nature of race prejudice and suggests the lengths of intellectual irresponsibility to which one must go to maintain the racist position. Critical scrutiny shows beyond all doubt the untenability of the entire network of assumptions upon which racial discrimination rests, and reveals the true character of racial bias as a device for rationalizing injustices. Modern scientific genetics offers an admirable empirical and conceptual base for affirming both human individuality and the essential unity of mankind. People of every nation, color, language, belief, and condition are now known to possess in their body cells trait factors drawn by an inconceivably complex sequence of intercombinations from a common "gene pool." The incontrovertible evidence of the cells is against all the racial divisions that prejudiced men have constructed and have sought to actualize by social regulation. At the same time, the gene story also shows how the virtually infinite number of possible chance combinations of the many factors that constitute a person's biological inheritance explain and support the idea of personal individuality and uniqueness. Thus, devotion to the truth about man, regardless of the consequences for traditional preconceptions about the races, leads the scientific inquirer to facts that sustain the grand democratic vision of a ground for fundamental human unity which is simultaneously the source of personal variety and singularity.

A clear understanding of the genetic history of mankind is important in coming to terms with the ultimate issue in race relations— namely, miscegenation. The supreme offense in the eyes of the racist is to marry a person of another race. All of the lesser taboos against associating with members of other races are justified as preliminary defenses against this final calamity. In a race-conscious society one can hardly overestimate the intensity of negative feeling generated in parents at the thought of their child's marrying a person of another race.

What is the cause of this horror of miscegenation among racists? Clearly, it is not an innate, inevitable psychological reaction, for there are many nations and societies where the mixing of the races is accepted without any question. For example, in Brazil and in France today racial intermarriages are considered proper and normal. Furthermore, breeding across race lines has been practiced throughout human history; that is how we came to have such a motley assembly of peoples on the earth today. Nor can any factual warrant be claimed for asserting the biological harmfulness of miscegenation—the alleged "contamination" of "superior" racial stock by crossing it with "inferior." On the contrary, there is evidence that close inbreeding brings out genetic defects in the progeny, and that outbreeding on the average is conducive to health and vigor of offspring.

The repugnance to racial intermarriage in a race-conscious society is a consequence of existing social divisions, which impose severe penalties upon persons who fail to respect them. Marrying a person of another race undermines the whole race system. It weakens and confuses the distinctions between races and thus renders insecure the entire structure of prerogatives, privileges, and priorities built upon these differences. The punitive effect on the partners in a mixed union is severe enough, but not as serious as the consequences for the children born to them. The parents choose to defy prejudiced custom and are presumably prepared to pay the price; their children have no choice in the matter and are not immune to the cruelties of biased men. When parents in a society with race lines look with apprehension upon the marriage of their child to a person of a different race, they have in view the indignities and disabilities which the unjust society will visit upon the couple and upon their children and their children's children. They also know that ordinary living imposes strain enough on a marriage, without inviting the additional difficulties occasioned by trying to bridge two subcultures which the majority of society are determined to keep separate. As a result, existing race divisions tend to be confirmed by the pressures against intermarriage, and the fiction of race purity is maintained by social forces opposing the free choice of mates, which would bring the whole arbitrary structure of race distinctions and discriminations tumbling to the ground.

The method of progress from injustice toward justice in intergroup relations is through persistent efforts at desegregation in all phases of cultural life. Segregation sustains racial stereotypes, facilitates identification by race, preserves traditional arbitrary racial taboos, and aids the suppression of those who would challenge the inequities of the existing system. While desegregation must proceed on many fronts simultaneously, in no segment of life is it more crucial than in education. Educational opportunity in a democracy should be the same for everyone, without regard to skin color, religious affiliation, national origin, or any other allegedly "racial" factor. These superficial and accidental traits which are taken as marks of race are in themselves educationally irrelevant and should be so treated in the allocation and conduct of schooling. As a result of prior injustices, members of disadvantaged racial groups may differ from the more privileged ones in ways that are educationally significant—for example, in health, manners, and intellectual competence. When this is the case, it may be unsound policy to effect complete indiscriminate desegregation in the schools at once; to do so might seriously impair the quality of education available to children of the more favored groups and might result in major social dislocations as the parents of the better-prepared children sought to forestall such impairment. The solution is to introduce minimal health standards, applicable to all, and a certain amount of ability grouping (without regard to race) to insure reasonable efficiency of instruction. In other words, during the transition from a racially segregated to a desegregated school system, it may be desirable to substitute for the previous racial groupings new kinds of educationally pertinent groupings, in which any deficiencies of the less favored race can be taken into account automatically, without reference to race as such.

Moreover, special efforts should be made in the schools to compensate for the effects of race prejudice. Often the child from a low prestige family receives little encouragement at home for doing well at school. In such cases teachers and guidance counselors have a special responsibility for helping the child use his abilities fully. It is the business of the schools to act as a countervailing force in a prejudiced society. If educators rate pupils according to the prestige scales used in the community generally and apportion opportunities correspondingly, racial bias will only be strengthened and perpetuated. Loyalty to the right requires that the educational pattern invert the measures of the unjust society and give special consideration and a larger proportion of resources to those who, because of neglect and frustration outside of school, need them most. The schools can and should be a principal agency for breaking the vicious circle of racial prejudice.

Racial desegregation in the schools cannot take place in isolation but must be part of a broad attack on bias in many directions. Since the assignment of pupils to schools is determined largely by place of residence, segregated housing conditions perpetuate school segregation. Separate schooling, in turn, prevents the establishment of common interests and sympathies which make residential integration normal and attractive. Racial discrimination in work opportunities tends to be reflected in schools, which carry so large a share of the task of vocational preparation. Parents in favored groups can give unusual educational advantages to their children and thus continue the privilege pattern from generation to generation. Desegregation in education helps to break this unjust system by preparing young people for positions on the basis of social need and personal ability alone, exclusive of racial considerations.

Since public education is controlled through agencies of government, racial justice in education depends upon equal political rights and responsibilities for all citizens regardless of color, religion, or national origin. Conversely, equal educational opportunity makes it possible for all citizens to exercise their civic duties intelligently. In the United States many Negroes have been prevented from voting by devices, such as literacy tests, which better education would have rendered ineffective. On the other hand, the excellent progress since World War II toward the conquest of civil disabilities for the Negro has been due in considerable measure to the emergence of a sizable group of well-educated Negro leaders.

The world-wide rising of submerged peoples to claim their just share in the good life puts the problems of domestic racial discrimination in dramatically fresh perspective, demonstrating so no one can miss it the urgency of the task of setting old wrongs right. The growing world consciousness in nearly every field of study and the increasing awareness of other culture patterns make apparent to students the indefensibility and untenability of discriminatory patterns and render most imperative the elimination of all racial criteria in education itself. The mass media of communication—the most potent new agencies of public education—are also helping to break down racial barriers by creating a single culture, open to all, from which no arbitrary social distinctions can exclude any person. Furthermore, well-prepared people of every race, through their contributions in such diverse activities as artistic creation, scientific discovery, and athletic performance, are demonstrating the falsity of racial stereotypes and revealing the new resources of cultural energy released when prejudices are transcended and personal potentialities are given full scope.

In education the very nature of intellectual life cries out for non-discrimination in matters of race. There is not one truth for white people and another truth for black people. Truth is one and universal. Inquiry is in essence a shared undertaking. The best possible thought and the widest possible range of experience are needed if the difficult problems of analysis and interpretation of modern knowledge are to be successfully solved. No irrelevant factors, such as those that are invented to mark off races, should be intruded to hinder the human intellectual adventure.

Truth is but one of the universal values to which education in a democracy of worth is devoted. All of the other values—of creativity, of conscience, and of reverence—are also independent of racial considerations and incompatible with racial segregation in culture and education. Dedication to truth, to qualitative excellence, and to the right are quite consistent with one kind of discrimination; in fact, they require it. But this is the discrimination of truth from error, of beauty from ugliness, of good from evil, and not the discrimination of one person from another on account of race. The well-educated person learns to make distinctions and to maintain standards, but they are not the arbitrary distinctions of the biased mind and the standards of traditional prejudice. A major goal of democratic education should be to inspire loyalty to universal values which dissolve artificial divisions between persons and unite all in common service of the good.

Some of the most urgent yet perennial problems for human conscience arise from the fact that the supply of most of the goods that people need or want is limited. It is therefore necessary to devise schemes for apportioning these limited goods among the people. Such allocation systems constitute the economic order of society.

In a plutocratic society the use and distribution of material goods, money, and labor is controlled by a special class of wealthy people. These privileged persons generally allocate a large share of the limited supply of goods to themselves, reserving for the much larger class of subordinate poor only enough goods to keep the latter in condition to perform services and to produce things for their overlords. In contrast to this type of social system, economic democracy aims at extending the control of goods and services to all the people. In a democracy the idea that a privileged class should determine the economic fate of all is rejected in favor of the principle that every person should have a voice in the allocation of the limited supply of goods.

In general, economic democracy is conceived on the basis of the desire motive. The fundamental assumption is made that each person wants to maximize his own share of the available goods—that everyone pursues his own economic interest, seeking the largest possible gain to himself.

There are three principal types of system according to which the acquisitive game in the democracy of desire can be played. The first is the system of *individual free enterprise*. Under it every person is regarded as free to pursue his own profit and advantage without interference. Each competes with all others in an open market, where material goods, money, and labor are bought and sold at prices determined by the balance of supply and demand. The highest rewards go to those who are most able and most diligent in the pursuit of gain. The mechanism of the market automatically determines the distribution of goods and services in a manner that is presumed by its advocates to fulfill the demands of justice. One of the great appeals of the free enterprise system is this conviction that the free market in consumer commodities, capital goods, money, and labor as it were, miraculously harmonizes the pursuit of gain and the pursuit of justice; that is to say, in the economic realm it is assumed that the democracy of desire and the democracy of worth are one and the same. This is why champions of free enterprise regard the profit motive as a command of conscience and seek for economic advantage with moral zeal.

Free enterprise accords with the democratic ideal of equality in the sense that everyone is subject to the law of the marketplace. No one is given any special privilege over another; each must win his own way in competition with everyone else. Other than this, there is no equality, for persons differ in their abilities and in their industry, and these differences are reflected in economic rewards. Thus, free enterprise promotes individuality within the broad principle of equality of opportunity.

An important feature of the free enterprise system is the institution of private property. The goods that one acquires and holds through labor, foresight, skill, and saving (renunciation of present enjoyments for the sake of future satisfaction) are for one's own use and disposition; no one else has a claim on them. Private property is the basis for one's personal security and autonomy, the guarantee that what has been won by the worker will be his to use and to enjoy. Property rights include the rights of gift and bequest, which introduce special privileges and inequalities into the free enterprise system, in that rewards are no longer in proportion to ability and effort alone but are also determined by the accidents of birth. In this way unrestricted private property rights tend to generate undemocratic hereditary economic inequities. On the other hand, private property serves the essential social function of permitting the accumulation of capital, which is applied to productive use, so that all goods will not be consumed at once.

Under the individual free enterprise system there are always some persons who because of illness or other incompetence are unable to compete successfully in the market. It is assumed that these unfortunates will be cared for chiefly by the voluntary benevolence of those who do succeed in the competitive struggle. However, proponents of this position would warn against allowing philanthropy to blunt the incentives for work in those who receive it, and thus would maintain charitable contributions at a subsistence level and require regular proof of need.

Supporters of the free enterprise system are also in favor of keeping government at a minimum, particularly in the economic sphere. Police power and military defense are doubtless necessary governmental functions, they hold, and for their support some compulsory tax assessment is required. The only function of government in economic life is to police the market to maintain free competition and exchange. This requires action against monopolies, price fixing, and other impediments to free trading.

The second type of economic system in the acquisitive society may be called *associated free enterprise*. This system is a logical development in the free market economy. Individual property owners generally lack sufficient personal capital to establish really large-scale enterprises, in which maximum profits may be made. Hence they associate with others to provide the required resources. In this way partnerships and corporations come into being. Individuals invest savings in stocks and bonds, in return either for dividends based on profits made by the company or for a fixed rate of interest. These companies may further unite in trade associations and combines in order to secure a better competitive position in the market. Such combinations may have the effect of destroying weaker competitors and thus of undermining the free market.

The movement toward association is also evident among those who sell their labor. Worker associations are, in fact, necessary even when productive facilities are individually owned, because of the disparity between the bargaining powers of the individual worker and the owner. Labor unions are even more imperative when corporations are organized, if the assumption of a free market is to hold. Such a market presupposes substantial equality of bargaining position, in which personal skill and diligence count, rather than initial preponderance of power. If the workers are not satisfied with the wages offered, the owners can refrain from hiring them, thus curtailing production. In such a case the owners can live on accumulated wealth, but the workers have no such choice. Since they must work or become destitute, they are at a great disadvantage compared with the owners. To equalize the bargaining position of workers and owners, workers find it necessary to combine forces so as to match the associated strength of the owners and thus to re-establish to some extent the conditions of a free market.

A similar associative effort is sometimes made by consumers, in order to protect their interests against either or both of the other two groups (owners and workers). The consumer may be victimized by excessive prices or by inferior products, in a situation where the complexity of the economic system, the technical problems of quality evaluation, and the preoccupation of the average individual consumer with his own pursuits make the price and product controls of the free market system ineffective. Consumer cooperatives, like the other two forms of association, help to restore some measure of equality of bargaining power in the market, thus re-establishing the conditions presupposed by the free enterprise system.

The third type of system is the *controlled economy*, in which the theory of automatic economic regulation by the free market is abandoned in favor of deliberate social control of economic processes. The purpose of the controlled economy is to distribute goods and services more equally than under the free market system. In actual operation the free market turns out to be an unstable system, because it tends to magnify inequalities. The rich and powerful have an advantage over the poor and weak in bargaining and thus are able to increase their relative strength still further. Freedom then becomes license for exploitation. The rich become richer and the poor become poorer. Economic classes develop, and groups of owners, workers, and consumers each unite in battle against the other interests. In reaction to these consequences of the free market system, the powers of government are invoked to mediate conflicts and to counteract the inherent instability of the system of competitive bargaining.

Furthermore, a controlled economy makes it possible to care for persons who through the accidents of fortune are unable to compete successfully, without requiring them to depend on the charity of others. Besides these social welfare benefits, in a complicated modern society many public services and facilities are best provided by government rather than by private enterprisers, who would normally make them available only to persons who could purchase them.

Deliberate social control of economic processes is possible only by the modification or abrogation of private property rights. Even under the associated free enterprise system the *management* of property comes to be more important than the fact of ownership. Under a controlled economy, government takes the place of voluntary associations in the management of property, and both privacy and free enterprise decline or disappear. In a socialist or a communist state private ownership of the major means of production is abolished. In state capitalism ownership may still be nominally private, but the uses of productive property are determined by government. The really important question in the economic sphere is who has the power to decide how property will be used. To the degree that decisions are made by government, either directly or indirectly, the property is public rather than private.

The economy may be controlled in many different ways. The government may directly eliminate market control by fixing prices, wages, and rates of interest. It may exercise control through buying and selling commodities in the market or through limiting the sale and purchase of certain commodities and services under a rationing system. Worker mobility may be limited, and outright labor conscription may even be adopted. The purchase and sale of goods may further be influenced greatly by regulation of the credit system. The most important of all means of economic control is taxation. A tax is an obvious and direct abrogation of private ownership in property. Once the general principle of taxation is granted, the right of private property in effect disappears, since even the property that is not collected for public uses remains with the owner only by courtesy of the state. Thus, the complexion of economic life is in principle determined by the system of taxation. Any desired pattern of distribution of goods and services can be achieved by levying appropriate taxes and allocating their revenues in a particular way.

The American economy never has been and is not now purely any one of the three systems described above. It is a mixture of all three. To some extent the free market and private property prevail. Associated free enterprise also flourishes, within limits, and to an increasing extent government control is being exercised. Moreover, our economic system continues to be the subject of wide disagreement, acrimonious discussion, and vigorous contests of strength. These conflicts are reflected in education, as partisans for the several economic philosophies vie with one another for the minds and allegiances of the young.

Most participants in the struggle over an American economic ideology assume the standpoint of the democracy of desire. Advocates of free enterprise and proponents of government control both affirm the democratic ideal of economic opportunity and self-determination for all the people. They also agree in the belief that the aim of economic organization is to satisfy the demand for material gain. They differ only in their convictions about the nature of the social system which will assure the maximum profit to all. In addition, the pursuit of material gain has become so predominant and unquestioned a motive in our culture that the acquisitive spirit has become suffused throughout the whole of life, entering spheres that are not intrinsically or properly economic at all.

This implicit elevation of economic motives to the position of ultimate principles aligns the exponents of the democracy of desire with the communists, for whom the economic determination of history is a fundamental tenet. The communists frankly assert that the drive for material satisfaction is the basic motive of life, and they endeavor to reconstruct all of civilization in accordance with that belief. They do this by adopting the controlled economy in its most extreme form, with all production and distribution of goods and services strictly governed by the state. In aim they are in full agreement with the most ardent free enterprise capitalists, for whom economic considerations are also ultimate. The communists and the capitalists differ, however, in their beliefs about how the maximum production can be achieved and how the resulting material goods should be distributed.

Under existing conditions in the modern world—with increasing populations, diminishing natural resources, and mounting specialization of function and complexity of social organization—it appears likely that if maximum material satisfaction remains the goal of economic life, the communist system or some similar system of socialization by force will win out over free systems. The free play of acquisitive motives, without subordination to the demands of moral conscience, leads by its own inexorable logic to social conflict, to the sharpening of class lines, and to the steady intensification of government controls. When the struggle for economic advantage finally becomes too intense for a free democratic government to control, the free political system is displaced by an absolutist regime, and social order is maintained by dictators backed up by the police power. In an increasingly crowded world of acquisitive people competing for limited supplies of goods, the police state with completely centralized control of economic life appears to be the only basis for social peace and order, without which life is not tolerable nor cultural progress possible.

Must we, then, accept the ultimate fate of communization? Is political and economic absolutism the final answer to the problems of production and distribution? If men insist on being autonomous and on seeking their own profit, they will eventually have to surrender their freedom altogether to powerful men who can keep them from destroying one another in their greed. The alternative to such unhappy servitude is to turn from the way of desire to the life of devotion. Eventual subjugation to tyrants is the price that must be paid for persistent neglect of the leadings of conscience. In the final analysis the necessary conditions for freedom are respect for the right and willing obedience to it.

The fundamental moral principle in the economic realm is that material goods and personal services are instrumentalities for the good life. Their possession, use, and distribution should therefore be determined by their contribution to excellence. The acquisitive outlook is dominated by quantitative standards; success is measured by the amount of wealth one has amassed. In its place we require a qualitative approach to economic life, in which material goods are sought in response to the demands of conscience and for the service of the right and the common good.

What kind of economic system would best serve the good of the human community? The ideal would appear to be a *mixed economy*, with different bases of ownership and control corresponding to the various uses of property. Individual private ownership should apply to: goods of a personal nature (such as clothing, books, and appliances), residential property used by the owner, small business property directly and personally operated by the owner ("small" could be defined by setting an upper limit on the number of auxiliary employees and on gross sales), portable tools used in the performance of an occupation, and personal savings. A sphere of individual privacy in property is important to provide a material basis for personal individuality and freedom. Such property should be limited to what the individual can actually use. Since its only purpose is to insure the person's own efficiency, it should not be allowed to expand into a means of controlling other people's economic lives. It is for this reason that individual private ownership should not be extended to large business enterprises.

Beyond this limited sphere of individual productivity, business should be conducted by cooperative private enterprises capitalized by invested private savings drawing a moderate fixed rate of interest. The work of these cooperatives would be done by professional managers and skilled workers, and policy would be determined by boards including representation from the investors, supervisory and production personnel, and the consuming public. These cooperatives would differ fundamentally from the typical corporation of the present time, in that control would be vested not entirely in the owners but in a broadly representative body, and in that profits would go not to the enlargement of owners' dividends but to capital improvements, higher-quality products, and lower prices. Among the cooperatives would be every sort of enterprise, including retail stores, manufacturing establishments, professional consultants' firms, and even private schools and colleges. The general adoption of such a cooperative enterprise system would amount essentially to the extension to all business and commerce of the principles governing existing nonprofit organizations which have vested control in widely representative boards.

One of the major purposes of the cooperative system would be to eliminate the split between labor and owners or managers by uniting them in a common undertaking for the general welfare. The motive of gain would be replaced by the professional pride in workmanship and the consciousness of being useful. Labor unions would no longer be necessary as a countervailing force against the concentrated economic resources of the owners, since the conditions of work would no longer be determined by an owner-controlled management with an eye to maximizing investors' profits. Thus, the social energies that are now dissipated in destructive competition for group and class advantage would be turned to concerted efforts for the well-being of all.

In addition to the individual and cooperative private ownership and use of property, there should be provision for public ownership and operation of property which is for the welfare of all the people. Included in the basic public services would be at least the following:

1. A defense establishment to protect the security of the nation against external aggression.

2. Agencies for constructive political, economic, and cultural cooperation with other nations.

3. A police force to maintain domestic peace and order, and a system of courts to administer justice.

4. Facilities for transportation, communication, sanitation, and utilities (light, heat, power, and water). These public facilities might be supplemented by individually or cooperatively owned facilities, but such essential properties for serving all the people as railroads, telephone networks, and power plants ought to be owned and controlled by all the people, since upon them depends the very survival of the community; their failure would bring speedy social disaster.

5. Basic medical services, including diagnosis, treatment by physicians and dentists, hospitalization, and prescribed drugs. Here also the public provision might be supplemented by private medical services. The public medical care should be so administered as to preserve the maximum freedom in choice of doctors. The essential point is that no person should be deprived of essential medical care for economic reasons.

6. Ample public recreation facilities, including national, state, and local parks, forest preserves, and wildlife reservations, together with the requisite personnel and program to make them interesting and effective.

7. A comprehensive social security program to insure at least subsistence support for the unemployed or unemployable, widows and orphans, retired people, and persons with physical or mental disabilities—these benefits to be available by right and not by charity. This broad program of social insurance might well be complemented by a wide variety of private individual and group insurance plans.

8. A public education system, with no tuition or with nominal tuition supplemented by scholarships for the needy students, extending from the nursery school through graduate school and even post-doctoral institutes, and including provision for education throughout life. These institutions of public education should be complemented by nonpublic schools of many kinds and at every level, to insure the freedom and variety of thought required for cultural vigor.

As mentioned earlier, a most important key to economic organization is the tax system. In a democracy built on the primacy of justice over profit, the following threefold tax structure would appear most equitable: (1) a progressive individual income tax; (2) a progressive tax on the net income of the cooperatives described above (which would be responsible for the major part of the society's business and industry); (3) very high estate and gift taxes. The income taxes would be progressive in order to reduce economic inequalities and to secure a larger proportion of necessary government revenue from those better able to pay. The rates should be high enough to sustain a strong system of essential public services, yet low enough to permit ample private capital and savings accumulations. Extremely heavy taxes, which would leave individuals and cooperatives only enough income to pay current bills, would quickly undermine the growth of productive enterprises, and this would necessitate further government intervention in economic affairs, probably including even the take-over of industries by government. Democratic freedom and variety are better served by limiting the sphere of direct government ownership and control to those critical services essential to all the people; for this limitation to be sustained, tax rates must not be allowed to increase to crippling levels. The imposition of high estate and gift taxes would equalize economic opportunity and prevent the establishment of hereditary privileged classes, on the principle that no person has a right to great economic power simply as a result of the chances of birth and relationship.

A single income tax on individuals and cooperatives should replace the complex system now used. Income taxes can be administered so as to take account of the actual abilities and obligations of every person and organization. Property taxes, general sales taxes, and special excise taxes, on the other hand, have only the advantage that they are relatively easy to collect. In general, they are not levied in accordance with principles of justice: ability to pay depends on income from property, not on ownership of property in itself. In any case property assessments are notoriously difficult to make and maintain equitably. Sales and excise taxes are also unrelated to ability to pay and tend to impose the greatest proportionate burden upon the lower income groups. Furthermore, it would be far more efficient, more honest, and more consistent with dedication to the right if taxes were collected in one open assessment and through one channel rather than in many different and often concealed ways. The people ought to know exactly what they are asked to pay for their public services, and they should willingly and directly pay it, instead of confusing and deceiving themselves by tolerating or even inviting a system of multiple and hidden levies.

A final essential feature of the type of economic organization here advocated would be agencies for both private and governmental maintenance of ethical standards in economic affairs. For example, a cooperative should not be permitted to acquire capital through the sale of securities without approval by an independent body of experts capable of appraising the soundness and probable prospects of the enterprise. Business and financial organizations should be subject to periodic independent audits and should be required to publish intelligible reports, to help insure the honest conduct of their affairs. Advertising and other representations of goods and services should be guarded against falsification, both through voluntary and governmental watchdog agencies.

The rationale for the economic scheme described above is the subordination of economic advantage to considerations of justice, by relating the ownership and control of property to its proper use. There is no inherent natural right in property. Material goods should be regarded as a trust to be faithfully administered in accordance with equity for all. The extent to which the disposition of labor and matériel can be left to the free determination of individuals or associations through the institution of private property depends upon the degree of private responsibility taken for their right use. If the motive of gain predominates, the sphere of privacy has to be limited, and the distribution of labor and property needs to be effected through direct political determination. On the other hand, if loyalty to the right is the rule in a society, a large degree of privacy in property is desirable. Private property and the free market are self-defeating in an acquisitive society. In a democracy of worth they serve the admirable purpose of providing for the continuous registration of the values of society.

One of the crucial economic problems of contemporary society is to determine how large a proportion of our available manpower and matériel should be spent for formal educational purposes. Limited goods and services, including those of formal education, should be allocated according to principles of truth, creative excellence, and good conscience. That is to say, economics is rectified only by reference to standards of worth that transcend (but also include) economic considerations. Schools, therefore, should be devoted not to the economic advantage of educators, nor to the efficiency of the economic enterprise generally, but to goodness alone. From this vantage point the educational community may supply criticism, inspiration, and leadership in society.

The basic principle of subordinating economic interests to criteria of worth has a variety of applications in educational policy and practice. Ideals of economic equity certainly make it clear that schooling should be available to everyone without regard to financial status. Educational leaders should also resist and counteract economic pressures on the curriculum, by keeping matters of detailed curriculum planning in the hands of teachers and by working for broad representation on boards of control. Educational policy should not be fixed by boards weighted in favor of one economic group in society (usually persons in the higher economic classes), nor should control boards be guided in their planning mainly by budgetary considerations. Educational leaders can show the way toward a more ideal economic program for society as a whole by organizing their own institutions along democratic lines, with boards of control including representatives of taxpayers (in the case of public institutions) or private benefactors (in the case of private institutions), parents, alumni, teachers, administrators, and possibly even students.

In school instruction, free discussion of economic issues should be encouraged. Students should be required to analyze critically contemporary or historical economic ideas and practices, in order that they may not simply reflect unthinkingly the positions of their own families. In order to assure freedom both to analyze these important issues and to consider without fear alternatives to the economic status quo, it is essential that the employment and tenure of teachers not be subject to the will and caprice of individuals or groups representing particular economic interests or convictions. Teachers must be held accountable for professional competence, not for conformity with the economic beliefs of influential persons or groups within the community. Professional organizations must be strong enough to guard this academic integrity against those who would threaten or injure teachers who do not accept their economic doctrine. Young people will be ill-prepared to cope with the momentous challenges of the contemporary world if their teachers are prevented, by fear of reprisal, from raising questions about the justification for various economic beliefs and practices.

Teachers, guidance counselors, and officers for admissions and placement should work to counteract the acquisitive motive by placing emphasis on the intrinsic values in learning, on preparation for the good life, and on the opportunities to engage in useful and interesting work rather than on the cash value of more education. Figures are commonly quoted to show how much more money a person may expect, on the average, to make over a lifetime by continuing his education through high school or through college; and it is estimated that each additional year of schooling actually yields a substantial additional life income. Such propaganda intensifies the tendency to make financial gain the ruling principle of life. It is the duty of all professional educators *and especially of parents,* who have such decisive influence in these matters, by their word and example to turn the young away from the prime concern for gain toward the cultivation of a worthy life in which economic matters will be seen in proper perspective.

Finally, school curriculums should not be organized—as they now largely are—primarily with a vocational orientation, thus importing into the whole educational system the patterns of prestige and power that characterize the acquisitive culture. The course of study should be aimed at the nurture of loyalty to truth and goodness and should include specific occupational preparation only within this framework of growth in human excellence. The central core of education should be liberal humane studies, in which the student discovers his universal calling to be a man through knowing and serving the good. Occupational specialization can then be rightly ordered in a contributory fashion around the general studies in which the fundamental values of life are taught.

We have thus far considered the meaning of democracy as a broad concept having relevance to every field of human interest and endeavor. We now turn to politics, the field in which the idea of democracy had its birth and in which it is still most naturally and commonly applied. Politics has to do with the way in which a society as a whole is organized and operates. It is concerned with the governance of all the people, with the structure of the public realm.

In matters political, democracy means—in Lincoln's words—government of the people, by the people, and for the people. It means self-government of a given body of people, as contrasted with non-democratic political systems in which rule is in the hands of a hereditary monarch, of a dictator, of an aristocracy (noblemen or intellectuals), of a class (rich people, the proletariat, or priests), or of a limited party.

Political democracy is based on the principle of political equality. The contrast between rulers and ruled, between sovereign and subject, is obliterated. The rulers and the ruled are one and the same people. The people are sovereign and subject to no other persons but themselves. In a democracy every man is a king.

But should the people govern themselves? Should not the best people govern, as the advocates of aristocracy propose? Why should the welfare of all the people be endangered by placing their destinies in their own hands, in view of the relative incompetence of the average man in comparison with the most able people? Can the general educational level ever be high enough to make the common people wise enough to rule themselves?

In the abstract it can be granted that the best people should govern. But who are the best people, and in what sense are they best? If "best" refers to high intellectual ability, personal dynamism, rhetorical eloquence, and the like, and if people with such powers are permitted to rule autonomously, they are likely soon to become tyrants. Democracy rests on the insight that no one—not even the "best" people—can in the long run and on the whole be entrusted with an unconditional grant of power over other people. Democracy did not come into being as a means of improving the quality of leadership by installing the common man as sovereign in place of the aristocrats. Democratic reformers have been under no illusions that the common man possesses any special wisdom which is superior to that of the exceptional man. Their insistence has rather been on the untrustworthiness of any person—"common" or exceptional—to exercise sovereignty over others without limitations and checks.

Popular rule may become as corrupt as autocratic rule. When self-interest dominates a society, the rule of the people becomes the tyranny of the mass, exercised through persons who hold authority in the name of the people. Such popular rule requires the suppression of minorities whom the majority do not consider consistent with their own best interest. Democracies based on the accommodation of competing interests are inherently unstable. As the pressures from dissatisfied elements within build up, and as the dangers of assault from without multiply, such a democracy is subject to weakness, frustration, and loss of morale, and ultimately to disintegration from within or conquest from without. There is widespread suffering due to the loss of social order, and the eventual result is an autocratic regime in which personal liberties are exchanged for the benefits of dependable authority.

Such are the consequences of building a political system on the principle of interest-satisfaction. The theory that human beings in pursuit of their own interests will automatically establish a harmonious society, provided everyone has an equal voice in political affairs, is no more true than the corresponding thesis in economic affairs. Furthermore, raising the educational level of the people offers no sure remedy for the corruption of a mass democracy. Education designed to further individual ambitions in fact intensifies the forces that make for the inefficiency and instability of popular democracy.

Democracy can be firmly established only on moral foundations. The democracy of desire contains the seeds of its own destruction. Only a democracy of worth possesses the resources for permanent growth and regeneration. The proper goal of democratic political life is the discovery and accomplishment of what is right. It is a great error to conceive of democracy in Utilitarian terms, as that form of government that affords "the greatest good to the greatest number," where "good" means pleasure, happiness, and the fulfilling of desires. The original democratic challenge to autocracy was mainly for the increase of freedom *in justice* and fraternal relations; this is still the proper goal.

Democracy is commonly thought of as a system for making effective the "will of the people." This idea assumes the democracy of desire, in which human autonomy is the governing principle. The proper principle of democratic responsibility is not the "will" of the people, but the fulfilling by them of truth and justice, regardless of what any person or group may will. Virtue is not guaranteed by majority vote. Real excellence is usually perceived and willed by the few rather than by the many. Then, should we abandon the democratic idea? By no means. Civic responsibility belongs to all the people because the people as a whole are the best custodians of the right, the safest guardians against the perversion of justice by the powerful few who would rule over others for their own advantage.

This subordination of the people's will is symbolized by the official American motto, "In God we trust." This motto is not an expression of an official national theism, for such a view would contradict the well-established principle of state neutrality in matters of religious belief and would imply that people who do not believe in God are not fully citizens. The motto should rather be understood as affirming that the nation stands under a judgment superior to any or all of the people—namely, that of the right itself. It means that the state is not supreme, nor are the people themselves the final standard by which everything is to be measured. The ultimate criteria are truth, goodness, justice, freedom—ideals of worth which may be approximated but never fully embodied in actual existence.

The nature of democratic authority is further clarified by considering the place of law in government. One of the cornerstones of democracy is that government is not of men but of law. The rule of law overcomes the anarchy of unbridled freedom and inhibits arbitrary action by persons in power. Political life must be conducted according to established rules and traditions which condition the liberty of all citizens, including government officials, for the sake of the common welfare. Indeed, laws are necessary in any society if the people are to have confidence and security and if public affairs are to be conducted with orderliness and predictability. Autocracies require laws as well as do democracies, and a democracy of desire as well as a democracy of worth. The differences between governments turn on the matter of the sources and sanctions of law. In autocracy, laws are made by the ruler and express his will. He can truthfully say, "I am the law," although for prudential reasons he usually suppresses this boast. In a democracy of desire, laws are made by the people and express their will. The people are then the law. They make laws to establish and conserve order and to maximize the satisfaction of special interests.

Under autocracy and the democracy of desire, government is really of men, not of laws. The laws are only tools through which men govern. In such societies the laws are constantly under challenge by subjected persons and by those who seek to improve their own position relative to others. Laws made by men are respected no more than are the men who make them, and laws that express the will of men will be broken without compunction by other men whose will, in the contest of interests, is opposed to that of the lawmakers. When laws have their source and sanction solely in human beings, therefore, resistance and defiance by those with opposite interests are to be expected. The only guilt is getting caught in the infraction of regulations. In fact, since success is considered the criterion of the good, taking advantage of the law without being apprehended is regarded as a mark of virtue. Thus, a thorough belief that laws are made solely by men engenders disrespect, disorder, and lawlessness.

Government by law rather than by men presupposes a sanction for law rising above human will. To be sure, all law is necessarily formulated by men; it comes through human channels. But if it is to inspire respect and obedience, there must be a belief that the law is an expression (albeit partial and imperfect) of what is good and right.

Respect for law as an approximation to the right must be carefully distinguished from legalistic absolutism. Legalists regard laws as unchanging, unchallengeable rules of conduct, as final, authoritative standards for human life. But nobody knows fully what is right, and no actual pattern of social life is a perfect exemplification of justice. The rule of law, then, does not mean that the people should follow only the established codes, remaining respectfully obedient to them and never criticizing or changing them. For authentic democracy the people must have respect for law, but not a slavish subservience to any existing code of laws. They should be alive to the need for improving existing codes and for making changes in them in the light of altered circumstances and wiser counsels. The young should be taught to obey the rules established by persons in authority and to have a respectful regard for the principles of conscience that those rules are meant to embody. They should at the same time be led to inquire into the justification for rules and instructed in the appropriate ways of bringing about changes in social regulations to make them more just.

In a democracy of worth, then, since law is viewed as an expression of the good, it is not only respected but it is also loved. The citizens do not obey the law only because they must, and they do not try to break it if their own advantage would be served thereby. They rather think of just laws as a sorce of human well-being, for which every citizen should be grateful. Laws are seen not as restricting life, but as means of promoting the good life for all.

Moreover, the connection between law and objective right is critically important in the adjustment of social conflict. If laws are believed to be entirely man-made, then power is the only criterion of right; differences between persons and groups can be adjusted only by domination and submission or by compromise agreement. It makes no sense to discuss the differences from a moral standpoint, for in theory the differences are solely a result of human will and preference. On the other hand, when laws are linked to the ideal of a universal moral order, a foundation for discussion is provided. Since the right may not be fully or certainly known, there is no assurance that conflicts can be successfully resolved. Nevertheless, cooperative exploration of differences is now a reasonable pursuit. Just as in scientific discussion, which makes no sense without a presupposed truth, moral inquiry has no point apart from a presupposed objective right. Thus, in the democracy of worth the grounds are provided for dealing with differences through a continuing dialogue rather than through contests of power which alienate disputants, instead of uniting them in a common search.

For the United States, the general structure of political life is set forth in the Federal Constitution. All acts of government and all decisions in law are ultimately referable to the Constitution. It is the Constitution that contains the law by which the people rule themselves. This is the instrument that saves the nation from the tyranny of individuals or of the mass. It is the gyroscope of the ship of state. The people do not feel free to assert their autonomous will; they consider first what the Constitution permits, and they make policy accordingly. Thus, the Constitution is the great conservator of civic wisdom, the preserver of the values of democratic polity.

The people may, of course, change the Constitution, and in this sense their will appears to take precedence over the supreme law of the land. But such amendments must be made in accordance with procedures set forth in the Constitution itself. Furthermore, such changes are made only after the most searching public deliberation and for the most weighty reasons.

This reverent regard for the Constitution, this willing submission to its provisions, this extreme caution in modifying it, and then only in obedience to its amendment regulations—these attitudes are not due to sentimental attachment or to absolutist legalism. A better explanation would be the assumption that the Constitution is a good approximation to the principles of justice to which the will of the people should be subordinate. When the people decide to amend the nation's charter, they do so because they believe the changes will make their Constitution an even more perfect instrument of the right, rather than because they think it will better serve them and their interests.

The political structure defined in the Constitution has three main components: legislative, executive, and judicial, each with explicitly defined functions. These three branches operate in parallel rather than in hierarchical fashion, according to the basic principle of the *separation of powers*. This separation makes possible the system of "checks and balances," in which the deliberative decisions of the

Congress are checked by the President; the actions of the President and his officers are in turn tested, challenged, and confirmed by the Congress; and the constitutionality of the acts of both the legislative and the executive branches is checked by the judiciary. The legislative branch has a further check-and-balance mechanism of its own, by its separation into independent House of Representatives and Senate, both of which must pass every measure that is to become law.

This system of separation of powers has two purposes: the negative one, through the checks and balances, of preventing the usurpation of power by any person or group of persons; and the positive one of affording independent approaches to what is for the good of all the people. In its negative function it minimizes the consequences of the power play that comes from construing democracy as the pursuit of autonomy. In its positive function it enhances the possibilities for knowing and doing the right. For effective government it is essential that the negative checking activity should not destroy the positive one. This is particularly important with respect to the executive power, which must be free for decisive leadership, without being frustrated at every step by an opposing legislature. A complex modern democracy is at a serious disadvantage in dealing with autocratic states as well as in expeditiously conducting its own internal affairs, unless it possesses strong executive powers which are not hedged about in matters of detailed policy and administration by legislative and judicial agencies. It is imperative that the executive be allowed to lead the people and to act quickly and flexibly in their behalf, within his defined sphere of responsibility, and that he be checked and balanced by the other powers of government mainly through regular review of his accomplishments and through the setting of long-term policy.

Besides the separation of powers, for the sake of freedom and individuality, the Constitution ordains a government with *limited* powers. In the American commonwealth the government is not omnicompetent. The spheres of political authority are explicitly set forth, and beyond these spheres the citizens are at liberty to decide for themselves. The individual's life is not to be controlled in all things by the collective power. Government is given sufficient authority only to accomplish necessary matters of public concern, leaving a wide range of decisions for the private sphere.

The most explicit statement of these limitations is in the Constitution's first ten amendments—the Bill of Rights—which guarantee freedom of religion, speech, press, assembly, and petition, the right to bear arms, protection against the obligatory quartering of soldiers, security from unwarranted search and seizure, the right to a grand jury, protection against double jeopardy and self-incrimination, the right of due process, just compensation for private property taken for public use, and speedy public trial by jury without excessive fines or bail. Finally, it is explicitly stated that rights and powers not delegated to the Federal Government by the Constitution are reserved to the several states and to the people.

By this limitation of powers a democracy committed to the right— that is, with a bill of "rights," not "conveniences" or "privileges"— is distinguished from a "people's democracy," in which the people rule. In a democracy of worth there is no majority rule, in the sense that the majority completely determine how life will be lived in the society. The majority is subject to the law of right, which includes the rights of minorities and the liberties of individuals.

The definition and limitation of powers also supports a policy of maximum local responsibility. The United States Constitution establishes a *federal* union, not a single monolithic nation-state. The nation as a whole is compacted of parts which retain their own proper governmental powers. The several states have their constitutions, executives, legislatures, and courts, generally modeled after the Federal system and in any event not inconsistent with the Federal Constitution. The states further delegate authority to local governments, thus keeping the responsibility for civic affairs as fully as possible in the people's hands. The several levels of government also check and balance one another, as do the separate branches of authority considered horizontally.

The most important constitutional principle for maintaining democratic civic responsibility is that of *representation*. The great problem for democracy in a complex society is to make the voice of each citizen count in the determination of public policy. The chief mechanism for solving this problem is the popular election of major government officials. These officials represent the people in guiding the affairs of state. In what sense do they "represent" the people? The answer depends upon the nature of the democracy in question. Under a democracy of desire, the elected officers represent the interests of their constituents, and the voters expect their representatives—whether in the legislative or executive branches—to help them secure what they want. Government then becomes an arena in which the champions of various interests in the society vie with one another for precedence, and the successful politician is one who can win the greatest benefits for his supporters.

Representation has an entirely different meaning in a democracy of worth. Here the elected official represents the people in the pursuit of civic excellence. He is not a politician whose only thought is to gain and hold political power, but a statesman whose central concern is for the right conduct of public affairs. He is a "representative man," in the sense that in his person he exemplifies some of the ideals toward which mankind aims. He is not a symbol of the average man— of commonplace mediocrity—but of what the average man in his better moments aspires to be.

In ideal democracy the statesman is a *leader* of the people, not their lackey. His task is not to get for them what they want, but to help them to do what is right. He is a servant of the people, and responsible to them, not for the satisfaction of their demands, but for guiding them more surely toward the goals that they have glimpsed in their finest hours. Statesmen should, therefore, be chosen from among the best of men and women, as persons of unusual wisdom, integrity, and vision. They should not be the common man writ large or people with whom the mediocre in character and ability feel comfortably equal. They should be persons to look up to, exemplars of the ideals of civility. The representative should be selected more for his difference from his constituents than for his likeness to them. He should be chosen more for his ability to transform the people than for his ability to confirm them, more to elevate them than to please them.

One other feature of American politics—namely, the party system— is worthy of mention as part of the mechanism for securing individual responsibility. Political parties provide a concrete basis for individual civic participation and decision on candidates and issues. In a time of de-personalization of life in the large community, they make a place for face-to-face associations between citizens in the discussion of affairs of state. Moreover, the two major American parties are not primarily competitive interest groups, with one, for example, representing capital and the other labor, or one reflecting rural interests and the other the interests of urban people. This contrasts with the multiparty system of many other countries, where the parties represent particular competing geographical, economic, or religious groups within the nation. The two main parties in the United States, on the other hand, constitute alternative *coalitions* for effective government.

This two-party system is consonant with the democracy of worth, in which both parties aim to serve the welfare of *all* the people, not to gain special advantage for a segment of the population. From this point of view party politics should be regarded not as a battle between opposing groups for precedence and power, but as a common pursuit, along somewhat different paths, for the common good. Both parties are in principle dedicated to the same goals—namely, justice in the nation and the welfare of all the people—but they have somewhat different convictions about what justice and welfare concretely mean and about how these benefits may best be secured. These differences make for deeper understanding and for more certain progress toward the right. They stimulate the continuing dialogue which is the *sine qua non* of wisdom and vitality in the community of free men. The point for emphasis is that these values may be realized only when the party system is predicated upon the objective reality of the good and loyalty to it, and not when parties are committed to a struggle for their own members' advantage.

The system of political organization in the United States is, of course, not the embodiment of civic perfection. It is not the only polity consistent with loyalty to the good. Its features are a consequence of the special history and conditions of the American Experiment, and hence cannot be taken uncritically as the ideal for nations with quite different traditions and circumstances. Nevertheless, in its general features the American political system is a marvelous achievement, exemplifying some of the fundamental characteristics of the democratic ideal. The main point in the present analysis is to show how the laws and polity of a society may exemplify the ideals of the democracy of worth, to indicate the dangers of a degraded conception of democracy, and to suggest the basis for the recovery of sound principles of government.

We turn now to a specific consideration of the bearing of political democracy on education. Democracy clearly requires educated citizens if it is to survive and prosper. It is for this reason that the state has, and should have, compulsory education laws. The right to ignorance is not recognized as one of the rights of man in a democracy, because ignorance is a form of slavery. A person cannot be free in his own person, nor can he contribute to the freedom of others, if he is at liberty not to learn what he needs to know to be a responsible and participating member of society. Hence, it is a matter of public law—not of private choice—that everyone shall receive education up to a specified age. To insure that this will be done satisfactorily, the state also should and does see to it that schools are provided for everyone, and that no one is deprived of an education for want of money or for any other reason. Free schools are one of the essential instruments of the general welfare which the Constitution aims to promote.

On the other hand, education belongs primarily to the family and not to the state. Public educational services are for the use and welfare of the people but are not obligatory upon them. If parents do not wish to have their children instructed in public schools, they may send them to nonpublic schools. This right was upheld by the United States Supreme Court, on constitutional grounds, in the celebrated "Oregon case" (*Pierce* v. *Society of Sisters*) in 1925. The government has no monopoly of education. It must make facilities available to all the children of all the people, and it must make sure that minimum standards are maintained in all schools, public and nonpublic, so that no one uses his freedom irresponsibly. Beyond this the proper authority of government over education does not extend.

The general principles of limited governmental powers and of local responsibility are clearly reflected in the relation of the several levels of government to education in the United States. As education is not among the matters specifically assigned by the Constitution to the Federal Government, it is by implication delegated to the states. While the states are thus officially charged with the public supervision of education, it has been the general pattern in the United States for the states to delegate detailed responsibility for the public schools to the local communities themselves. In this way the control and support of public education have been made an immediate and visible responsibility of all the people. This localism has been preserved in the interests of freedom and variety in a pluralistic society distrustful of high centralization of power, particularly in a field such as education, where individual persuasion is paramount.

Still, the predominance of state and local responsibility for education does not exclude the Federal Government entirely from the sphere of education. Certain phases of education, such as the conduct of programs connected with the military establishment or with diplomatic missions, are a direct Federal responsibility. Furthermore, under the general welfare provision of the Constitution, the Federal Government offers financial assistance to states and local communities for a variety of educational purposes, ranging from subsidies for school lunch programs to salaries for teachers of agriculture and loans for school building construction. The Federal Government by substantial financial aid also can help to counteract the differences in the ability of the states to supply educational facilities for their citizens. In this way the ideal of equality of opportunity may be furthered, the more favored sections of the nation helping to lift the heavier educational burden of the less affluent sections. The same functions of educational equalization are also served by a system of state financial apportionment among the local communities.

Local control of education is always subject to state supervision. School boards are not free to conduct their affairs autonomously; they can act only within the limitations and in accordance with the standards and requirements set forth by the state. In matters of education the states in turn are subject to Federal law in relation to constitutional rights. The most celebrated example of Federal intervention in state and local school affairs is the 1954 racial desegregation decision of the United States Supreme Court. Since the Court found that state and local educational policy were in conflict with fundamental democratic rights as expressed in the Constitution, it ruled that local self-determination in respect to segregated schools must be overruled by national policy.

The school desegregation story illustrates the general principle that to the degree that control of education is not exercised with a sense of responsibility for justice, Federal control will be introduced. Local autonomy is not an absolute right. It is a grant of freedom which may be enjoyed only so long as it is not abused. On the other hand, the Federal Government is not necessarily just either; we may not assume that centralization of educational control would make school policy right in all respects. The genius of a balanced system of limited, reserved, and delegated governmental powers and of defined civil rights is that the connection between freedom and responsibility is kept constantly in view. Furthermore, in the continuing tension between levels and branches of political authority, the distrust of unrestricted autonomy is expressed, and the need for common loyalty based on objective principles of justice is made plain.

Freedom is important in a democracy so that in the long run the citizens may more nearly approach what is right. For the perfecting of freedom, government must as far as possible be persuasive rather than coercive. But persuasion is the work of education. From this it follows that education is the foundation of democratic freedom. Because the institutions of education are the prime agencies of persuasion in society, they should as far as possible be separate and independent of the ordinary channels of political power. If the schools, colleges, and universities are to serve as the mind and conscience of society, if they are to be sources of criticism, creativity, and guidance, it is imperative that they not be embedded in the regular administrative structure of government. Politics is the realm of collective action; it is the art of the practicable; and the practicable is never the ideal. Education is the realm of individual exploration and creation; it is the transformation of practicality in the light of ideal possibilities. Accordingly, academic freedom, supported by a high degree of administrative and fiscal independence, helps to sustain democratic liberty.

One useful method of separating the educative function from the other administrative functions of government is to have special school districts organized without direct reference to other political subdivisions, separate special elections for school boards, and provision for raising capital funds and operating expenses by special school bond issues and earmarked tax revenues, so that educational statesmanship may not be compromised by direct involvement in the struggle for political power. Furthermore, when appropriations for education are made directly from the public treasury, they should be granted to politically independent agencies so that government financial support does not become a means for political domination of education.

The ultimate safeguard for the integrity and freedom of education is in the conscientious assumption of responsibility by professional educators. If they prove themselves worthy of public confidence by maintaining high standards of competence, if through professional associations and voluntary accrediting agencies they discipline themselves in matters of knowledge, skill, and character, independence of political control can be assured, and unwarranted interference and coercion can be successfully resisted.

The grant of a high degree of freedom in education is, of course, for the sake of political democracy itself. Teachers are not at liberty to teach in a manner that undermines the very foundations of the free society. It is for this reason that teachers and other school officials who actively oppose the principles of free democracy as expressed in the Constitution (especially the Bill of Rights) should be excluded from positions in education. This is not to say that a loyalty oath should be required of all educators; such a procedure does not in fact separate the loyal from the disloyal and has the effect of driving some sensitive and conscientious persons out of teaching. There are other ways of detecting people who openly promote and labor for the subversion of the free society, and these people should be excluded by action of the teaching profession itself from work in education.

In a closed society, typified by communist and fascist countries and by states in which the agencies of government are in the hands of absolutist ecclesiastical authorities, the preservation of the social order requires that the schools be under political control, in order that the official dogmas may be taught and the will of the controlling parties may be implanted in the minds of the young. In a free society, on the other hand, the ideal of education is persuasion through dialogue —through open and continuing discussion of issues—on the assumption that there is truth to be known and right to be done, but that since no one can claim full and final possession of these objects, inquiry must go on. In any kind of society, only those persons can be accepted as teachers who abide by the fundamental premises of the society. In the closed society the authorities will see to it that only persons loyal to the official doctrine may teach. In a free society the same is true, but the official doctrine is one of responsible freedom rather than of unquestioning compliance to fixed orders. Only persons who adhere to that doctrine, of the duty to seek truth and do justice through unrestricted disciplined investigation of the same, are fit to teach in an authentic democracy.

Democratic political values may be taught in many ways. The academic study of government is one approach. Every American student, by reading, discussion, and observation, should be thoroughly acquainted with the fundamentals of the political system of his country. Through a study of the history of our political institutions he should become aware of the price at which liberty has been bought, and gain insight into the continuing faithfulness and vigilance required to preserve it. Some knowledge of the history and forms of political organization of other nations is also desirable, as a source of suggestions for improving American governmental processes and of warnings about tendencies to be avoided, and as a basis for understanding the different ways of people with other traditions, resources, and problems. Of special importance in democratic education is thorough and fair-minded instruction in the politics of nondemocratic nations, including the communist autocracies (for example, the U.S.S.R.) and the fascist dictatorships (such as Spain).

But far more effective than such academic civics teaching are the political lessons learned by actual participation in the life of the home, school, and community. Verbal instruction in democracy is not convincing within a social context that contradicts the principles taught. Home, school, and community life should be organized democratically, with respect for every person and with a grant of freedom in proportion to social maturity. Regulations in family and classroom can be used as a basis for developing a high concept of law, when they are presented as approximations to right—not as arbitrary impositions, not as expressions of superior power, not as absolute rules which can never be questioned or modified. Parents and teachers can teach the democratic principle of the limitation of powers by carefully defining the areas of adult responsibility for the young and by making plain the widening dimensions of liberty for those who learn to accept the disciplines of responsible freedom.

School life affords excellent opportunities for gaining practical executive, legislative, and judicial experience through student government organizations. Students can learn the meaning of leadership by seeing that the proper criteria for selecting their representatives are not popularity, eloquence, social status, or influential connections, but ability to serve the common good and to embody the common aspiration for the ideal. Special care should be taken to discourage young people, who in their search for personal identity tend to be conformists, from interpreting and practicing democracy as majority rule, in disregard of individual and minority rights and careless of the proper subordination of the will of the group to the principles of justice. To this end, the regular practice of minority criticism should be encouraged, and constructive, thoughtful nonconformity should be welcomed.

Teachers and parents can reinforce the lessons of democracy by their own example of civic responsibility. The principles of academic freedom and of relative independence for education within the political structure do not exclude or excuse those who teach from active participation in political life. If their elders remain aloof from civic affairs, at most engaging in detached observation and criticism of the politicians, it is hardly cause for wonder that the young should learn to leave the decisions of state to others and thus prepare the way for the loss of their liberties. Educators are often repelled from politics because compromise and concession are necessary; the neat perfection of contemplated ideals cannot be achieved, and so the teacher may seek refuge in ideas and feel he is doing his duty by decrying the greed, corruption, and ignorance of the politicians.

A democratic teacher's calling is rather to seek to bring the ideal into vital relation to the actualities of political life, by encouraging young people to consider the high and honorable vocation of statesmanship and by faithfully and visibly engaging himself in civic affairs. In a democracy politics is everybody's business, and from this assignment the educator especially is not exempt.

Finally, the organization and the administration of the schools have an influence on what pupils learn about democracy. Talk about freedom does not carry much conviction when school personnel have to work within an autocratic system. The rule of law, rather than of men, ought to hold good for schools as well as for communities and nations. School boards, superintendents, principals, and teachers ought also to be related to one another in a scheme of authority and subordination with carefully articulated limitation and separation of powers, checks and balances, means of representation, individual and minority rights, and maximum delegation of responsibility. The principles of true political democracy do not only belong to governmental organizations. They are principles of universal human relevance, applicable to all social institutions, including homes and schools. In short, effective teaching of democratic values requires the practice of democracy by those who teach and a democratic structure in the institutions of education.

It is not enough, in the present age, to promote justice in the local community and in state and nation. Events and peoples beyond our borders can no longer be regarded simply as subjects for inquiry by the adventurous and the curious. The world has become a neighborhood.

Thus, the idea of one world, of the family of mankind, is today not merely a prophet's vision. In one sense it is an accomplished reality. But it is a fact forced upon us by technology, rather than a moral achievement. Morally we still live in many separate worlds. We are fearfully unprepared from a personal standpoint for the technical unity which the progress of modern knowledge has presented to us. As in so many other realms, our knowledge has outrun our virtue.

This unification of the world through science has been accompanied by a diffusion of democratic ideas among peoples of every land. Men everywhere are demanding equality and independence. The old assumption that one nation may hold sway over another is now universally challenged. "Colonialism" and "imperialism" today have unqualifiedly evil connotations, particularly in countries struggling for national self-determination.

The spread of the idea of freedom throughout the world is essentially a consequence of education. Through the diffusion of information by modern methods of travel and communication, democratic ideals are transmitted from one people to another. When people in one nation are given knowledge of better ways of life in other nations, they have a basis for aspiring toward equal benefits and opportunities for themselves. The subjugation of a people can be maintained in the long run only by keeping them in ignorance of their rights, potentialities, and means of emancipation. Now that enlightenment is within reach of everyone everywhere, the demand and expectation of freedom and opportunity are also universal.

The results of these world-wide movements toward independence are nevertheless ambiguous. On the one hand, new hope and vigor are in evidence over wide areas of the earth. The long sleep and silence of oppressed and exploited peoples are at an end. Within a generation, cultures are being transformed from the level of the stone age to that of the atomic age. People who only recently were nobody are now treated with the greatest seriousness. The attention of the whole world is fastened upon the struggles of new republics to be born, to survive, and to grow to some degree of political maturity. Such events provide an atmosphere of expectation and exhilaration for the many peoples who see their own fortunes in the ascendancy.

On the other hand, these revolutionary changes have been accompanied by unprecedented fear and violence. The precipitous plunging of people from the life of nomads, peasants, and forest dwellers to that of urban industrial workers has had catastrophic effects on morale. The rapid assumption of prominent positions in international affairs by politically immature people has made for a high degree of instability in relations among the nations. The meeting and the mixing of cultures have caused the dissolution of traditional values without any satisfying framework of meaning to take their place. Thus, hope and enthusiasm in wide segments of the earth's population are compounded with anxiety, confusion, conflict, and suffering probably without parallel in the history of man.

Out of this complex of aspiration and desperation has arisen the greatest of all enemies to human welfare, total war. War is nothing new in man's history. Men have perennially battled with one another, whether for sheer love of contest or for lust of conquest. But modern total war is something new under the sun. War is no longer a limited engagement at arms between selected members of the population. Today war between nations involves everybody, soldiers and civilians alike. It is a comprehensive effort to destroy the enemy by any and all practicable means. Every available resource of materials and manpower is poured into the struggle, and all of the treasures and traditions of civilization are sacrificed for the one supreme goal of military victory.

The crushing burdens of war must be carried not only during the actual armed conflict but also when there is no open combat. Preparation for war is essential to success in it, and the intervening times must be used to make ready for engagements to follow. Thus, it is no longer customary to speak of alternating war and peace, but of "hot" wars and "cold" wars. "Peace" is, then, merely the preparatory phase of war, a phase that makes the ensuing struggle all the more deadly because of the greater power accumulated during it.

Modern war is total in three respects: in involving everyone and everything in waging it and in suffering from it; in absorbing the energies and concern of the nations perpetually; and in the destructiveness of modern weapons. Technical discoveries have also made available the means to effect the speedy annihilation of humanity and civilization. Atomic bombs, now stockpiled in abundance by the major contending powers, can desolate cities within a few moments and blanket the earth with radioactive dust which would make it completely uninhabitable. Biological weapons could quickly destroy whole populations by spreading fatal infections across the land. Or the enemy could use certain gases to destroy the people's will to resist and so could take his victim without a struggle.

Included among the resources marshaled for the conduct of total war are those of education. When civilization is clouded over by the threat of armed conflict, everything that is done to prepare the young for the future tends to have some reference to the needs of national defense. Science and engineering are emphasized at the expense of the humanities. Control of education is centralized in order to enable the national government to meet the continuing emergencies of full or partial military mobilization. In the totalitarian nations every agency of instruction and communication is enlisted in the government's service, to educate the people in the requirements of national security. Under conditions of international military rivalry, the free nations, too, become more and more regimented, and liberty in teaching and learning are suppressed in the national interest. Thus, war and the threat of war make education in all nations subordinate to considerations of military strength.

The desperate world situation which modern warfare has now created makes the pursuit of peace mankind's number one objective. Since war has at last become an all-consuming evil, no human achievement of any kind is possible unless war is prevented. Knowledge, art, and social invention—all of the works of civilization—depend for their realization upon the elemental securities of existence. Human life and its products cannot endure without a hospitable environment. Total war creates a totally inhospitable environment for man and all his works. None of the other values—of intelligence, creativity, conscience, or reverence—that education ought to promote has any meaning at all apart from the basal fact of human survival. Modern war makes all judgments of better or worse pointless in comparison with the primordial "to be or not to be" which determines whether there shall be anything at all to appraise. The questions of autocracy and democracy, of desire and worth, of mediocrity and excellence in education—all of the matters that have concerned us in these pages—have significance only on the assumption that war does not consume us all. It is in this sense that world peace is today the value of values.

How has our present international predicament come to pass? The most obvious factor has already been noted—namely, the progress of science and invention, by which the world has been contracted and united and weapons have been made totally destructive. But such knowledge and skill are not in themselves evil. Our perilous condition is due to the conjunction of these technical factors with the moral and personal factor of self-centeredness. The present fearful state of the world is a result of combining the human tendency to strive for autonomy with the vast powers now at man's disposal through science and technology. In other words, what today threatens to extinguish the light of civilization altogether is a union of the democracy of desire with vast technical capability.

The upsurge of nationalism all over the world is not simply a struggle for justice. It is not only an attempt to redress the wrongs of colonialism and imperialism. It is also a clamor for autonomy, a demand for absolute liberty, for full self-determination. So insistent are the pressures that even peoples who are not yet prepared to assume the responsibilities of self-government claim their independence and then pay a heavy price in internal chaos and strife, with the likelihood of having to settle for order by dictatorial power rather than by consent. Thus, the irresponsible demand for independence characteristic of the democracy of desire tends at length to autocracy and police coercion, which actually diminish the people's freedom.

The widespread revolutionary movements of the time are also due to the popular demand for a larger share of material goods. The "have nots" are rising to challenge the "haves," usually with scarcely any conception of the necessary economic, political, and demographic conditions required to produce a high standard of living. Impoverished people in underdeveloped agrarian societies, newly aware of the abundance enjoyed by the people of advanced industrial societies with a long history of civilized development, are demanding at once the benefits of civilization without creating the instruments necessary to produce them.

These insistent demands for more power and possessions contain the roots of war. Nations fight for markets, for territory, and for prestige as well as to defend themselves against other countries which seek such things at the expense of their neighbors. The explosive insecurities of our time follow from the general acceptance of the principles of the democracy of desire—namely, that the goal of life is to have maximum liberty and to acquire as much power and as many things as possible.

No lasting solution to world problems can be achieved apart from widespread conversion from the life of acquisition to that of devotion. Yet under modern conditions of weapons capability, even the acquisitive philosophy is incompatible with war, for in total war nobody can win. On purely practical and prudential grounds, apart from any considerations of justice or excellence, armed conflict no longer pays, for anybody. War is not now, as it once may sometimes have been, a way of gaining desired ends. In a nuclear holocaust the difference between victor and vanquished would disappear in the abyss of universal destruction and suffering which would ensue. A clear assessment of the facts of modern warfare makes it evident that armed conflict is no longer defensible on any view except that of nihilism.

A primary objective of education today, in homes, in schools, and through the mass media of communication, should be the full and forceful dissemination of knowledge about the extreme destructiveness of modern weapons of war and about the awful consequences for everybody which would result from their use in any large-scale conflict. The false sense of security in the possession of a stockpile of powerful weapons must be dispelled, and a proper fear must be engendered of the heightened danger to which all the nations of the world are exposed through the arms race. Even from the standpoint of national advantage, the citizens must be encouraged to work for a reduction in arms. An atomic build-up cannot be risked, because of the ease with which a nuclear war could be initiated by accident if not by design. At present there is a balance of terror through the possession by each of the world's major antagonists of the means to inflict mortal damage on the other. Such a balance is dangerous and precarious. The minds and wills of all the people must be prepared by education to find some way, not yet apparent, out of the collective insanity into which our compounded knowledge, fear, and hostility have led us.

Wars will not cease from the earth until the universal demand for autonomy is subordinated to the search for truth and justice—that is, until democracy is founded more in devotion than in desire. What, then, are some of the ideals for a democracy of worth in the sphere of international relations? What are some of the goals of education for world responsibility?

A first objective is the renunciation of war as an instrument of national policy. This position must now be taken even on strictly practical and prudential grounds. It ought also to be supported on an ethical basis. The mass extermination, in warfare, of persons and of the means of livelihood is a moral enormity. War violates every canon of right. It contradicts the ideal of human worth. It silences the voices of reason and of conscience. For the slow and patient work of creation it exchanges swift annihilation. In place of civilized persuasion it exalts barbaric force. Instead of sensitivity it promotes indiscriminate callousness. It displaces love and understanding concern by hatred and indifference. Every strategy of trickery and deception is allowed in war. Truth is subordinated to success in battle, and honor is regarded as merely one of the conditions of mutual assistance.

In earlier times warfare may have had its noble aspects. It sometimes engendered courage, loyalty, and endurance. It provided a field for the exercise of skill and imagination. It was a training ground for leaders and a powerful impetus to patriotism, national unity, and civic cooperation. But recent technical developments have so transformed the ways of warfare that whatever nobility it may have had in the past no longer maintains. While it is true that the necessities of national defense still provide a powerful stimulus in a variety of technical and educational fields and still serve to unite citizens in a common struggle against enemies within and without, the end toward which these efforts point is so evil that their virtue is negated. Thus, in our present predicament perhaps the most fundamental of all moral tasks is the abolition of war.

The renunciation of war as an instrument of national policy can be effected only if nations also abandon their claim to absolute national sovereignty. The idea of full national sovereignty belongs to the philosophy in which autonomy is the highest good. National sovereignty means unrestricted national self-determination. It means that the nation is believed to be subject to nothing beyond the pursuit of its own interests. When interests conflict, it is natural to resort to force, since it is assumed that there is no higher authority to which appeal can be made for settlement of differences. If, on the other hand, the controlling principle of national life is doing what is right, then the nation is no longer autonomous and self-sufficient; its policies are determined and judged by reference to the superior authority of what is right. The nation is regarded not as the source and criterion of all good, not in itself as an object of unconditional loyalty ("my country, right or wrong, my country"), but as an instrument and channel for goodness.

To relinquish complete national sovereignty is not to eliminate the nation as such. It is frequently urged that the existence of nations is the cause of wars, or in any event that the creation of a single world political community, without separate independent nations, would insure world peace. Such a scheme is not practicable in the foreseeable future, nor would it appear desirable from a democratic standpoint. Just as the democratic nation should be comprised of free and diverse individuals, with maximum personal and local responsibility, so a democratic world community should be made up of independent and distinctive nations, severally and regionally responsible for the universal good. Every nation has its own special history, traditions, culture, and purposes. The citizens of each country have their unique capabilities, national characteristics, and styles of life. These differences in nature, custom, and outlook from country to country enrich the life of mankind.

Nations organized in independence and freedom are as essential to world democracy as free and independent persons are to a democratic community. But such a world of free nations presupposes the subordination of national will to the sovereignty of justice. If nations continue to assert their independence of all higher authority, the end will be either war to the death (for all) or the emergence of a single dominant world power which will maintain by force the minimal order necessary to insure the survival of civilization. National integrity and independence in a democratic world community are contingent upon acceptance and practice of national responsibility for the pursuit of justice and the relinquishment of the principle that the nation is a law unto itself. Vigorous nationalism and devoted patriotism are thus not incompatible with world democracy. The progress of mankind does not lie in the destruction of national identity and the denial of patriotic pride and devotion—any more than civic virtue would be improved by undermining family loyalties. The best citizens of the world are those who are also conscientious individuals, devoted members of families, responsible citizens of the community, and loyal patriots.

If war is to be eliminated as an instrument of national policy and if absolute national sovereignty is to be abrogated, matters in dispute among the nations must be dealt with by persistent and patient negotiation. If, as here contended, there is an underlying assumption of rightness to be discovered, negotiation becomes a means of cooperative exploration. The search for an acceptable solution to disputes is not simply a contest for maximum advantage. It is rather an attempt through discussion and persuasion to satisfy the requirements of justice. Negotiation between democracies of worth is a quest for mutuality founded on common loyalty to the right.

Implicit in the negotiation of disputes according to principles of justice is the acceptance of international law. It is by this law that the sovereignty of nations is limited. This is the higher authority to which they ought to be subject. This law is the criterion of judgment between nations in conflict with one another. By this rule the procedures for equitable relationships and for meaningful persuasion are established. Such international law must be regarded as an approximation to the right, since laws that are held to be only convenient conventions will be ignored when important national interests require it. Force is the only resort in disputes over vital interests when the principles of justice are believed to be solely man-made agreements for purposes of mutual accommodation.

International law comprises the basic rules for ordering the relations between nations. It covers such basic national rights as security against invasion, the control of entrance and exit of persons, the ownership of property, the extradition of criminals, and honorable treatment of ambassadors. Ideally, international law should also extend far beyond these traditional provisions for preserving the integrity and independence of sovereign states, into the domain of universal human rights. Just as there are laws within a nation that forbid a person to misuse his liberty, so there should be laws under which the irresponsible use of a nation's powers over its own citizens could be judged; that is to say, the rights of self-determination by the nation should be subordinate to the fundamental rights of man. For example, under extended international law no nation should be allowed to maintain a system of slavery or to cause its citizens to suffer loss of life, health, or property without just cause. Eventually a universal bill of rights should emerge, containing the basic principles of justice with which all law, both within and between the nations, should be compatible.

A meaningful system of international and universal law requires organized machinery for adjudication—an international court system. It further presupposes some sort of world legislative and executive bodies by which procedures could be formulated and authority exercised. An international police power is also needed to keep order and insure compliance with fundamental world law. Such a force should eventually take the place of the huge military establishments now maintained by the separate nations, under a world order in which war and preparation for it would be abandoned as intolerably burdensome, impractical, immoral, and suicidal.

World courts, legislatures, executives, and police forces constitute a world government. Universal law cannot operate effectively among the nations without concrete instrumentalities in which certain of the powers now held by sovereign nations are surrendered to a world governing agency. But for the sake of national freedom, the powers assigned to the world authorities ought to be clearly defined and strictly limited. A world state with comprehensive powers would weaken or altogether destroy the nations and would raise the threat of a world tyranny more absolute and destructive of liberty than any of the imperial tyrannies of history. The democratic principle of limitation of powers is therefore even more essential in world government than in the political organization of the individual nations. Some sort of world commonwealth there must be, if mankind is to continue to live in a single world of radical interdependence. Some visible instrumentalities are necessary if a common allegiance to certain elemental principles of universal justice is to be more than a pious sentiment. But the vast preponderance of governing power belongs within the free nations of the world community, and not to any world body. International political organization should have jurisdiction only in matters essential to basic peace and justice among the nations and to the preservation of certain universal human rights everywhere.

Much progress can be made toward a world commonwealth, apart from the actual ceding of certain national powers to a world government, by the strengthening of voluntary international cooperation. For example, the United Nations provides a forum for continuing discussions of world problems and even for cooperative police action as a substitute for traditional warfare. Postal services, telephone, telegraph, and broadcasting facilities, monetary exchange, and the regulation of trade all require administrative cooperation across national boundaries. In such activities a kind of world government exists *de facto*, and in these practical ways a basis is provided for the eventual formation of a limited world government *de jure*.

World democracy may also be furthered by the more advanced and prosperous nations providing economic and technical assistance to underdeveloped nations. The inequities of national privilege due to historical and geographical circumstances should be removed by assisting the less fortunate peoples to develop their own material and cultural potentialities. This cannot be done by making indiscriminate gifts of money, nor by seeking to remake other nations according to the details of the governing pattern of the would-be benefactor nation. The United States, for example, cannot effectively help other nations simply by pouring out dollars and by persuading other people to adopt American institutions and culture. It can best serve the cause of world democracy by helping supply the means for the less developed nations to fulfill their own unique aspirations, without attaching to the aid any conditions of military, economic, or political alliance, conformity, or dependency. To insure equity and freedom in aid programs it is desirable to utilize such cooperative international agencies as the World Bank, instead of one nation's contributing directly to other nations. The establishment of a world government with well-defined and strictly limited powers would further facilitate the just and impartial allocation of economic and technical assistance.

Finally, for a world established in liberty and universal equality of opportunity, free exchange of goods, persons, and culture is essential. In a world-wide federation of free nations there is no place for protective tariffs and other forms of trade restriction, which subsidize inefficiency and prevent the people of certain nations from reaping the benefits of their special skills. Every nation should be encouraged to use its resources and the capabilities of its citizens most efficiently, and this requires open channels for the exchange of goods and services. Temporary hardships caused in certain industries by competition from foreign producers should be alleviated by direct economic assistance and by helping in plant modernization or the retraining and reallocation of displaced workers, and not by the imposition of import duties which prevent able and industrious people from reaping the rewards of their efforts.

Free movement of persons is another goal for a democratic world. At the present time, because of the great economic and political disparity among the nations of the world, complete freedom of immigration is not practicable or desirable. The economic and political structures of a nation are hard-won achievements of responsible citizens who have fashioned their careers in relation to these structures. Large numbers of people from other nations cannot then be brought into any country without placing great strains on its own people and institutions. The difficulties of quickly accommodating substantial numbers of new citizens are great. Ultimately, however, as the cooperation of the interdependent nations of the world brings about more complete equality of privileges, and particularly as measures are taken to bring population growth under control and in balance with available natural resources, it should be possible to permit persons to live and work under whatever flag they may choose and to fulfill their human vocations as loyal citizens of whatever nation most fully commands their devotion.

A practical and productive approach toward a democratic world can be made through cultural exchange. Travel and residence in other lands (apart from transfer of citizenship) is one important means of intercultural association. Regular exchanges of teachers and students should be arranged, so that direct personal experience of other peoples may be an integral part of the organized program of education. Seasoned and well-informed interpreters of the world's cultures should be employed to make of foreign travel something more significant than a pleasure tour, and persons who travel abroad should be encouraged to regard themselves as responsible representatives of their country to other nations and to behave accordingly.

International conferences in every field of human endeavor including business, sports, the arts, and science are helpful in keeping open the channels of communication between the peoples of the world. Books and periodicals should be regularly exchanged, both in the original languages and in translation, in order that the widest possible reading may be assured. Care should also be taken to insure that cultural products sent abroad are reasonably representative of the sending nation and are not a caricature of it, as has unfortunately too largely been the case with American motion pictures circulated in other countries. Serious efforts should likewise be made to secure for foreign service in government and commerce men and women who are capable and dedicated, who will inspire confidence, respect, and affection in the people among whom they sojourn, and who will identify sympathetically with these people in attitudes and way of life rather than create little outposts of the home country in a foreign land.

None of the major human purposes can any longer be fulfilled apart from a world perspective. All of the values discussed in this book clearly presuppose universality and world outlook. Truth knows no national boundaries, nor does esthetic excellence. Scientific knowledge is not validated without the concurrence of inquirers everywhere, and the fund of human knowledge, skill, and beauty needs replenishment from men of genius in every land. We shall not have learned true civility in manners until we have passed beyond conformity to local and national custom and learned through our actions to symbolize our respect for every person everywhere. Work can be no true vocation while it is turned directly or indirectly to the forging of instruments of destruction, nor can play be more than momentary escape from the abiding fear of violence so long as the nations are related to each other in hostility or uneasy alliance.

As it is with the values of intelligence and creativity, so is it with conscience. Conservation is a world problem. Since supplies of essential raw materials are usually highly localized geographically, international trade is necessary for their proper distribution. Moreover, the ways and rates of use of scarce materials are matters for international decision and control. The population explosion is likewise a problem for everybody and can be solved only by world-wide education. There is no hope for peace and civilization unless the pressures for the earth's limited resources are relieved by responsible social planning; and, conversely, there is no hope for dealing constructively with resources and population as long as war and the fear of war govern the decisions of nations. Public health is another world concern. Disease is no respecter of nations, and the talents and resources of all nations are needed to eradicate it, coordinated through such agencies as the World Health Organization. World tensions and anxieties are certainly harmful to mental health, and the physical ravages of war spread sickness, injury, and death everywhere. In short, for wholeness of mind and body in its inhabitants, a whole world—that is, a world healed of its mortal disease of war—is necessary.

Even right relations in the family are correlated to world understanding. The exigencies of war disperse and dislocate families. Young people are exposed to loneliness, stress, and compulsion, which are not conducive to healthy love and marriage relationships, and the attitudes of hostility and habits of violence which war breeds ill prepare them for secure and stable sex and family life. In like manner, hostilities between the nations intensify estrangement between social classes and racial groups within the nation, especially where some of the groups are of foreign origin. An open, cooperative, peaceful association among the nations, on the other hand, makes for corresponding constructive relationships in families and between class and racial groups. Of special importance for world democracy at the present time is the decisive rejection of the white man's dominance of the world, as people of every shade of skin assume places of leadership in the councils of the nations. The new democratic world-mindedness, despite pockets of bitter resistance, is bringing a sense of the worth of all people and exploding the racist illusions that long supported arbitrary privilege and unjust subjugation.

Finally, in this interdependent world it is evident that economic and political democracy cannot be achieved in isolation. When one nation suffers material hardship, other countries are affected also. When certain people in a nation prosper at the expense of others, the people of all countries are impoverished. The equitable distribution of labor and materials is not a task for each nation alone, but one for the whole family of nations, working cooperatively to administer justly man's natural estate, which is entrusted to all men for the right use and service of all. Political democracy, too, must transcend individual nations. Tyrannies abroad beget defensive reactions at home, which threaten liberty. The necessities of war and of defense make political democracy difficult, since the great power that must be mobilized and directed by centralized authority against enemies abroad is easily turned to the suppression of inconvenient freedoms at home. The rule of law under which free men live is not a matter only of national tradition and preference. It is a universal principle, an objective right which should order the lives of men in every country.

For education, the inculcation of a world outlook is a clear imperative. A prime objective of the study of modern history should be to make vivid the story of the emergence of one world and the spread of the hunger and hope for freedom to people everywhere. Scientific and technical studies should also be presented in the light of their essential contribution to the creation of a single world, in the annihilation of space and time effected by machines for transporting and communicating. Through study units in regular courses and through special lectures, discussions, conferences, and seminars people of all ages should be given full and frank instruction in the causes, character, and consequences of modern warfare. Especially important in supplying such information are books, magazines, newspapers, radio, and television, through which the public can best be kept continually abreast of developments and possibilities both in weapons technology and in efforts toward armament reduction and control, and can be made aware of the nature and scope of the peril in which the world stands so long as war remains the ultimate resort in the settlement of international differences.

In schools and colleges every subject of study should be treated with regard to its world basis and implications. All fields of knowledge, from archeology to zoology, can claim distinguished contributors from many lands, and all studies have important applications to world understanding, whether it be an inquiry into the archeology of the Middle East, once the cradle of civilization and now a focus of cultural and industrial renaissance, or an analysis of the zoology of malarial infection, which has sapped the energies and influenced the destinies of millions in tropical areas around the globe. Today there is no justification for teaching any subject from a purely national or regional standpoint—not even American history, which can be rightly comprehended only as a phase within world history. Neither man nor nation is an island, isolated and self-explanatory. A country's very essence, the meaning of its national character and destiny, are defined in part by its interconnections with other countries.

World responsibility in education further entails serious attention to the teaching of foreign languages, beginning in the early years of school, when children can quickly and naturally learn another tongue in the same fashion as they learned their native language. The backwardness of Americans in giving attention to foreign languages is nothing less than a national disgrace. In most other countries the educated people have been instructed in at least one language other than their own, and many of them have attained a considerable fluency in it. If Americans are to play their parts as world citizens with full responsibility, they must speedily extend and intensify the program of foreign language instruction, not only in the traditional fields of Latin, French, German, and Spanish but also, for large numbers of citizens, in Russian, Chinese, Japanese, Arabic, and other non-European languages.

With more thorough preparation in foreign language, both written and spoken, American students will be in a better position to learn effectively from travel and residence abroad as part of their educational preparation. Such foreign study, under a broad program of regular international exchange of teachers and students, should increasingly become a normal feature of formal education for mature young people.

Finally, in homes, schools, and community affairs a new emphasis should be placed on patriotism, no longer as exclusive loyalty to the sovereign nation, but as devotion to country as the organized agency of articulate relationship with all mankind. The central symbols through which love of country is expressed should cease to be those of military might and should more and more come to celebrate those distinctive national aspirations and traditions that prefigure the reign of freedom and justice everywhere.

PART 5 * REVERENCE

Having now treated the values of intelligence, creativity, and conscience, we come to reverence, the last of the four pivotal values by which civilization and education should be formed. This is a unitary and consummatory value, which comprehends and animates all the rest. On this account, a consideration of the grounds and relevance of reverence furnishes at once a summary and a fresh interpretation of the values already discussed.

Reverence is the most characteristic feature of the religious consciousness. Here the word "religious" is intended to signify the attitude and practice of sincere devotion to what is supremely worthful. This definition excludes much that commonly goes by the name of religion. We are reserving the name of *religion* in the present analysis for a reverential orientation to what is of ultimate value. Beliefs or practices that do not express devotion or that refer to objects of less than supreme worth are by this definition not religious.

Irreligion stands in diametric opposition to religion. It consists in self-seeking orientation. It is the denial of any object of supreme worth beyond the self. It is founded upon the conviction that man himself is the source of values, that human beings do not discover the worthful but themselves create and decide whatever is to be counted as good. Furthermore, since from this standpoint man is the measure of goodness, his wants, preferences, and interests become the criteria of value judgment. The irreligious life is directed toward the goals of satisfaction, acquisition, security, and power. It is founded on the premise that the proper end of man is to become independent and autonomous.

A third orientation, which may be called *idolatry*, stands intermediate between religion and irreligion. Idolatry is devotion toward that which is less than supremely worthful. It partakes of the nature of both religion and irreligion. It is like religion in being a form of devotion. The worshiper to some degree transcends his egocentric craving and offers himself in service to what he deems valuable. But idolatry is also like irreligion, because when the object of loyalty is less than ultimately worthful, dedication to it circumscribes, excludes, and impoverishes life in the same fashion as self-serving.

Idolatry is even found in what commonly goes by the name of religion. Whenever any persons, institutions, rituals, dogmas, or writings are regarded as worthy of ultimate loyalty, idolatry is present. Doctrinaire, exclusive, absolutist "religions" result from ascribing finality to what are in fact less than final goods. Authentic religion cannot exist without finite symbols to serve as channels for devotion to the infinite. Religion becomes idolatrous when the symbols of perfection are worshiped as though they were the ultimate itself: when founders, prophets, and seers are deified, when infallible authority is ascribed to certain organizations and books, and when the performance of rites is taken as a guarantee of salvation.

In religious fanaticism the drive for power and for self-justification is bolstered by attachment to what is believed to be divine. This is the explanation for the evils that have been committed in the name of religion throughout human history. Persecution, war, injustice, superstition—many are the wrongs and great is the human misery caused by idolatrous religionists. The power to do evil is never greater than when it is fired by a conviction that God commands it. Hence, a fundamental religious virtue is humility, born of the persuasion that no man and no human institution can rightly claim the authority of God himself, but that all are under an authority toward which each may at best help to direct his fellow seekers after truth.

Much of what is called religion does not even have the objective reference and the active loyalty of idolatry. It is explicitly oriented toward satisfaction of selfish wants. In other words, it is essentially irreligious. For example, when people pray for success, prosperity, or victory in battle, they are indistinguishable from persons who are centrally concerned with promoting their own interests in other ways. The use of religion to bring "peace of mind" and physical health may also easily deteriorate into self-seeking. Mental and physical well-being are proper objects of petition, provided they are not sought simply for personal ease and comfort, rather than for the sake of God and for the better service of fellow men.

Much popular religion is a direct expression of the democracy of desire. In a hard and cruel world, with many competitors for earth's honors, riches, and privileges, most people lose out. In fact, so insistent are human demands that nobody feels himself a complete and permanent winner. Furthermore, in the end everybody, rich and poor, of high station and low, is defeated by the last enemy, death. Under these conditions it is not surprising that every society should have developed systems of belief and practice which attempt to counteract and compensate for these partial and ultimate frustrations of human desire. The usual content of these faiths is that another world exists wherein all the disappointments and denials of the present world will be made good. Religion of this sort has the effects of sanctifying selfishness and of blunting concern for excellence here and now. For if everything will be made right in the future world, it is not really essential that full justice be done now.

The religion of reverence is opposed to these popular faiths. Religion as devotion to the highest overcomes the self-centeredness of desire and attachment. In authentic religious faith the direction of concern is shifted from the striving, seeking self to the valued other. The errors of idolatry are also corrected by the perpetual judgment rendered on every finite good as never exhausting the infinitude of goodness. The religious person is saved from fanaticism both by the humility that prevents him from identifying himself and the objects of his wants with the supremely worthful and by his recognition that every attained or any conceivable good falls short of absolute and final perfection. Thus, the objections made by thoughtful people to religion as it is commonly practiced properly apply to the perversions of religion and not to its pure and mature forms. In fact, the criticisms of corrupt religion made by secularists and humanists, as well as even more vigorously by prophets, saints, and reformers within the traditional religions, are themselves evidence of ultimate concerns for truth and right, which express the authentic spirit of the religion of reverence.

Undemocratic conditions in any sphere of human affairs are symptoms of irreligion or idolatry. Injustices, the demand for privileges, arbitrariness, prejudice, exclusiveness—all of the forms of oppressive behavior in which individual freedom and worth are denied—are a consequence either of deliberate self-seeking or of absolutizing limited goods, such as membership in a particular social class, nation, or family. Democratic movements, on the other hand, reflect a religious spirit, when in the name of truth, equity, and universal rights the idols of race, class, economic privilege, party, and nation are tumbled down. As we have already observed, however, democracy is not necessarily religious in motivation. It becomes corrupt when the democratic concern for worth degenerates into an acquisitive free-for-all, when the cry for justice turns to the demand for popular autonomy. The democracy of desire rests on the principle of human self-determination and self-sufficiency, which is the antithesis of the principle of reverence upon which democracy should be founded.

Irreligious and idolatrous cultures may take many forms, from the pure self-seeking of irresponsible individualism, through the various types of more or less organized pursuit of advantage, to the collectivistic autonomy of a totalitarian "people's democracy." The communist societies, for example, afford a clear contemporary illustration of fanatical idolatry. That doctrinaire communists are dedicated to what they believe to be of supreme worth is evident. Their willingness to labor and to sacrifice for the Cause, and their devotion to what they are convinced is absolutely and irrevocably true, are also beyond question. In these respects the communist faith appears to be religious in nature. That it is in fact idolatrous is evident from the finitude of its ultimate goals, the closedness of its rigid and exclusive membership and belief system, and its ruthless denial of many of the elemental rights of man in the struggle to reach its goals. Not only does communism but utopian social systems generally tend to be idolatrous. Any scheme that is taken as a final and complete blueprint for human felicity functions as an idol, for no such plan can possibly encompass the fullness of excellence, and no humanly contrived pattern or program can embody the ultimate meaning of human existence.

Genuinely religious cultures, too, may take many forms. Devotion to the supremely worthful can be expressed in ways without number. No single doctrinal formula can fully capture and contain infinitude. No system of ritual uniquely and exclusively qualifies as a vehicle for affirming devotion through symbolic acts. No one code of conduct contains the last word on the holy life. No religious institution can rightly claim exclusive and final divine authority. The worship of the most high takes place through countless channels. The object of supreme devotion has many names—or, perhaps better still, no name at all, for to name is to limit and confine and thus to negate the very ultimacy one seeks to affirm. There is a boundless wealth of habitual acts that may be used individually or corporately to express religious faith. The holy life, too, can be lived according to many different patterns, and any number of institutional forms may be devised to give body, structure, and continuity to religious conviction.

A religious person is one who in intention and in deed is devoted to the supreme, the infinite, the perfect, the true, the completely excellent, regardless of the words, acts, or institutions through which he expresses his dedication. This is not to say that all doctrines, rites, and social organizations are equally true or serve equally well as channels for the ultimate. Some forms are more easily turned to idolatrous and irreligious purposes than others. Actually, many ideas and practices that purport to be religious contradict the fundamental requirement of every religious symbol that it at one and the same time reflect the ultimate and affirm its own finitude. The best religious creeds, rituals, codes, and institutions are those that both powerfully evoke sustained loyalty to the most high and at the same time repel attempts by the faithful who fall into idolatry to make the symbols themselves into objects of worship.

Just as no religious forms are fully adequate to the supreme object of devotion, so also do all persons fall short of complete religious dedication. Everyone has the propensity to live for his own advantage, and everyone succumbs to some extent and at some times to the temptations of idolatry. These acts of disloyalty to what is of ultimate worth constitute what in the religions of the West is called "sin."

Perfect reverence is an ideal that no one wholly attains. By weakness, ignorance, and fear all are prone to live for self and to snatch after such satisfactions as come within their grasp.

It is mainly because of this self-centeredness that the social forms of democracy are necessary. Since every person tends to ascribe to himself more importance than he accords to others, some scheme of balance and limitation is required. Since each looks upon his relationships from the standpoint of his own interests, it is important, for the good of all, to devise measures that will insure a degree of universality and equity. If all people were by nature completely disposed toward the good, it would be necessary only to inform them of it, and the good society would be assured. This view overlooks the universality and gravity of self-centeredness. When democracy is founded on faith in the natural innocence of man and when human wants are taken as the measure of what is good, the ground is prepared for anarchy, conflict, and mass tyranny. A realistic appraisal of human nature leads to a view of democracy as a dyke against the flood of self-interest, as a means of approaching basic justice in relationships between people who are by nature inclined toward injustice because they look first to their own advantage.

It follows that a democracy of desire strengthens and encourages irreligion and thus undermines the only foundations upon which any democracy can rest—namely, those of objective, impartial, and universal justice. A democracy of worth, on the other hand, is founded on the religious premise of the primacy and reality of right. Yet it is not presupposed in a democracy of worth that everyone is fully devoted to what is good and true. On the contrary, it is assumed that because every person to some extent seeks first to satisfy his own wants, democratic principles, commitments, symbols, and structures are needed to remind one of the universal good he ought to serve.

The foregoing analysis invites the conclusion that the central task of education is *religious conversion*. This is not to be understood in the conventional sense, as securing commitment to a specific organized church or acceptance of one of the traditional creeds. What is meant is the inner transformation of purpose and motive from self-regarding irreligion and the idolatrous service of limited goods to reverent service of the most high. Such conversion may well lead one to institutional affiliation with others of similar intention and to the use of certain verbal formulations of faith, since the inward reorientation needs *some* social and symbolic embodiment. Many outward expressions are suitable, the appropriate one in any given case depending on personality type and on the person's social and cultural situation.

Whatever its visible forms, the important goal is the redirecting of life from finite attachment and acquisitiveness to the active love of the good. To accomplish this change is the supreme end of all teaching and learning. All increase in knowledge and skill that confirm one in his lust for autonomy is loss, not gain. From this standpoint much of what is taught and learned in present-day education misses the mark. Studies that increase the power to exploit the earth and other people, that arm one for the struggle for privilege, that prepare one to pursue his advantage more successfully, destroy rather than edify a person. The sovereign test of all education is whether or not it is religious—that is, whether or not it tends toward conversion of the person to unconditional commitment to truth and right.

This central religious task is inherent in all teaching, regardless of the field of study. It is the end that should govern instruction in mathematics and in literature, in mechanical arts and in modern dance, in biochemistry and in law. Every study, theoretical and applied, elementary and advanced, formal and informal, is an appropriate vehicle for teaching the fundamental lesson of loyalty to what is true, excellent, and just. Every institution of education—the home, the school, the church or temple, the industrial shop or laboratory, the museum or library, the mass media—can be and ought to be an agency of religious instruction, engaged in the one saving work of emancipating persons from bondage to selfish desires and idolatrous attachments and of directing them toward the life of devotion to that in which their being and well-being are grounded.

Thus "religion" is not to be regarded primarily as a special subject of study, parallel to geography and physics, but as a life orientation to be effected in and through all special studies. To be sure, religion is *also* a field of intellectual inquiry and practical skill, and it is possible and desirable to give instruction in religious history, philosophy, beliefs, and institutions as well as to arrange for practical experience in religious affairs. But valuable as these lessons may be, it should not be thought that such explicit religious education exhausts the

244 REVERENCE

obligation to teach religion or is even the principal part of it. Religious faith is relevant to every aspect of education and to every subject of study, and is to be mediated through the whole life of teaching and learning.

The situation is somewhat parallel to the teaching of logic and rhetoric. While these are properly regarded as special subjects of study and are taught as separate disciplines, skill in reasoning and in the use of language is also a necessary aspect of every other intellectual discipline. For example, a teacher of physics necessarily teaches logic and rhetoric, while one who teaches logic or rhetoric as a special discipline does not necessarily teach physics. Right ordering and expression of ideas is a task for both specialists and everybody, *especially* for everybody. So it is with religious instruction. "Religion" is an important and legitimate special study, but more important still is the fact that instruction in every field promotes either autonomy or reverence. The present book is a case in point. This chapter deals with religion as a particular facet of education in a democracy, but more significant is the fact that all of the preceding chapters set forth a religious point of view by demonstrating what the life of ultimate devotion means in a wide range of human concerns.

In our pluralistic society, constituted of people with all kinds and shades of religious belief and disbelief, the advocacy of religiously oriented education presents serious difficulties. One obvious way out is to place education under the auspices of organized religious institutions. This way has the advantage that the ideas and practices of religion can be infused throughout the instructional program without the confusions and restrictions imposed by having to take account of diverse religious traditions. Against this approach two principal objections must be lodged. First, religious schools tend to breed idolatry, by identifying a particular tradition with the ultimate. Young people come to accept the religious forms and structures which they are taught as the substance of religion itself. In the second place, sectarian schools lose the religious values implicit in the confrontation and interplay of different ways of faith. Their students and teachers are not driven to the deeper levels of devotion which bridge (but do not obliterate) the differences between traditions. They are likely to neglect the fundamental lesson of democratic faith—that, prior to all other commitments and uniting people of many forms of belief and practice, is our common vocation to love and serve truth, excellence, and justice.

What, then, of teaching religion in public schools? Surely, no official state religion ought to be taught. This is clear from the First Amendment to the Federal Constitution, in which the Congress is denied the power to make any "laws respecting an establishment of religion or prohibiting the free exercise thereof." Such a regulation is necessary if the ultimacy of religion is to be preserved. Since government is necessarily finite and fallible, it cannot define the object of ultimate loyalty. The state must be "under God"—that is, subject to the higher judgment of righteousness-in-itself; the state is never itself the true standard of perfection. Freedom of religion is an essential feature of democracy, since the state is not an end but a means.

Since matters of faith cannot and should not be legislated, irreligion and idolatry as well as all forms of religion have a right to exist in democratic society. No one should be penalized or coerced because he holds any particular view about the ultimate. Of course no citizen is completely at liberty to act in any way he pleases, even though his religious convictions require it. Some lines must be drawn, at the points where public safety and welfare are endangered. Thus, persons fanatically committed to doctrines of class warfare and subversion of free institutions (communists, fascists, racists) would have to be prevented by the police power of the democratic state from putting their ultimate commitments into practice. So also would religious opponents of medical treatment normally have to be overruled when the public health was endangered by neglect of treatment.

On the other hand, it is a mark of mature democracy when provisions are made for exempting conscientious objectors from military conscription. Having in view the question of national security, this contribution to the practice of freedom of conscience can be made only because the great majority of citizens are willing to bear arms in defense of their country. Conscience sometimes drives citizens to certain actions—for example, nonpayment of taxes—which cannot be condoned and against which sanctions must be brought. Even in such cases there may be lessons to be learned from the nonconformists, and these may in later times be embodied in new social regulations. It belongs to the open society not only to give the widest practicable freedom to its members' consciences, but also to be sensitive to the social message that may be contained in the deeds of prophets, seers, and reformers who now are caused to suffer for their radical non-conformity.

The duty of the democratic state and its agencies, including the public schools, is, then, to recognize and promote freedom of religion. Government is not the arbiter of faith. Yet neither can the state be neutral with respect to religion. While it is not within the province of government to determine who is religious and who is not, nor to discriminate between the different forms of religion, irreligion, and idolatry, except where public security is at stake, it is the function of the democratic state to persuade and encourage its citizens toward religious faith and away from irreligion and idolatry. They are not to be coerced or penalized for failure to be religious, because it is given to no man to judge the faith of another and because compulsion is incompatible with reverence. But the duty of the state to promote religion (in the fundamental sense) remains. This is not an obligation to support religious organizations as such, but to encourage in the citizens a life of loyalty to what is supremely worthful.

It is thus not right to conclude from the constitutional guarantee of religious liberty that the public schools have no business dealing with religion. The question of fundamental life orientation cannot be avoided. At issue are the ruling presuppositions which affect every-thing which is taught and learned. It is not a purely private affair whether or not a person is religious. Religion as ultimate loyalty is profoundly relevant to public life, and the institutions of public ed-ucation ought to promote it actively and explicitly. From the stand-point of the democracy of worth, the basic aim of public education is to inculcate reverence, propagate true faith, and expose and oppose irreligion and idolatry. This is the one crucial objective of instruction, in comparison with which all accumulation of knowledge and acquisi-tion of skill are insignificant, and through which alone these special accomplishments may be made meaningful. The goal of education is the formation of good character, whose measure is the habit and attitude of devotion.

Public education can be religious in this sense without violating religious liberty and without teaching sectarian doctrines as official public dogma. The content of such public religious instruction should be twofold. First, in every domain of teaching the following essentials of religious faith should be emphasized and demonstrated in the teacher's own outlook: That the world, man, and his culture are neither self-sufficient nor self-explanatory but are derived from given sources of being, meaning, and value. That the supremely worthful is not finite or limited but transcends all human comprehension and every human achievement. That the life of selfish ambition, the struggle for autonomy, acquisition, and success, and attachment to finite goods lead in the end to misery, conflict, guilt, despair, boredom, and frustration. That every individual has a personal calling to turn from following after desire to a life of loving and grateful dedication to what is of ultimate worth.

Second, these fundamentals of faith should be brought into relation to the historical patterns of faith in the civilized tradition. The many ways in which religious faith has been expressed should be recognized. But, first, each student should be taught to understand and appreciate the religious tradition in which he was reared, and to see how it may be used maturely and responsibly as a vehicle for ultimate devotion. Included among these religious traditions should be ones of protest as well as of affirmation. Thus, many critics of religion— self-styled atheists and freethinkers—are frequently more devoted to ultimate truth and righteousness than are the nominal adherents of the more traditional religions. In public education, then, the initial aim of instruction in the religious heritage is to help adherents of each tradition—Christians, Jews, Muslims, Ethical Culturists, Religious Naturalists, and all the others—to realize to the full the resources for the embodiment of religious faith available in their tradition at its best.

Along with this deepening of faith through each student's own heritage should go a broadening of perspective through continuing conversations with persons of other traditions. It should never be assumed that all of the historical religions are equally good or that a person should always remain within the tradition to which he was born. Religions differ greatly in the power and purity of the devotion they evoke. It is within the province of public schools not only to see that students are correctly informed about religious matters, but also to provide a setting in which older young people may learn to recognize and sift out irreligious and idolatrous tendencies and perversions in the various religious systems of mankind. They should be encouraged so to grow in knowledge and power of discriminative judgment that each person will at length be competent to choose for himself the forms of belief, celebration, and conduct that best express and sustain the dedicated life.

Religion is not a matter for uncritical acquiescence, nor are religious traditions simply to be accepted or rejected. Of all the concerns of life, religion is the one that supremely calls for active inquiry, growing insight, and continual redefinition and decision. If out of fear or ignorance any real consideration of religion is excluded from the school curriculum, the educational program is thereby trivialized and the school fails in its central educative mission. Worse than that, religiously sterilized schools actively spread the virus of autonomy and irreverence, for the absence of any reference to the claims of faith or to its historic expressions communicates the idea that they are unimportant or at least irrelevant to whatever is studied in school. By removing the wide segments of knowledge and skill with which the school ordinarily deals from all explicit relation to religion, the meaning of religion is falsified; by being made a specialized concern, it is robbed of its essential comprehensiveness, and the school studies become occasions for propagating the gospel of autonomy and self-sufficiency.

It is easy to understand how zeal for public harmony in a religiously plural society has led to the secularization of American public schools. Since it is not possible—or perhaps even desirable—for everyone to agree on the forms of religion, it is concluded that the common schools must exclude religion altogether. In support of this position the famous Jeffersonian doctrine of the "wall of separation" between church and state is regularly invoked. While this approach eliminates some difficulties, it does so at the expense of fundamental educational and democratic values. The secularization of public education has done serious damage to the cause of basic religion—though perhaps not to that of conventional or nominal religion, which prospers well enough—and has encouraged a philosophy of life that undermines the moral basis of democratic civilization. An enduring and progressive democracy rests on common loyalty to a law of truth and right which is found and given, not constructed by human decision; and for the propagation and health of such democracy an educational system centered around this religious principle is required.

The state and its agencies, including the public schools and colleges, can be true to the principle of religious liberty without giving up their primary obligation to promote the religious life, in the fundamental sense of reverent devotion. Freedom of religion is itself a religious principle, since it rests on the conviction that no man, group of men, or institution can claim final and authoritative knowledge, perfection, or righteousness. If a wall of separation is erected between religion and the state (and its schools), that wall will prove to be a tomb in which church, state, and schools will decay with a civilization that has lost its soul. Schools that are purged of all religious concerns become agencies for the propagation of irreligion or idolatry —for the feeding of selfish ambitions or training for subservience to secular utopias. If religion is understood in its elemental sense, and not merely in its sectarian expressions, it is entirely practicable for the public schools to educate religiously without violating any ideals of religious freedom, without partisanship for any historical tradition, and without transgressing the principle of persuasion, not compulsion, in all matters of faith.

If the institutions of public education fail to teach for religious commitment and thereby both make education personally superficial and effectually promote irreligion or idolatry, it will be necessary, for the well-being of society, to have the instruction of the young carried on in nonpublic schools under the auspices of religious organizations. Although such schools doubtless have certain merits even under ideal conditions, they are neither religiously nor democratically desirable as an alternative to a public school system. Public schools, with young people from a variety of religious backgrounds, provide the optimum setting for growth in mutual understanding and for that continuing disciplined dialogue in which differences deepen insights and correct errors, instead of confirming prejudices and sharpening divisions.

For public schools to be able to deal responsibly with religion, two conditions must be met. First, teachers must be properly selected and prepared. No teacher can communicate reverence if he does not have it himself. The character of the teacher is of prime importance. Knowledge and skill are necessary, too, but they are subordinate to the fundamental requirement of personal devotion to the good. In addition to religiously oriented character (whether or not it is expressed in conventional religious terms), every teacher should have a working knowledge of the major religious traditions of mankind as well as of the principal idolatries. This requirement is no more unreasonable than expecting every teacher to know in broad outline the major forms of political and economic organization and the principal types of personality structure. No teacher should be or need be at a loss to deal intelligently and fairly with most religious issues that might arise in public schools in a pluralistic society, and every teacher can be and ought to be prepared to grasp the religious dimensions in any subject of study and to use sectarian differences to clarify issues and enrich the learning of all.

The second prerequisite for responsible religious instruction in public education is a strong teaching profession, which can withstand the pressures of organized religion outside the schools and colleges. Religion is everybody's concern; official "religious" bodies have no monopoly of it. The greatest present bar to a mature religious orientation in public education is the assumption that the church and the synagogue are the only appropriate channels for religion, and that anything done about religion in the schools must be accomplished through these channels or at least with the official approval and sanction of the recognized religious officials.

Thus, religion is regarded as a delicate subject, like sex, politics, economics, and all other important matters about which people differ sharply and feel strongly, and which for those reasons are in greatest need of careful study and cooperative inquiry. Students' questions about religion are usually handled with the utmost caution and are referred back to parents and ministers for answering, for fear of reactions by representatives of organized religion to any treatment of religious matters by teachers of another affiliation. The only cure for this crippling influence is a strong and independent organized teaching profession, whose members are protected against outside interference in the performance of their professional functions and who recognize and accept their responsibility for dealing knowledgeably and impartially not only with the proximate issues of life but also with the ultimate concerns of faith through which the particulars of life gain their deeper significance.

That education is for reverence has been the common theme of all the chapters in this book. Each element in the curriculum for a democracy of worth exemplifies the religious aim and furnishes occasions for fulfilling it. In intellectual matters, religious faith means devotion to truth, keeping inquiry open, foregoing the demand for absolute certitude yet not despairing of progress, striving for universality, publicity, and objectivity in knowledge, and being thankfully obedient to the disciplines of reason and of empirical evidence. In the use of the mass media of communication, reverence is manifest in the aim of creating a blessed community, bound together in the truth, through media of public education devoted to the common good rather than to propaganda and profit for the advancement of selfish interests. In esthetic education, religious faith is revealed in persistent dissatisfaction with the second-rate and in the constant yearning for creative perfection. Good manners, too, have a religious foundation; considerateness, respect for others, a sense of fitness, grace, humility, gentleness, and dignity all grow when reverence displaces self-assertion. Work performed with a sense of calling is religious in quality, and reverence informs education for any occupation that creatively incarnates excellence. One who learns the disciplined joy and self-forgetfulness of play therein also learns the power of worship to make old things new by acts of re-creation.

Without religious devotion to the right, no secure basis can be laid for proper regard for nature and responsible control of procreation, so that the earth may be a secure dwelling place for all the generations to come. Education for health is ultimately religious also, for health is wholeness, and one cannot be whole while he lives in autonomous alienation from the sources of his being. True love and enduring marriage are rooted in a faithful covenant which transcends the ebb and flow of feeling, considerations of advantage, and the contingencies of fortune. Similarly, only a transcendent devotion can surely dissolve the barriers of class and race by teaching men to know themselves equals and brothers in the sight of God and for his sake. Finally, religious faith is present whenever material goods are regarded as a trust to be administered for the right rather than as a treasure to be grasped, and whenever the affairs of politics within the nation and between the nations are seen as occasions for discovering and obeying the universal law of right to which all are subject and in which the ends of life are fulfilled.

This is the one supreme purpose which unites all the lesser purposes of education: to engender reverence. Reverence is the mark of perfection in character. Devotion to what is supremely worthful is the one aim of the curriculum, to be worked out in all of the special areas of instruction. The quality of life which springs from this ultimate commitment is the soul of democracy and the consummation of education for the common good.

SELECTED BIBLIOGRAPHY

CHAPTER 1 * TEXT AND CONTEXT

Jaspers, Karl, Man in the Modern Age (New York, Anchor Books, Doubleday, 1957).

Lippmann, Walter, The Public Philosophy (New York: New American Library of World Literature, 1956).

Tillich, Paul, The Protestant Era (Chicago: University of Chicago Press, 1948).

Ward, Barbara, Faith and Freedom (New York: Doubleday Image Books, 1958).

Weaver, Richard M., Ideas Have Consequences (Chicago: University of Chicago Press, 1948).

CHAPTER 2 * TWO DEMOCRACIES

Becker, Carl L., Freedom and Responsibility in the American Way of Life (New York: Vintage Books, Random House, 1955).

Bell, Bernard Iddings, Crowd Culture (Chicago: Henry Regnery, 1956).

Ortega y Gasset, José, Revolt of the Masses (New York: W. W. Norton, 1932).

Riesman, David, The Lonely Crowd (New York: Anchor Books, Doubleday, 1953).

Whyte, William H., Jr., The Organization Man (New York: Anchor Books, Doubleday, 1957).

CHAPTER 3 * INTELLECTUAL EXCELLENCE

Bronowski, Jacob, Science and Human Values (New York: Harper Torchbooks, Harper & Brothers, 1959).

Ruby, Lionel, The Art of Making Sense: A Guide to Logical Thinking (Philadelphia: Keystone Books, J. B. Lippincott, 1954).

Sertillanges, Antonin G., The Intellectual Life (Westminster, Md.: Newman Press, 1956).

Stebbing, Susan L., Thinking to Some Purpose (Baltimore, Md.: Penguin Books, 1939).

Sullivan, J. W. N., *The Limitations of Science* (New York: New American Library of World Literature, 1949).

CHAPTER 4 * THE MASS MEDIA OF COMMUNICATION

Barnouw, Erik, *Mass Communication: Television, Radio, Film, and Press* (New York: Holt, Rinehart, & Winston, 1957).

National Society for the Study of Education, *Mass Media and Education*, 53rd Yearbook, Part 2 (Chicago: N.S.S.E., University of Chicago Press, 1954).

Schramm, Wilbur, *Responsibility in Mass Communication* (New York: Harper and Brothers, 1957).

Seldes, Gilbert, *The Public Arts* (New York: Simon and Schuster, 1957).

Wright, Charles R., *Mass Communication* (New York: Studies in Psychology, Random House, 1959).

CHAPTER 5 * ESTHETIC EXCELLENCE

Dewey, John, *Art as Experience* (New York: Capricorn Books, G. P. Putnam's Sons, 1958).

Edman, Irwin, *Arts and the Man* (New York: W. W. Norton & Company, 1939).

Lynes, Russell, *The Tastemakers* (New York: Harper and Brothers, 1954).

Mumford, Lewis, *Art and Technics* (New York: Columbia University Press, 1952).

Read, Herbert, *Education Through Art* (New York: Pantheon Books, 1958).

CHAPTER 6 * MANNERS

Creel, Herrlee G., *Confucius and the Chinese Way* (New York: Harper & Brothers, 1960).

Free, Anne R., *Social Usage* (New York: Appleton-Century-Crofts, 1960).

Hadida, Sophie C., *Manners for Millions* (rev. ed., New York: Barnes & Noble, 1956).

Montagu, Ashley M. F., *Education and Human Relations* (New York: Grove Press, 1958).

Nicholson, Harold, *Good Behaviour* (Boston: Beacon Press, 1960).

CHAPTER 7 * WORK

Arendt, Hannah, *The Human Condition* (New York: Anchor Books, Doubleday, 1959).

Calhoun, Robert L., *God and the Day's Work* (New York: Reflection Books, Association Press, 1957).

Donohue, John W., *Work and Education* (Chicago: Loyola University Press, 1959).

Mumford, Lewis, *Technics and Civilization* (New York: Harcourt, Brace, 1934).

Steere, Douglas V., *Work and Contemplation* (New York: Harper & Brothers, 1957).

CHAPTER 8 * RECREATION

Denney, Reuel, *The Astonished Muse* (Chicago: University of Chicago Press, 1957).

Huizinga, Johan, *Homo Ludens: A Study of the Play Element in Culture* (Boston: Beacon Press, 1955).

Kaplan, Max, *Leisure in America: A Social Inquiry* (New York: John Wiley & Sons, 1960).

National Education Association, Department of Health, Physical Education, and Recreation, *Education for Leisure* (Washington: N.E.A., 1957).

Van Doren, Mark, *Liberal Education* (Boston: Beacon Press, 1959).

CHAPTER 9 * THE USES OF NATURE

Brown, Harrison, *The Challenge of Man's Future* (New York: Compass Books, The Viking Press, 1954).

Glass, David V. (ed.), *Introduction to Malthus* (New York: John Wiley and Sons, 1953).

Osborn, Fairfield, *Limits of the Earth* (New York: Little, Brown, 1953).

Sax, Karl, *Standing Room Only: The World's Exploding Population* (rev. ed., Boston: The Beacon Press, 1960).

Wrong, Dennis H., *Population* (rev. ed., New York: Studies in Psychology, Random House, 1956).

CHAPTER 10 * HEALTH

Allport, Gordon, *Becoming* (New Haven: Yale University Press, 1955).

Dicks, Russell L., *Toward Health and Wholeness* (New York: Macmillan, 1960).

Fisher, Irving, and Emerson, Haven, *How to Live* (8th ed., New York: Funk & Wagnalls, 1950).

Fromm, Erich, *Man For Himself* (New York: Holt, Rinehart, and Winston, 1947).

Slaughter, Frank G., *Your Body and Your Mind* (New York: New American Library of World Literature, 1958).

CHAPTER 11 * SEX AND FAMILY LIFE

Hiltner, Seward, *Sex and the Christian Life* (New York: Reflection Books, Association Press, 1957).

Mead, Margaret, *Male and Female* (New York: New American Library of World Literature, 1955).

Watts, Alan Wilson, *Nature, Man, and Woman* (New York: New American Library of World Literature, 1960).

Weatherhead, Leslie D., *The Mastery of Sex* (Naperville, Ill.: Alec R. Allenson, 1960).

Winter, Gibson, *Love and Conflict* (New York: Doubleday, 1958).

CHAPTER 12 * SOCIAL CLASS

Goffman, Irving, *The Presentation of Self in Everyday Life* (New York: Anchor Books, Doubleday, 1959).

Hollingshead, August B., *Elmtown's Youth: The Impact of Social Classes on Adolescents* (New York: John Wiley & Sons, 1949).

Mills, C. Wright, *The Power Elite* (New York: Galaxy Books, Oxford University Press, 1956).

Tawney, Richard H., *Equality* (New York: Capricorn Books, G. P. Putnam's Sons, 1960).

Warner, W. Lloyd, *American Life: Dream and Reality* (Chicago: University of Chicago Press, 1953).

CHAPTER 13 * RACE

Allport, Gordon W., *The Nature of Prejudice* (New York: Anchor Books, Doubleday, 1958).

Benedict, Ruth, *Race: Science and Politics* (rev. ed., New York: Compass Books, Viking Press, 1959).

Dunn, L. C., and Dobzhansky, Theodosius, *Heredity, Race, and Society* (New York: New American Library of World Literature, 1946).

Handlin, Oscar, *Race and Nationality in American Life* (New York: Anchor Books, Doubleday, 1957).

Rose, Arnold, *The Negro in America* (Boston: The Beacon Press, 1956).

CHAPTER 14 * ECONOMIC LIFE

Childs, Marquis W., and Cater, Douglass, *Ethics in a Business Society* (New York: New American Library of World Literature, 1954).

Polanyi, Karl, *The Great Transformation* (Boston: Beacon Press, 1957).

Tawney, Richard H., *The Acquisitive Society* (New York: Harvest Books, Harcourt, Brace, 1946).

Veblen, Thorstein, *The Portable Veblen*, ed. by Max Lerner (New York: The Viking Press, 1948).

Ward, A. Dudley (ed.), *Goals of Economic Life* (New York: Harper & Brothers, 1953).

CHAPTER 15 * POLITICAL ORGANIZATION

Dewey, John, *The Public and its Problems* (3rd ed., Denver: Alan Swallow, 1957).

Lasswell, Harold D., *Politics: Who Gets What, When, How* (New York: Meridian Books, 1958).

Niebuhr, Reinhold, *Moral Man and Immoral Society* (New York: Charles Scribner's Sons, 1932).

Smith, Thomas V., and Lindeman, Eduard C., *The Democratic Way of Life* (rev. ed., New York: New American Library of World Literature, 1951).

Wilson, Woodrow, *Constitutional Government in the United States* (New York: Columbia University Press, 1908).

CHAPTER 16 * WORLD RESPONSIBILITY

Butterfield, Herbert, *International Conflict in the Twentieth Century* (New York: Harper & Brothers, 1960).

Hocking, William Ernest, *The Coming World Civilization* (New York: Harper & Brothers, 1956).

Lefever, Ernest W., *Ethics and United States Foreign Policy* (New York: Meridian Books, 1957).

Toynbee, Arnold J., *Civilization on Trial* and *The World and the West* (New York: Meridian Books, 1958).

Ward, Barbara, *Five Ideas that Change the World* (New York: W. W. Norton, 1960).

CHAPTER 17 * RELIGION

Barker, Ernest, *Church, State, and Education* (Ann Arbor, Mich.: University of Michigan Press, 1957).

Cogley, John (ed.), *Religion in America* (New York: Meridian Books, 1958).

Dewey, John, *A Common Faith* (New Haven: Yale University Press, 1960).

Smith, Huston, *The Religions of Man* (New York: New American Library of World Literature, 1958).

Whitehead, Alfred N., *Religion in the Making* (New York: Meridian Books, 1960).

INDEX

Ability grouping, 165, 172 f., 184
Absolute, 27
  never attainable, 6, 11, 203, 239
Absolutism, 194, 214
  in law, 205, 206
  in religion, 238
Abstraction, 5, 61
  classification as, 162
Academic freedom, 43 f., 200, 213 f.,
  216
Acquisitiveness, 13, 25, 72, 93, 128,
  193 f., 200, 222, 243
Adult education, 57, 109 f., 135, 197
Adulteration, food, 140
Advertising, 65, 198
  liquor, 143
  and the mass media, 55, 58
Age, special problems of, 135
Age grouping, 164 f.
Agreement, on moral issues, 5, 6, 7, 10
Alcohol, and economics, 143
Alcohol education, 142 f.
Alcoholic beverages, 141 ff.
Alcoholism, 142
Aims of education, 6, 8, 10, 13, 15,
  19, 76, 103, 124
  in the democracy of desire, 25
  in the democracy of worth, 26
  in race relations, 179
  in recreation, 112
  refinement as, 90
  as religious conversion, 242, 246 f.
  supreme, 252
American Dream, 160
American society, 20, 23
American way of life, 26
Analysis, 40
Appetite, 86, 139, 140 f.
  sexual, 152, 153
Aristocracy, 90, 165, 201
  and esthetic life, 62 f., 64, 65
  of knowledge, 37
  and liberal education, 112
  and manners, 79 f.
  and recreation, 108
  and work, 92, 93
Art, 5, 66, 67, 70
  and morals, 73

speaking as, 83, 85
study of, 76
and utility, 71
work as, 92
Atomic energy, 130, 220
and war, 223
Augustine, St., 9
Automobiles,
and drinking, 142 f.
proper use of, 136 f.
Authoritarianism, 88
Authority, 111
arbitrary, 13, 15, 23, 34, 151, 152
divine, 238
of government, 207 f., 211
infallible, 238, 241
intellectual, 37
of justice, 225
of law, 205, 225
need for, 166
parental, 151
of the people, 202
respect for, 90
responsible, 151
of teachers, 89, 151 f., 171 f.
traditional, 38
of truth, 36, 37, 38
of values, 10
Automation, 93
Autonomy, 9, 14, 24, 25, 28, 53, 90,
  122, 127, 129, 238, 240, 248
and communism, 100
and creativity, 65
in free enterprise, 189
intellectual, 36
local, 212
and the mass media, 48, 51
money as symbol of, 94
and national sovereignty, 224
in political affairs, 202, 203
and war, 221, 223

Bacon, F., 127
Balance, 90
between work and recreation, 134 f.
in diet, 139
esthetic, 68, 70
Behavioral sciences, 12